SHERIDAN'S SECRET MISSION

SHERIDAN'S SECRET MISSION

How the South Won the War
After the Civil War

ROBERT CWIKLIK

HARPER

An Imprint of HarperCollinsPublishers

HarperCollins books may be purchased for educational, business, or sales promotional use. For information, please email the Special Markets Department at SPsales@harpercollins.com.

FIRST EDITION

Designed by Michele Cameron

Library of Congress Cataloging-in-Publication Data has been applied for.

ISBN 978-0-06-295064-2

23 24 25 26 27 LBC 5 4 3 2 1

FOR JULIE

CONTENTS

SHERIDAN'S SECRET MISSION

THE BEST, THE BRAVEST, AND THE PUREST

General Philip H. Sheridan, late hero of the Civil War, made a splash on his arrival at the magnificent St. Charles Hotel in New Orleans on the night before New Year's Eve 1874. Along with his usual phalanx of aides and minders, the notorious Yankee commander was squiring "a party of ladies," including Miss Irene Rucker, the Army quartermaster general's willowy twenty-two-year-old daughter, who was soon to become the great Sheridan's fiancée.

Sheridan was dressed in a plain civilian frock coat and swore to anyone who would listen that he and his companions were merely tourists stopping in the Crescent City en route to Cuba and the "Land of Flowers." Locals were skeptical. In a New Year's Day headline, the *Daily Picayune* mocked the hard-eyed military man with an allusion to "The Raven," Edgar Allan Poe's famous poem about a disturbing midnight visitation:

> *Purely a Pleasure Trip, Only This and Nothing More.*

Like many Southerners, the *Picayune's* editors had raw memories of Sheridan, whose troops had torched homes, barns, and crops in

Virginia's Shenandoah Valley during the war, in a campaign known as "The Burning," to transform the region into "a barren waste" so residents could no longer provision Confederate forces. "If a merciless deed has to be done," a contemporary writer noted, "everyone expects Sheridan to do it."

Louisianians also had firsthand experience of Sheridan's ways and means. Installed as military governor of occupied Louisiana after the war, Sheridan scandalized many residents with his attitude toward former slaves, or "freedmen," backing their demands to ride on streetcars with white passengers and allowing them to serve on juries weighing the fate of their former masters. When the idea of black voting rights moved from the radical fringe to the center of federal Reconstruction policy in the Republican-controlled Congress, Sheridan was the point man in Louisiana, registering new black voters, who became a majority of the state's electorate, and disqualifying ex-Confederates from the voting rolls. The new majority-black electorate chose a slim majority of black delegates to write a new state constitution, producing one of the most progressive charters of a remarkably progressive period during Reconstruction, establishing, at least on paper, universal public education, integrated schools, and the rights of black men to vote and hold office. Congressional Republicans also engineered the adoption of the Fourteenth and Fifteenth Amendments, establishing birthright black citizenship and prohibiting the denial of voting rights on account of race, to address work left undone after the abolition of slavery with the Thirteenth Amendment.

Sheridan's peripheral involvement in this work hardly made him a civil rights hero. He shared most of the prejudices against black people harbored by white Americans in those days. But he appreciated the courage of black men who fought in the Union Army during the Civil War, encompassing about 10 percent of Union forces, and he believed that since the U.S. government had emancipated the freedmen, it was duty bound to secure for them "a fair chance in the battle of life."

The advent of black voting rights in Louisiana and other Southern states greatly benefited Republican candidates, black and white, and the party of Lincoln and emancipation took power in states across the South. Although in some Southern states with smaller black populations white conservatives had gradually regained control, helped by the return of some former Confederates to the voting rolls, as of January 1875 Republicans maintained their hold on the Louisiana state government thanks to powerful support from black voters. The *Picayune* held Sheridan "more responsible" than any other man for what it viewed as Louisiana's postwar misfortunes because he helped congressional Republicans "subject the State to a negro Government," affixing "chains from which we have never been able to escape."[1]

The *Picayune*'s editors strongly supported efforts of white conservatives to "redeem" Louisiana by wresting control of the state government away from Republicans put in office with the help of black votes. The newspaper lavished glowing coverage on the Crescent City White League, the New Orleans chapter of a Democratic Party–aligned paramilitary group unhinged by black voting and office-holding, whose stated mission was "to re-establish a white man's government."

White League operatives terrorized black and white Republican officials in the state's country parishes during the summer of 1874. Then thousands of White Leaguers swarmed New Orleans, Louisiana's capital at that time, on September 14, killing a dozen black police officers and injuring dozens more, to chase the white Republican governor, William Pitt Kellogg, out of office.

Kellogg was one of many former Northerners who resettled in the South during and after the war seeking opportunities to improve their lot, and who tended to vote Republican. Democratic newspaper editors branded these migrants as "carpetbaggers," alluding to a cheap travel satchel to portray them as wandering grifters scheming to profit from the South's adversity. Native white Southerners who allied themselves politically with freedmen and carpetbaggers were scorned as "scalawags," which meant something akin to "worthless traitors." A majority of so-called carpetbaggers had served in the Union Army, but their numbers also included businessmen, teachers, and employees of the Freedmen's Bureau, an agency established in the War Department to help former slaves adjust to new circumstances. Many carpetbaggers and scalawags won political office with the backing of newly enfranchised former slaves. Freedmen often viewed Yankee Republican transplants like Kellogg, a Vermont native and former Union Army officer, as natural allies.[2]

The White League's high-profile exploits targeting Republican officials might have inspired white insurgents elsewhere in the region scheming to seize power in places with large black electorates. White vigilantes in Alabama ambushed freedmen near polling stations on election day, November 3, 1874, driving down black turnout to help Democrats carry the state, thereby securing its "redemption." In early December, armed white militants in Vicksburg, Mississippi, drove a black Republican sheriff from office and slaughtered scores of freedmen in the aftermath.[3]

The citizenship and voting rights of former slaves were among the most consequential fruits of the Union victory in the Civil War. Republicans were reckoning with the possibility that gangs like the White League, made up mostly of former Confederate soldiers and winked at by Democratic officials, could turn back the clock and nullify the freedmen's hard-won gains of recent years.

President Ulysses S. Grant sent federal troops to New Orleans within days of the September White League assault to disperse the insurgents and reinstate Kellogg, and bluecoats were still there in force when Sheridan arrived months later on his "pleasure trip." Sending soldiers to put down flagrant vigilante violence in previous years had often boosted Republican political fortunes in the North. But in Grant's December 1874 annual message to Congress, he acknowledged that such troop deployments were now "repugnant to public opinion." Disenchantment with the September Louisiana intervention, and with the administration's Southern policy more generally, likely contributed to the Republicans' smashing defeat in the fall 1874 congressional elections, when Democrats won control of the House of Representatives for the first time since before the Civil War. But despite the public's mounting impatience with the use of federal troops in the South, Grant vowed in his December annual message to enforce the rights of former slaves "with rigor." Citing the threat from heavily armed "White Leagues and other societies," he said that failure to intervene in the face of insurgent violence would make the entire project of enfranchising the freedmen "worse than mockery and little better than crime."

As the *Picayune*'s editors evidently suspected, Sheridan's return to their city had little to do with any "pleasure trip." In a Christmas Eve telegram, Grant had asked Sheridan to visit New Orleans, Vicksburg, and other Southern trouble spots to learn "the true condition of affairs" in the region, and to devise a plan for dealing with the new paramilitary threat. Grant suggested that Sheridan bring family and friends along and act like he was on vacation, perhaps unsure how much federal interference in a Southern state the public would tolerate. But Grant authorized Sheridan, in case trouble broke out, to assume command of U.S. forces stationed in the region, at the general's sole discretion.[4]

This was far from the first time Grant turned to Sheridan in a crisis. In July 1864, about a year after federal forces halted Confederate general Robert E. Lee's invasion of the North with a decisive triumph at Gettysburg, Union commanders were confident of their ultimate victory over the Southern Confederacy. But a series of raids against Union armies in Virginia's Shenandoah Valley led by Confederate general Jubal Early had profoundly unsettled the Northern public, especially when Early marched his men to the back porch of Washington, D.C., itself. Northerners primed for a long-awaited final assault on Confederate headquarters in Richmond were disheartened to learn instead of Rebel raiders poised to sack the Union capital. This reversal fueled a crisis of morale in the war-weary North that threatened to demolish President Abraham Lincoln's campaign for reelection in the fall, a defeat that likely would have upended the Union war effort itself—and emancipation along with it—as the new president sued for peace with the Confederacy. Lincoln himself expected the worst. "I am going to be beaten," he told an Army officer, "and unless some great change takes place badly beaten."

To confront this emergency, Grant tapped an aggressive young cavalry commander whose pluck and resourcefulness had so impressed him in the war's Western Theater; he asked thirty-three-year-old Phil Sheridan to lead an army into Virginia and dog Jubal Early's steps "to the death." Grant's military advisors in Washington looked askance at sending such a young, hotheaded commander on so vital a mission. But Sheridan more than vindicated Grant's faith, ultimately dealing a smashing defeat to Early's army. Sheridan's Shenandoah Valley successes bolstered Northern morale and furnished inspiring fodder for Lincoln's ultimately victorious reelection campaign, as well as "the germ of one of the most beautiful friendships in history," according to Grant's wartime aide-de-camp and biographer Adam Badeau. From that time forward, Badeau writes, Grant "relied on Sheridan" as completely as he relied on his other great friend General William Tecumseh Sherman, whose victorious march through Georgia also helped to resuscitate Lincoln's reelection campaign.[5]

A wiry and excitable young commander during the war, Sheridan, at forty-four years old, with the generous girth of a prosperous burgher, was among the Army's highest-ranking officers as he set forth in New Orleans on his latest mission for Grant. But at five feet, five inches tall, he was still known as "Little Phil," and he was still excitable.

True to form, Sheridan outed himself soon enough. A few days after his arrival in New Orleans, just blocks from his hotel, as the state House of Representatives convened to seat the winners of the recent election, Democrats ambushed the proceedings. Although Republicans had apparently won enough seats in the election to maintain their majority, Democrats seized control of the House chamber, through a blend of trickery and intimidation, with help from mysterious armed operatives. Republicans, whose ranks included twenty-nine black House members, claimed this coup was the work of the White League.

Sheridan was sitting in with the local commander of U.S. forces as the legislature convened, and advised him that Governor Kellogg's request for military assistance to put the situation right should be honored. Soon a squad of U.S. bluecoats with fixed bayonets entered the House chamber and removed five Democrats illegitimately sworn in during the coup, returning control to Republicans. But the incident enraged Sheridan. In a telegram to Secretary of War William Belknap in Washington, he condemned the "spirit of defiance to all lawful authority" in Louisiana, and announced that he was assuming command of U.S. troops in the region. Then he leaked the telegram to the newspapers. So much for tourism.[6]

The day after the incident in the legislature, demonstrators crowded the public parlors of the St. Charles Hotel to protest Sheridan's insults to their state in his telegram. He responded with another blistering telegram, also leaked to the press. "I think that the terrorism now existing in Louisiana, Mississippi and Arkansas could be entirely removed and confidence and fair-dealing established by the arrest and trial of the ringleaders of the armed White Leagues," he wrote to Belknap. Sheridan offered to perform these chores himself, applying the swift justice of military tribunals instead of courts. "It is possible that if the President would issue a proclamation declaring them banditti," Sheridan said of White League leaders, "no further action need be taken, except that which would devolve upon me."

Sheridan's suite was steps away from the busy rotunda of the St. Charles Hotel, a circular grand parlor of marble floors and frescoed walls where city residents mingled with visitors. Prominent White Leaguers strolled there often. A rumor swept the rotunda that Sheridan "would soon make a demand upon the White League for their arms."

News of federal bayonets in the Louisiana legislature and Sheridan's "banditti dispatch" rocketed across the nation. The incident generated howls of outrage, more than validating Grant's assessment of public opinion. The *Picayune* condemned Sheridan for targeting "the best, the bravest and the purest citizens" of Louisiana. The *New Orleans Bulletin*, a White League mouthpiece, blasted the expulsion of Democrats from the state legislature as "the most disgraceful scene ever witnessed in a free country." But many Northerners also sympathized with the White League view of things. The Republican *New York Times* fretted that Sheridan's plan to haul "banditti" before military tribunals would take the U.S. to a dark place, the New York *World* branded Grant "a traitor and a tyrant," and the *New-York Tribune* called for his impeachment.[7]

The period after the Civil War known as Reconstruction, when federal and state policymakers erected a new regime of civil and political rights for African Americans, is often spoken of as a tragic failure. But that description is profoundly misleading. The White League and other paramilitary groups didn't launch a violent insurgency because those policies were failing, but because they were succeeding. Former slaves were voting and holding office; their children were attending public schools.

The White League's revolt against Louisiana's Republican government was part of a postwar Southern insurgency that toppled so-called Radical Reconstruction, ultimately denying full citizenship to African Americans for nearly another century. Although Reconstruction and its violent undoing constitute a chapter of surpassing importance in the larger drama of the Civil War and the end of slavery, episodes of the war proper, like Sherman's March through Georgia or Sheridan's Shenandoah Valley campaign, have gained far greater purchase in the nation's collective memory.[8]

Today's relatively dim public awareness of Reconstruction and its demise is partly a legacy of responses to the Southern insurgency in real time. When Sheridan arrived in New Orleans to take the White League's measure, Southern Republicans were near despair over the lack of public engagement with their predicament. The "butcheries" routinely inflicted on freedmen and their allies were met with "stolid indifference" by Northerners, who often seemed persuaded that reports of White League outrages were "manufactured out of whole cloth" to rile up Republican voters, just as Democrats claimed.[9]

The White League and other vigilante groups drew a considerable amount of press attention. But Southern Republicans believed that newspaper accounts minimizing the crimes of such groups, published in Democratic organs North and South, were largely responsible for the North's apparent apathy toward the plight of freedmen and their allies in the South, and the consequent lack of public support for military assistance to help them. In our own day, when an assault on the U.S. Capitol by a mob of thousands is portrayed as an innocent meander of tourists by partisan news outlets, despite exhaustive photographic evidence to the contrary, the complaints of Southern Republicans about 1870s press coverage might be easier to credit.

This Reconstruction-era pattern of minimizing vigilante violence preceded the White League and their ilk. Democratic newspapers in earlier years routinely played down outrages of the Ku Klux Klan, a precursor of the White League that terrorized freedmen and their allies to drive them away from the ballot box. Democratic newspapers, and some moderate Republican organs unsympathetic to Radical Reconstruction, not only minimized Klan outrages but at times denied the group's existence outright, insisting it was merely a hobgoblin invented to frighten Northerners into supporting punishments for the South. Such trivializations and denials flouted mountains of evidence of Klan crimes, including a congressional report running to thirteen volumes compiling extensive eyewitness testimony.

Grant addressed this sort of information warfare in his December 1874 annual message to Congress. Lamenting that "White Leagues" and other groups were spreading "terror" among those whose political action they sought to suppress, he conceded that one side of the partisan divide tended to "magnify wrongs and outrages," while the other side tended "to belittle them." He suggested that Congress might wish to assign a committee to determine whether "the alleged wrongs to colored citizens" were real, or "reports thereof were manufactured," seeming confident that such an investigation would confirm recent accounts of widespread vigilante violence.[10]

Some Republicans trying to make sense of the threat from White League–style vigilantes found new relevance in a peculiar idea floated years earlier. As the nation hurtled toward civil war and Southern states were debating whether or not to secede and join the rebellion, Virginia governor Henry A. Wise argued that they should stick inside the union to wage their fight, to keep their grip on levers of power within it. Wise was known as a bit of an eccentric. Tall, bony, wan, and whiskerless, with flowing mane and fierce, flashing eyes, he called to mind "a corpse galvanized." Southerners mostly greeted his idea of "fighting in the Union" with polite bewilderment. "I never could exactly understand how we could do it," said Eppa Hunton, a judge and delegate to the Virginia secession convention.[11]

But after the war, when former Confederate states were back in the union and Ku Klux Klan operatives unleashed a campaign of terror against freedmen and their allies, some Republicans believed that Wise's strategy had been adopted. Frederick Douglass, the celebrated abolitionist author and orator who had escaped from slavery as a young man, warned that the South, "having failed to gain its ends by a war outside of the Union, has adopted the advice given at the beginning of that war by Henry A. Wise to carry on the war within the Union." This type of war—"[c]overt, insidious, secret, striking in the darkness of night while assuming spotless robes of loyalty in the day—is far more difficult to deal with than an open foe," Douglass wrote.[12]

Federal raids and prosecutions smashed the Klan, assisted by a temporary grant of extraordinary power from Congress to the executive branch in the Enforcement Act of 1871. But Republicans in 1875 believed the White League and similar groups were picking up where the Klan left off, functioning as the military wing of the Democratic Party and waging an undeclared "war in the union" targeting freedmen and their white allies in the South with "threats, intimidation, murder and violence." Meanwhile, Democrats minimized reports of White League crimes as exaggerations or inventions of Republican "outrage mills" intended to inflame Northern opinion, and challenged the president's authority to send troops to the South to confront nonexistent threats.

Klansmen had generally kept to the shadows, but White Leaguers basked in respectability. They swore fealty to the Stars and Stripes and didn't hide their identities under hoods. Democratic newspapers chronicled their exploits in the cause of regional self-defense and compared them to heroes of the nation's founding era.[13]

Republicans in the South found themselves in a rapidly collapsing position at the start of 1875, confronting a "standing army" of terrorists at least ten thousand strong, including Louisiana White Leaguers and cognate groups in other states determined to nullify the postwar amendments by robbing the votes of black men and their white allies through murder, intimidation, and fraud.[14]

Between 1869 and 1874, white conservative rule had been restored in six Southern states, most with relatively small black populations, largely through consolidation of the white vote as ballot restrictions on former Confederates were relaxed, including: Arkansas (25 percent black), Texas (31 percent black), North Carolina (37 percent black), Tennessee (26 percent black), Virginia (42 percent black), and Georgia (46 percent black). Conservative Democrats in these states were already devising creative ways to curtail black suffrage without running afoul of the Fifteenth Amendment's prohibition against denying the right to vote "on account of race."

After Alabama, with its 48 percent black population, was "redeemed" with help from violent white vigilantes in November 1874, white conservatives fixed their sights on the four Southern states with the largest black populations, which remained under Republican control: Florida (49 percent black), Louisiana (50 percent black), Mississippi (54 percent black), and South Carolina (59 percent black). With white insurgents apparently "preparing to overrun" some of these states, Southern Republicans weighed the likelihood of the violent overthrow of Reconstruction, and spoke openly of their fears that freedmen could be returned to a status little better than slavery. Many of them believed that the next few months would offer the best and possibly only chance to prevent such outcomes.[15]

Southern Republicans pleaded with their allies in Washington for help against the emboldened white vigilantes of their region, and stressed that time for effective action was running out. Democrats would assume control of the House of Representatives on March 4, mere months away, putting them in position to block funds for federal enforcement of black voting rights. Republican leaders agreed to seek swift passage of a two-year Army appropriations bill and a new enforcement act that would again give Grant the extraordinary power to suspend the writ of habeas corpus, a power he had used in the federal campaign to subdue the Ku Klux Klan. Republicans would also make a last-minute push to fulfill the promise of the Thirteenth and Fourteenth Amendments with the passage of a new civil rights bill, to outlaw racial discrimination in public accommodations, transportation, entertainment, and public schools across the nation.

Lucius Q. C. Lamar, a prominent Democratic congressman from Mississippi, largely agreed with the assessment of Southern Republicans about their vulnerability. Writing to a friend just before Christmas, Lamar gloated that "Grant is lost & the Republican Party is lost unless he can plunge the South into war & get this Congress to arm him with extraordinary powers & money before the 4th March."[16]

As Lamar's appraisal of the political landscape suggests, when Sheridan returned to New Orleans just before New Year's Day 1875, the circumstances bore striking similarities to those of his 1864 Shenandoah Valley campaign, when the Northern war effort and emancipation itself seemed to hang in the balance. The stakes in 1875 were again monumental: to maintain the new regime of black civil and political rights, or surrender those dearly won gains to yet another Southern insurrection. Once again, the mood of a Northern public disillusioned with endless sectional strife promised to play a pivotal role, and the time for taking effective action was fleeting.

Sheridan's return to New Orleans brought him back to the place where Reconstruction began in 1862 amid a still-raging Civil War. After Northern forces captured New Orleans, the South's largest, most cosmopolitan city, Lincoln assigned agents to encourage union loyalists there to write a new state constitution that did not permit slavery, so he could engineer the rapid readmission of a "reconstructed" Louisiana into the federal union. Ultimately Louisiana's readmission had to wait until the war was over, but Lincoln had hoped his maneuver would create a prominent beachhead of Southern buy-in for a reunited nation, signaling to the world that the Confederacy was doomed and hastening the war's end.

Culturally rich Louisiana was also the place where Reconstruction's promise "soared highest and fell hardest," according to historian Lawrence N. Powell. He attributes some of the state's soaring promise in that moment to the so-called free people of color in New Orleans, part of a sizable population of mixed-race, often light-skinned Louisianians of African descent who had been free since well before the Civil War. Although white people still treated these "free negroes" as members of an inferior caste, many were prosperous and well educated, and used their advantages to promote the cause of black rights after emancipation. Louis Charles Roudanez, a free Negro physician in New Orleans who had studied medicine in Paris, founded the *New*

Orleans Tribune, the nation's first black-owned daily newspaper and a major voice in the era's revolutionary politics. Roudanez and other free men of color were "the driving force" behind Louisiana's remarkable 1868 constitution, Powell writes, including its pioneering integrated-schools clause.

Former slaves also sustained the soaring promise of Reconstruction in Louisiana. Henry Adams cofounded a group of intrepid freedmen who roamed the region gathering intelligence on plantation working conditions to help job-hunting former slaves avoid abusive placements. Adams also put his life on the line as a scout for federal soldiers seeking to contain white vigilante violence.

So-called carpetbaggers played a constructive role as well, despite the insults heaped on them by white Southerners. Vermont native Marshall Twitchell commanded a company of United States Colored Troops during the Civil War, moved to New Orleans to launch a branch of the Freedmen's Bureau, then helped to establish a flourishing community along the Red River in north Louisiana, where he pursued numerous real estate investments and was elected to the state senate with overwhelming support from black voters.

Despite his successes, Twitchell was fastened with a wretched fate during a particularly gruesome episode of white backlash, the sort that plagued Louisiana whenever the promise of Reconstruction soared there. Such episodes generally took the form of flagrant election tampering and terrorism by white vigilantes, including two of the ugliest outbreaks of mass political violence in American history, the legacies of which redound to this day: the New Orleans Massacre of 1866 and the Colfax Massacre of 1873, "the bloodiest single instance of racial carnage in the Reconstruction era," according to historian Eric Foner.[17]

As Reconstruction buckled in Louisiana after a series of assaults by white vigilantes in 1874 and early 1875, Sheridan's return to New Orleans stirred hopes that its promise might soar anew. This was not entirely wishful thinking. About eighteen months earlier, after a similarly bleak period of backlash and despair, Reconstruction's prospects had risen abruptly to previously unseen heights, and the state appeared to be poised for a happy ending to this most turbulent era after all.

CHAPTER 1

THERE IS LOVE ENOUGH

When construction was completed on Exposition Hall in 1871, the striking Renaissance-style edifice was a bulletin in brick and mortar from the New Orleans business elite, announcing that the city was moving on from the Civil War's wreckage. Its "spectacular" interior space, bathed in light from nearly wall-to-wall windows, was designed to showcase the latest household and workplace products, from "magic curtains" raised and lowered with the yank of a cord, to fireproof safes and deodorizing "earth closets." Such marvels roosted in kaleidoscopic vistas, framed by twin staircases spiraling upward to a concert hall that ranked among the nation's grandest.[1]

On the evening of July 15, 1873, the so-called Unification Movement convened at Exposition Hall for a public meeting that was also something of a new-product rollout. Unification was a campaign for cooperation between black and white Louisianians backed by many leaders of the New Orleans business community. While racial brotherhood was not likely to become one of the state's top exports, the movement had preoccupied the local press for weeks and was steadily gaining converts. A "vast throng of people" showed up for the public meeting, despite the evening's oppressive heat. Many seemed to believe this gathering could shape the future of the state, if not the nation. A banner draped above the speaker's platform bore the motto:

Equal Rights—One Flag—One Country—One People

The *New Orleans Times* reported that white people outnumbered black people in the audience four to one; the *Picayune* counted more black attendees, if just barely. But all agreed that for several weeks prior to the July 15 meeting, fifty white leaders had huddled periodically with fifty black leaders—at first in secret, then in public—to hammer out a program for unifying the races. Some of those leaders were seated on the speakers platform. The results of their work had been presented to the public in a series of resolutions published in newspapers under the heading "An Appeal for the Unification of the People of Louisiana."

The jagged period since the end of the Civil War in Louisiana had been consumed in political strife and racial violence, and disfigured by a pair of mass atrocities. In July 1866, a white mob in New Orleans butchered forty-four black men and wounded over one hundred others, alerting the nation to grave unfinished business in the former Confederacy little more than a year after the war ended. In April 1873, just twelve weeks before the Unification meeting, white militiamen in the town of Colfax, Louisiana, slaughtered about seventy black men, many of whom were their prisoners.[2]

The Unification Appeal addressed these apocalyptic trends in its opening lines, warning that "Louisiana is now threatened with death in every vital organ of her moral, material and political being." Blaming "unnatural divisions" for this state of affairs, the appeal also asserted "an abiding faith that there is love enough for Louisiana among her sons to unite them."

The meeting's first speaker was Isaac N. Marks, a prominent businessman and perhaps Unification's chief visionary. While Marks had backed secession, and his sons fought in the Confederate Army, he believed it was time for white Southerners to accept the "accomplished facts" of black rights. Among his many civic commitments, he ran a charity that ministered to families of deceased firefighters. He now pursued a broader ministry, calling on the crowd "to lay upon the altar of our country all the prejudices of the past; to recognize all the citizens of the United States as equals before the law." Marks asked his listeners "to unanimously ratify" the remarkable resolutions developed by leaders of both races and lately published in the press.[3]

In the name of unification, the resolutions called for upholding, once and for all, the political and civil rights of black Louisianians. While their rights had been written into state and federal law to some extent in the wake of the Civil War, such enactments often became dead letters in the face of white resistance. The Unification resolutions promised to combat that resistance by mobilizing a cadre of Southern white champions for black rights: "We shall advocate by speech, and pen, and deed, the equal and impartial exercise by every citizen of Louisiana of every civil and political right guaranteed by the Constitution and laws of the United States, and by the laws of honor, brotherhood and fair dealing."

The resolutions promised a campaign for the rights of all Louisianians to frequent "places of public resort," to travel "on all vehicles of public conveyance" on equal terms with other passengers, and to send their children to "any of our public schools." Some resolutions even called for steps toward black economic equality, including recommendations that banks, insurance companies, and other public corporations concede black shareholders' right to sit on boards of directors; that foundries and factories hire black mechanics and workmen; and that large landowners in rural districts sell plots to aspiring black farmers, fostering "a political conservatism which is the offspring of proprietorship." The resolutions also promised to advocate for "an equal distribution" of public offices among black and white candidates, and condemned "all acts of violence," with the carnage at Colfax still raw in memory.[4]

As Marks read the resolutions aloud, he was stopped by a shouted question from the crowd: "Will you send *your* children to public schools?" The Unification-friendly audience responded with "an uproar of hisses and other demonstrations," the *New Orleans Times* reported.

The city desegregated its public schools to a significant extent for several years during Reconstruction, a feat that would not be matched elsewhere in the South until 1954 and was rare even in the North during the 1870s. The effort represented Louisiana's attempt to begin implementing the schools-desegregation provision of its new state constitution, and was viewed as something of an experiment by state officials.

Intense public resistance greeted the rollout. White parents pulled their children out of the city's public schools en masse and new, all-white private schools quickly proliferated to accommodate them. But roughly half of the white students remained in public schools with their new black classmates, and many white students who initially fled gradually returned. About a year into the experiment, overall attendance was up and racial disturbances were few in the city's public schools, according to Thomas W. Conway, the state superintendent of education, who launched the desegregation push. "The children were simply kind to each other," Conway reported. Even some bitter foes of the policy revised their opinions, including the conservative *Daily Picayune*, which reported in September 1872 that many classrooms found to be "thinly attended" during the previous school year were now "quite full." Overall the paper detected "the strongest indications of the continued and deep affection of the people for our public school system."[5]

Despite the prevailing equanimity in the city's public schools, white anxieties about desegregation and the potential for "social equality" with black people persisted in New Orleans, as the shouted Exposition Hall comments suggested, and such feelings were much more powerful in rural Louisiana. Still, misgivings about Unification seemed to be receding in the city. The mostly white business community largely backed the movement, for pragmatic rather than humanitarian reasons, seeing it as the best way to wrest power from the alliance of Republican "carpetbaggers" and black voters that controlled the state government. "It is our only hope of salvation," a prominent white businessman told the *New Orleans Times*. "The negroes, unless drawn over to us, will constantly elect carpet-baggers. Their election means increased taxation, and this means total and absolute ruin."

While Unification championed policies cherished by the Republican Party, many Republicans were initially wary of the movement. "Is It a Trick?" editors of the *New Orleans Republican* asked when Unification first stirred, correctly surmising that white proponents were trying to drive a wedge between freedmen and carpetbaggers allied with them. If those pushing Unification truly backed black rights, the editors said, "Let them join the Republican Party, by whom all the rights and privileges of citizenship have been given to the negro."[6]

Despite such misgivings, Unification made rapid progress in the city. The business-friendly *New Orleans Times* was an early booster, running interviews with movement figures in its "Round About Town" column. Unification notched another influential backer when the conservative *Daily Picayune*, despite its frequent complaints about "negro rule," lavishly endorsed the movement in early June. "Let there be a union, then, on terms of the broadest liberality," the *Picayune* said. "Let there be an end of prejudice and proscription, and for the future let there be no differences of opinion dividing our people except upon questions of governmental policy."[7]

When the Unification resolutions were unveiled in mid-June, even the deeply skeptical editors of the *New Orleans Republican* let down their guard and embraced the movement. "The barriers of prejudice have been swept away by a mighty effort," the editors gushed, while also boasting that Unification was an epic "surrender" to Republicans, a signal that the party's mission was accomplished.[8]

Unification had clearly established a beachhead in New Orleans, but the Louisiana countryside was far less receptive. "[W]e abhor it in every fibre of our being," the *Ouachita Telegraph* wailed, its editors

proclaiming their "natural disgust" that such measures to benefit Negroes had been contemplated. The *Shreveport Times* also spoke from
the viscera, finding the Unification movement "repulsive" and its leaders "absurdly ignorant" of sentiment in country parishes. Some Republicans sided with the critics. A correspondent in the party stronghold
of Baton Rouge said Unification's leaders promised more than they
could deliver and had "no sympathizers in this district."[9]

The Unification movement seemed to be banking on its biracial
roster of high-profile backers to sway public opinion. None of these
leading citizens was more admired than former Confederate General
P. G. T. Beauregard, chairman of the movement's Resolutions Committee, whose stature in the South approached that of the revered
Robert E. Lee himself.

Pierre Gustave Toutant-Beauregard grew up on his wealthy family's plantation in St. Bernard Parish, just south of New Orleans, an
area settled by Frenchmen in colonial times that remained "fiercely
French" when he was born there in 1818. Like other so-called French
Creoles, Beauregard spoke French exclusively as a child and lingering traces of an accent contributed to his aura of romance. At five
foot seven, 145 pounds, he was known as "Little Creole," among other
nicknames. Dark and handsome, with an olive complexion, prominent
cheekbones, and large, soulful eyes, Beauregard was trailed by rumors
of extramarital liaisons, "most of them baseless," according to his biographer. An investigator looking into potential treason charges against
prominent Confederates after the war discovered that Beauregard's
personal papers "consisted mainly of mash notes from the general's
female admirers."[10]

Beauregard's warm relationship with the Southern people began to
blossom even before the war's first shots were fired. After he assumed
command of Confederate forces at Charleston, South Carolina, in
March 1861, tasked with confronting the Union garrison at nearby
Fort Sumter, it soon became clear that the local populace was smitten

with its dashing new general. "It is no exaggeration to say that he was regarded as a demigod," his biographer reports.

Beauregard worship swelled across the Confederacy after his capture of Fort Sumter and subsequent victory at Manassas, or Bull Run, in Virginia. He was the South's first great hero of the Civil War. Newspapers extolled his grit and peerless generalship, although Sumter had largely been a fireworks display—with no casualties—and Manassas was an accidental victory, achieved despite "grave errors" by Beauregard that could have brought disaster. An astute Richmond editor dubbed him Beauregard *Felix*, affixing the Latin word for lucky to his name.[11]

Babies were named after Beauregard, as were steamboats, racehorses, and a silk cape for women. After the war, his fame doubtless helped him find a level of success in business that eluded many career soldiers. He also weighed invitations to serve in foreign armies, an option pursued by other former Confederate officers. Rumors of such arrangements were common press fodder. The *New Orleans Crescent* quoted "a gentleman of position" in July 1866 concerning whispers that Beauregard might accept a leadership role in the Italian army. "If so," the gentleman said, "there would be some hope for Italy."[12]

Unification was not Beauregard's first excursion into politics. He had joined conservative white businessmen in 1872 to launch the Reform Party, which mainly sought tax cuts and lower government spending, but also supported the rights of black Louisianians, hoping to attract enough of their votes to topple the state's Republican "carpetbagger" government. Black voters felt little enthusiasm for the Reform Party's vague promises to secure their rights and the fledgling enterprise flopped. Beauregard was well positioned to apply lessons from this failure the following year as his committee drafted the groundbreaking Unification resolutions. Newspapers often referred to them as "the Beauregard resolutions."

As Unification's most celebrated proponent by far, Beauregard naturally drew fire from the movement's critics. "General Beauregard must be crazy," the *Ouachita Telegraph* raged. Did he suppose that Louisiana could prosper as "a Negro state" after his Unification scheme took effect? Editors of the *Morning Star and Catholic Messenger* deduced that if Beauregard had truly read the Unification resolutions, if he had actually endorsed them "with full knowledge" of their "galling" provisions, then "the glory that rose around his name on many a proud battle-day has gone down forever."[13]

The Confederacy's legendary *beau sabreur* was unaccustomed to such rough handling. In an address "to the people of Louisiana" published in newspapers across the state, Beauregard answered his critics. Stung by their "ungracious and illiberal" comments, he offered a pragmatic defense of Unification, calling it simply "a candid and frank acknowledgement" of the established "legal facts" that black citizens now possessed the same "rights and privileges" as white Louisianians. But Beauregard insisted there was power in this simple acknowledgment: it would remove the impetus for black Louisianians to work with carpetbaggers, undercutting those "unscrupulous adventurers" from other states to restore "faithful administration" of Louisiana government.

Ridding the state of carpetbaggers might not have satisfied white critics of Unification deranged by the idea of an approaching "social equality" of the races, who worried that Beauregard's program was a shortcut to that dreaded destination. Beauregard actually shared their prejudices about black people, but he dismissed their concerns about social equality, claiming that only "malice or stupidity" could detect anything in the Unification resolutions that would interfere in private social relations. When we travel or dine in restaurants, we often share public spaces "with thieves, prostitutes, gamblers and others who have worse sins to answer for than the accident of color," Beauregard explained unflatteringly, but "no one ever supposed that we thereby assented to the social equality of these people with ourselves."[14]

One of the most prominent black leaders of the Unification movement, Dr. Louis Charles Roudanez, also sought to defuse the explosive "social equality" issue. "We do not ask for social equality," he said in the spring of 1873, as Unification was first stirring. "We know that the thing is impossible. But we do insist on having equal civil rights." Roudanez believed that once black rights were accepted, social relations between the races "would soon adjust themselves quietly."[15]

Although he was regarded as a member of the vilified Negro caste, the light-skinned Roudanez was about one-eighth black. Born free before the war, he was one of thousands of so-called free men of color in Louisiana, perhaps the wealthiest, best-educated "free negroes" in the antebellum United States. Also known as "creoles of color," they were mostly descendants of unions between enslaved black women and French or Spanish men in Louisiana's colonial past. White men in such relationships, under prevailing customs of French and Spanish culture, often gave the women and children their freedom and bequeathed property to them, sometimes including slaves, a level of familiarity unheard-of in English colonies. White men were legally prohibited from marrying slaves or free blacks everywhere in the United States, but these coupling patterns persisted after Louisiana became a state under a system of sanctioned concubinage known as *placage*, whereby a white man agreed to provide financial support to his live-in black mistress. The practice contributed to a gradual "whitening" of the free-Negro community as mixed-race girls from such unions grew up and bore children with white men.

Roudanez's father, Louis, a white man of French heritage, immigrated to Louisiana as a young boy with his prosperous family, from the French colony of Saint Domingue following the Haitian Revolution there in 1791. A free woman of color, Aimée Potens, gave birth in 1815 to Louis Roudanez's first son, Jean-Baptiste, in New Orleans, and in 1823 she delivered his second son, Louis Charles Roudanez, in St. James Parish.

Louisiana's free-Negro population was the largest in the lower South in 1860, numbering around 18,000, with about 10,000 clustered in and around New Orleans. Louisiana's antebellum free people of color had more liberty than free blacks in other states, including the right to marry, testify in court, and learn a profession. Roudanez made the most of it, attending private schools in New Orleans and studying at the prestigious Faculté de Médecine de Paris, where he earned his MD degree in 1848. He had been operating a successful medical practice in New Orleans for years.

Roudanez and Beauregard were remarkably similar in some ways for leaders on opposite sides of the racial divide. Both were prosperous and exceptionally well educated—Beauregard graduated at the top of his class at West Point. Both were trim and handsome, Beauregard strikingly so, while the taciturn Roudanez's good looks were more a matter of sturdy symmetries. Both were native French speakers who understood the racial ambiguities of the Louisiana creole experience. While light-skinned free men of color like Roudanez were routinely taken for white, Beauregard was also known to sow racial confusion. Shortly after the Civil War, an apparently drunk former Confederate soldier hollered at the olive-complexioned general: "I believe you are a damn nigger."

Despite the relatively privileged status of Louisiana's free people of color, even someone as accomplished as the handsome and dignified Dr. Roudanez suffered routine slights and insults. At the theater, he was seated among riffraff in "a cock-loft against the ceiling," he bitterly recalled for a reporter. Hotels assigned him lodgings "that a deck-hand would indignantly decline."

A lifetime of such humiliations fed Roudanez's political activism. He had great hopes for Unification, if it could manage to avoid the Reform Party's big mistake: failing to incorporate "equal rights" for all citizens of African descent into its platform. If Unification truly embraced those rights, it would "sweep the state like wildfire," Roudanez predicted, and carpetbaggers would become "a thing of the past."[16]

Roudanez himself, as a member of Beauregard's committee, had a hand in shaping the Unification movement's extraordinary resolutions, which went further to accommodate the interests of black people than any other agreement by white Southerners of the era. The public was asked to ratify those resolutions at the July 15 meeting in Exposition Hall, which was seen as a make-or-break moment for Unification. As Isaac Marks, the evening's first speaker, completed his presentation to the overflow crowd, he made his pitch: Louisiana would know "neither peace, nor prosperity, nor good government" until the Unification resolutions were put into "practical effect."

A leader of the previous year's failed Reform Party push, Marks now called himself an "unswerving advocate" of the Unification manifesto, declaring: "I religiously believe that it is the only means left to us to rescue our state."[17]

Warm applause greeted the announcement of the next speaker, former judge William Randolph, a gifted orator beloved for his light-hearted style. But as the crowd watched the stage expectantly, the judge failed to appear. It was said that he was confined to his bed with a sudden malady. Judge Randolph was among the most prominent of the fifty white leaders on the Resolutions Committee and his perspective would be missed. But he was not to be the only eminent no-show on this night. Voices in the crowd were soon whispering that yet another white leader would not be in attendance, a man of vastly greater fame than anyone else on the rostrum, whose very name was synonymous with the Unification Movement—the beloved Beauregard himself. No reason would be given for the great man's absence.[18]

Apart from a brief, apologetic statement by a stand-in for Judge Randolph, there would be no further remarks from Unification's white leaders on this most essential evening, despite their solemn pledge to "advocate by speech, and pen, and deed" for the movement's agenda.

Several black Unification leaders were still expected to address the crowd, although Roudanez would not be among them. The taciturn physician was not known as a strong public speaker, and well-off freeborn men of color like him were thought to hold little sway with struggling former slaves in any case. But Roudanez would play a role before the evening was over, perhaps fittingly. Many white Louisianians saw Unification as a trade-off to contain the state's newly ascendant black voters, and few had done more than Roudanez to put ballots in their hands.[19]

Roudanez's campaign to secure black voting rights had begun over a decade earlier, focused at first on extending the franchise to free men of color like himself.

After Union forces captured New Orleans in April 1862, the atmosphere crackled with revolution. Enslaved African Americans from nearby plantations swarmed Union Army bivouacs seeking asylum or the chance to take up arms in the righteous war on their so-called masters. Free people of color also seized the moment. Members of the Louisiana Native Guard, a free-black militia, flouted Confederate orders to abandon the city and offered their services to General Benjamin F. Butler, commander of Union occupying forces, who was preparing for a Rebel counteroffensive. Butler soon overcame his wariness about the free-black militiamen and invited them to join the Union war effort, assuring his superiors in Washington "they will be loyal."

The First Regiment of the Louisiana Native Guard, composed of free-black militiamen and former slaves, was mustered into service on September 27, 1862—less than a week after Lincoln issued the preliminary Emancipation Proclamation—forming the U.S. Army's first officially sanctioned all-black unit. On the same day, determined to play an active role in the political changes roiling Louisiana, Roudanez and other prosperous free men of color launched *L'Union*, the South's first black newspaper. "We inaugurate today a new era in the destiny of the South," editor Paul Trévigne wrote in *L'Union*'s debut issue. Published twice a week, in French, the language of its target audience among Louisiana's free people of color, *L'Union* called for the abolition of slavery and beseeched readers to enlist in the armed struggle against the Confederacy as a demonstration of manhood, to bolster their case for political equality.[20]

Operating a black newspaper in the Confederacy's largest city carried its own element of physical risk. Planters "spoke openly of ransacking the printing plant and destroying the house" where *L'Union* based its operations, recalled one former editor, who said the paper "formed the center around which the boldest colored men of New Orleans rallied."[21]

On the front page of its debut issue, *L'Union* condemned the institution of slavery for nullifying the humanity of its black victims, reducing them "to the level of a farm animal." The privileged free men of color in *L'Union*'s orbit believed their fate was linked to slavery, and that its demise would topple barriers of prejudice blocking their own progress. They yearned above all for the right to vote, viewing it as a fulcrum for attacking racial injustice more broadly.

The agenda of federal officials in the occupied portion of Louisiana seemed to offer free men of color a feast of potential voting opportunities. Lincoln wanted loyal white "Unionists" there to organize a new state government without slavery, which federal authorities could then recognize as the "free state" of Louisiana, welcoming it back into the Union's embrace. This effort would involve elections for delegates to write a new state constitution, elections for approving that constitution, and elections for choosing officials to run the new state government. *L'Union* urged free-black leaders "to demand finally a place at the political banquet which the Unionists of Louisiana are now preparing."[22]

In November 1863, free men of color in New Orleans sent a petition to General George F. Shepley, military governor of Louisiana, asking to be registered as voters so they could take part "in the reorganization of civil government." The petition was signed by one thousand free blacks, including entrepreneurs and artisans who paid taxes on millions of dollars of assessed wealth. Many of the petitioners had put their lives on the line serving in the Union Army. The free blacks also sent their petition to General Nathaniel P. Banks, the new commander of U.S. forces in the region. Neither General Shepley nor General Banks bothered to reply.

The New Orleans free men of color decided to go over the generals' heads and convey their petition directly to President Lincoln himself. At the end of February 1864, they dispatched a two-man delegation to Washington, including wine merchant Arnold Bertonneau and Jean-Baptiste Roudanez, an engineer who was also publisher of *L'Union* and the older brother of L. C. Roudanez.[23]

When the Louisiana envoys arrived in Washington for their interview with the president, they met first with a group of congressional Radicals, including Senator Charles Sumner of Massachusetts and Representative William Kelley of Pennsylvania. These two would emerge as strong advocates for extending the franchise to freedmen, in part as a political counterweight against hostile former Confederates after the war. Within days of this meeting, the Louisiana envoys attached an addendum to their petition seeking voting rights also for black men who had been born into slavery, although white advisors in New Orleans had counseled that such a step was politically premature amid significant prejudice against extending the franchise to "ignorant" former slaves. Perhaps to quell such objections, the addendum stated that "qualifications" for the right to vote, presumably such as basic literacy, could be included as long as they were applied equally to "white and colored citizens."

Bertonneau and Roudanez found Lincoln to be a sympathetic listener. But he could not endorse their petition unless doing so was a "military necessity"—something that would help to end the war and reunite the country. It was easy to imagine Lincoln's endorsement having the opposite effect, since even abolitionists were divided on whether the time was ripe to push for black suffrage.

Although Lincoln denied their request, the free-black envoys from New Orleans seem to have made an excellent impression on him. The day after their visit, he wrote to Michael Hahn, who had recently been elected governor of the "free state" of Louisiana, after New Orleans free men of color had petitioned unsuccessfully for the right to vote. White delegates to the state's approaching constitutional convention would soon write a new state charter, deciding things like who could vote in future elections. "I barely suggest," Lincoln wrote to the governor, "whether some of the colored people may not be let in" as voters; "for instance, the very intelligent, and especially those who have fought gallantly in our ranks. They would probably help, in some trying time to come, to keep the jewel of liberty in the family of freedom." Lincoln closed his letter by clarifying that his thoughts on these matters amounted to "only a suggestion, not to the public, but to you alone."

Delegates to the constitutional convention had little sympathy for granting voting rights to black men. But under pressure from Governor Hahn, they took a step in that direction, empowering the legislature to enfranchise black men "deemed entitled" by "intellectual fitness," wealth, or military service, but not requiring lawmakers to do so.[24]

Knowing nothing of Lincoln's back-channel efforts on their behalf, the free-black envoys from Louisiana left Washington believing their mission had failed. But if they were disappointed by their encounter with the president, their earlier meeting with Radical Republicans in Congress was apparently bearing fruit, nudging them toward regarding the freedman less as pathetic victims and more as essential allies.[25]

Soon L'Union's pages showed a new solicitude toward former slaves. The paper had sometimes addressed them in patronizing tones, as when it warned that freedom was no excuse for "anarchy and laziness." Now L'Union proclaimed for the first time that former slaves might also be granted voting rights and called for "harmony among all the descendants of the African race."[26]

The free black men in L'Union's orbit were not impressed with the constitutional convention's decision to allow some future legislature to grant certain black men the right to vote. They believed their suffrage rights should have been inscribed in the constitution itself. But as the convention finished its work, L'Union faced more pressing concerns. Financial problems threatened to silence the paper's distinctive voice. Acting swiftly to address the crisis, L. C. Roudanez decided to start a new publication, effectively reinventing L'Union to face the battles ahead. He purchased the struggling newspaper's printing equipment, and two days after *L'Union*'s final issue appeared, Roudanez launched the *New Orleans Tribune*.

L'Union had been moving toward a closer engagement with the broader black population and the *Tribune* picked up where it left off, vowing to continue its predecessor's mission as an "organ of the oppressed class." Published in English, the language of most former slaves, as well as French, the *Tribune* appeared three times a week at first, but became the first black-owned U.S. daily newspaper before the year was out.[27]

Roudanez hired the remarkable Jean-Charles Houzeau, a white Belgian astronomer, naturalist, and frequent *L'Union* contributor, to take over as the *Tribune*'s editor. While a white European intellectual might not seem like the ideal choice to run the first black-owned U.S. daily newspaper, Houzeau's recent experiences demonstrated a capacity for cultivating topics of concern to formerly enslaved Louisianians. When his pro-democracy political views cost him his job at the Royal Observatory in Brussels, Houzeau embarked on a U.S. sojourn to research and write. Along the way, he helped a group of fugitive slaves escape to Mexico from Confederate Texas after a "Vigilance Committee" there got wind of his abolitionist sympathies, forcing him to flee for his life. Houzeau wrote a short book about his brush with "The White Terror in Texas," and followed it up with a book on slavery in the United States and the case for abolition.[28]

Houzeau saw Roudanez and the prosperous free men of color clustered around the *Tribune* as a "vanguard of the African population of the United States," who would help the nation "deal with the consequences of this great reform"—the abolition of slavery. He took over as editor in November 1864 and set about helping Roudanez to reimagine the *Tribune* as "the organ of five million black and brown-skinned men." Houzeau's top priority was transforming the *Tribune*'s English-language section from a "cut and paste collection" of items from other newspapers into the paper's "major weapon of attack and defense."[29]

To secure maximum impact for the *Tribune*'s thrusts, Houzeau sent copies of the paper to Northern editors and public officials, including members of Congress, some of whom salted their speeches with quotations from its pages. He also staffed the *Tribune* with "an extraordinary group of black, brown and white workers," including talented holdovers like Paul Trévigne, formerly *L'Union*'s top editor, and newcomers like the versatile J. Clovis Laizer, son of a free woman of color and a Swiss immigrant, who was fluent in French, Spanish, and English.

Operating from a dowdy French Quarter townhouse, Houzeau and his crew rapidly raised the *Tribune*'s profile. Historian John Rose Ficklen, a Southerner with little sympathy for Reconstruction Era radicals, described the *Tribune* as "a very dangerous organ of opposition" to Louisiana's ruling conservatives, "vigorously edited in the interests of the negroes" and wielding "immense" influence in Washington.[30]

The *Tribune* crusaded for the desegregation of schools and streetcars, and equal access to restaurants, theaters, and other public places. It attacked federal authorities over their so-called Free Labor Plan, devised by General Banks to harness the state's agricultural output, which tied freedmen to yearly labor contracts restricting travel, socializing, even whiskey consumption, all enforced by the Union Army. Lincoln regarded the Banks system as a temporary expedient allowing planters and former slaves to "gradually live themselves out of their old relation to one another," with benefits for all: planters secured a stable workforce; freedmen received wages, however meager, and schools for their children. But the *Tribune* likened the Banks plan to antebellum slave codes, with freedmen confined in their old plantation quarters after dark, requiring written permission to visit friends or "take a walk in the neighborhood." The plan classified black laborers as "freemen," but the *Tribune* understood that "any white man" subjected to such constraints "will certainly call himself a slave."

The *Tribune*'s proprietors believed that progress on its many battlefronts ultimately depended on the paper's signature cause: the right to vote, and the political leverage that came with it. Roudanez and the *Tribune* fully embraced voting rights for freedmen. Apart from the matter of simple justice, it was a question of security. If freedmen weren't registered as voters, Louisiana Unionists would be swept from power by Confederates returning to the ballot box after the war, handing control of the state government to "open foes of the Union."[31]

W. E. B. Du Bois, the pioneering historian of African Americans' role in Reconstruction, credits Louisiana's free men of color with elevating the issue of black voting rights in national politics at a time when "negroes" were dismissed as "ignorant field hands," absurdly ill-suited for responsibilities of citizenship. If Lincoln's first experiment in Reconstruction had been attempted anywhere but Louisiana, with its assertive free-black population, "it is possible that the whole question of Negro suffrage would not have been raised then or perhaps for many years after," Du Bois writes.

Congressional Radicals blocked Louisiana's effective readmission into the Union largely because Lincoln's Reconstruction plan did not deliver black voting rights. By April 1865, even Lincoln felt compelled to address the matter publicly.

He chose a uniquely joyous occasion: the evening after Grant accepted the surrender of Confederate General Robert E. Lee at the courthouse in Appomattox, Virginia, all but ending the Civil War. As the happy news spread, a festive throng accumulated on the North Lawn of the White House, erupting in wild cheers when the gangly president appeared at a second-story window to speak. After thanking "General Grant, his skillful officers and brave men," and voicing "hopes of a righteous and speedy peace," Lincoln abruptly pivoted to the rather trying topic of Reconstruction in Louisiana.

Lincoln made the case for welcoming Louisiana back into "proper practical relations" with the Union. Alluding to the unhappy Radicals in Congress who were blocking that very outcome, he acknowledged that some found it "unsatisfactory" that Louisiana had not granted voting rights "to the colored man." Lincoln then made a historic revelation, stating that he personally favored conferring the right to vote on two classes of black men: "the very intelligent" and "those who serve our cause as soldiers." No U.S. president had ever before publicly called for extending the franchise to black men.

Of course, Lincoln was merely repeating suggestions about black suffrage he had offered to the governor of Louisiana months earlier, after meeting with J. B. Roudanez and Arnold Bertonneau, free men of color from New Orleans. On that occasion, during an election year, Lincoln had asked the governor to keep those suggestions private. Perhaps the now safely reelected president, Confederate surrender in hand, viewed the risk of triggering a political backlash with an open endorsement of black suffrage as more manageable.

But Lincoln's words triggered at least one observer in the joyous crowd outside the White House. "That means [black] citizenship," a startled John Wilkes Booth snarled to his companions. The handsome young actor and fierce Southern partisan then issued a fateful promise: "That is the last speech he will ever make." Three days later, Booth strolled into the Presidential Box at Ford's Theatre and shot Lincoln in the back of the head.[32]

Radicals had long foreseen trouble in Lincoln's free state of Louisiana when former Confederate soldiers returned home after the war, especially if voting rights were not extended to black residents so they could help protect Union war gains—and themselves. With Lincoln out of the picture, the postwar reality proved even worse than the Radicals feared. Lincoln's vice president, former U.S. senator from Tennessee Andrew Johnson, had famously proclaimed that leading Confederates were "traitors" who "must be punished." But when Johnson assumed the presidency after Lincoln's death, his surprisingly lenient amnesty and pardon policies allowed former Confederates to quickly re-enter the political system as voters and candidates.

Lincoln had endorsed limited black voting rights just before his death, apparently agreeing with Radicals that it would help secure Union war gains against former Confederates returning to Southern voting booths. But Johnson opposed black suffrage. A former slave-holder who spent most of his career as a Democrat before he became Lincoln's second-term vice president on a National Union Party ticket, Johnson was deeply racist and fought Republican efforts to expand the rights and opportunities of freedmen.

James Madison Wells, the Unionist who succeeded Hahn as governor of Louisiana weeks before Lincoln's death, chose to ride the state's new political currents. He catered to returning Rebels and conservative planters, awarding them coveted appointments as judges, mayors, and district attorneys, among many other posts. The *Tribune* mockingly published a list of the signers of Louisiana's secession ordinance to help Wells locate the best traitors to fill government jobs.[33]

The return of ex-Confederates to Louisiana was accompanied by a wave of violence against former slaves and Union loyalists. Corpses of black men were found floating in the Red River and hanging from trees near Shreveport, some with their throats slashed. Former Confederate soldiers swelling the ranks of the New Orleans police meted out "violence and injury upon the freedmen almost without limit," recalled Thomas W. Conway, then a Union general who served as assistant commissioner of the Louisiana Freedmen's Bureau.[34]

Union loyalists began to feel as if they had been on the losing side of the late war, while ex-Confederates strutted like conquerors. In the November 1865 statewide election, former Confederates who had fought to destroy the Union could vote, but black men who had fought to save it could not. Former Rebels easily took control of the legislature, winning every parish but one.

In the new, Rebel-dominated legislature, the doorkeeper wore a Confederate uniform and lawmakers rushed to enact so-called Black Codes, which had already been adopted in Louisiana municipalities and other former Confederate states. These laws were often attempts to push freedmen into agricultural labor by requiring them to be employed, but limiting their options for work beyond the plantation. A freedman found without proof of employment could be arrested for "vagrancy," and while he served a sentence of forced plantation labor, his children could be "apprenticed" to a white planter until the age of eighteen for females, and twenty-one for males. Other laws forbade freedmen from carrying weapons or holding public meetings.[35]

Many Northerners condemned Black Codes as attempts to restore a form of slavery and upset the war's verdict. After Congress reconvened in December 1865 for the first time since Lincoln's assassination, Republican majorities won passage of a bill giving the Freedmen's Bureau more power to protect the rights of former slaves. They also passed the Civil Rights Act of 1866, which defined native-born freedmen as citizens and codified the basic rights of all U.S. citizens, regardless of race, including "equal benefit of all laws and proceedings for the security of person and property."

The Civil Rights Act represented the first attempt by Congress to define in legislation the freedoms afforded by the Thirteenth Amendment, which abolished slavery. Embodying the belief, generated by the Civil War, that the national government could name and protect basic rights of citizenship, the bill honored the traditional primacy of states in law enforcement, while offering former slaves avenues for redress in federal courts when confronted with discriminatory state enactments. But the bill deployed no national police or troops to enforce its terms, and was primarily aimed at official acts of injustice, even as freedmen faced a plague of random violence. The Civil Rights Act also did not address black suffrage, a topic Republican moderates still found troublesome when almost all Northern states did not extend voting rights to black men.[36]

Although the Freedmen's Bureau and civil rights measures enjoyed broad support among congressional Republicans, Johnson vetoed both. He denounced the Freedmen's Bureau as an "immense patronage," arguing that Congress had never authorized spending on such a program for "our own people." If this was too subtle, Johnson amplified the sentiments in his veto message for the Civil Rights Act, condemning it for centralizing power in Washington and somehow discriminating "against the white race" by extending citizenship privileges to black Americans.

Republicans had come to view black citizenship rights as fruits of victory in the Civil War, and they mustered the required two-thirds majorities in both houses of Congress to enact the civil rights bill over Johnson's veto in April 1866. But as Johnson's antagonism grew more manifest, Republicans sought to place the fruits of victory beyond the reach of vetoes and future hostile majorities. In June 1866, Congress approved the Fourteenth Amendment to the Constitution, granting citizenship to "all persons" born in the United States and forbidding states to deny "equal protection of the laws" to anyone within their jurisdiction.

In sending the proposed Fourteenth Amendment to the states for ratification, Republicans were also finally addressing black suffrage, if only indirectly, in part to avoid further empowering white Southerners at the expense of former slaves. Before the war, only three-fifths of slaves were counted toward congressional apportionment. But all former slaves were included in apportionment calculations, so Southern states were now poised to gain clout in Washington, even as they continued to deny freedmen the right to vote. Partly to block this perverse result, the Fourteenth Amendment mandated a reduction in congressional representation in proportion to the number of male citizens denied the franchise. Republicans thus settled for incentivizing Southern states to extend voting rights to black men, while still lacking sufficient support to enfranchise them directly.

But an aggressive new push for black voting rights soon emerged from a very surprising source: Louisiana governor James Madison Wells. As former Confederates relentlessly consolidated their power in his state, defeating the governor's New Orleans allies in snap municipal elections, they seemed less like political assets and more like wolves swallowing Louisiana whole. When reports of secret armed clubs of former Rebels stirred fears of political violence, Wells decided to join a desperate push to defang the ex-Confederate threat.

Wells had been elected in November 1865 as an opponent of black suffrage. But by the summer of 1866, the ever-flexible governor found himself agreeing with Radicals that enfranchising loyal black men was the only way to rescue Louisiana from the clutches of ex-Confederates. He and a group of free-state Unionists cooperated in a scheme to reconvene the 1864 state constitutional convention to amend the charter and award voting rights to black men, while also barring former Confederates from the ballot box.[37]

The lawfulness of this undertaking was far from clear. The Convention of 1864 "has no legal existence in 1866," the conservative *Picayune* thundered, condemning the project as "revolutionary." Even that Radical champion of black suffrage, the *New Orleans Tribune*, seemed queasy, expressing "sympathy and support" for the proposal's authors, while withholding approval of the means chosen to achieve a cherished goal.[38] New Orleans authorities, now replete with former Rebels, threatened to arrest attendees of the "illegal" convention. But General Absalom Baird, acting commander of U.S. forces in the region, cautioned that the delegates had every right to assemble and discuss public affairs. If their conclave indeed lacked "the legal right to remodel the state government," Baird advised city officials to treat it as a "harmless" joke. In any case, such questions were best left to the courts, Baird admonished, since the paramount task of both military and municipal authorities during the convention was "the maintenance of perfect order and the suppression of violence."[39]

In the days leading up to the convention, it would appear that New Orleans police made meticulous preparations to do precisely the opposite.

Over one hundred black men, most of them former Union Army soldiers, marched to the Mechanics Institute in New Orleans a little after noon on July 30, 1866, to support the cause of universal suffrage at the constitutional convention opening there that day. City police had worked furiously all weekend to arrange a proper greeting. Beginning in the early morning hours, almost all uniformed officers abandoned their beats to assemble at staging areas near the institute. Normally armed only with nightsticks, today they also carried pistols and bowie knives. Many had turned the ribbons on their uniform Panama hats inside out to conceal their badge numbers.

The Mechanics Institute, an imposing downtown landmark, was in those days home to the state House of Representatives, which met in the sweeping center hall on the main floor. The state Senate convened downstairs on the ground floor, a few doors away from the governor's office. But even the proximity of such consequential tenants would not restrain police on this day from transforming the premises into an abattoir.[40]

On the streets near the institute, fights broke out between some black marchers and rowdy white onlookers crowded nearby, many of whom were armed, as were some marchers. Gunshots were exchanged. Soon fire alarm bells rang out across New Orleans in a distinctive twelve-strike pattern, a prearranged distress signal last used in 1862 when Union occupiers broke through the city's defenses. This time police sprang from their staging areas to swarm the Mechanics Institute.[41]

Black marchers and black spectators scrambled to escape, with police and armed white civilians pursuing as if in tandem, firing their weapons with abandon. In previous days, police had enlisted the assistance of scores of white civilians for this operation, as well as armed firemen and members of secret Rebel societies. Some black men were hauled out of shops and trolleys and attacked on the street. One wounded and hobbled black fugitive was jumped by a policeman striking him flush in the head with an ax and screaming "you black son of a bitch."

Some black men sought refuge inside the Mechanics Institute, where convention delegates had been preparing for an afternoon session in the center hall. Police and the white mob shot out the institute's windows, broke down the door, and charged into the hall, firing at delegates and black spectators, even those emphatically attempting to surrender. Some victims were shot as they leapt from windows to escape the carnage.[42]

The belated arrival of General Baird with a contingent of U.S. troops around 3 p.m. finally halted the violence. He had mistakenly concluded that his presence would not be needed until later that evening, and only reached the scene hours after trouble began.

An estimated forty-four black men were killed in the Mechanics Institute assault and an additional sixty were severely wounded. Much more forbearance was shown to white convention delegates and attendees, of whom three were slain and eight were severely wounded. The police and their helpers suffered one death, likely inflicted by their own side, and ten minor injuries.[43]

The conservative New Orleans press promptly blamed the principal victims. "The riot was commenced in every instance by negroes," who were "spurred on" by white radicals in a "treasonable scheme to overturn the State government," the *New Orleans Times* proclaimed, while actually praising the police for "quelling" the violence.

General Philip H. Sheridan, the commander of U.S. forces in the Gulf of Mexico region, had been out of town during the so-called riot, but after returning to his New Orleans headquarters the next day he wired his own rather different assessment to General Grant in Washington. "The more information I obtain of the affair of the 30th in this city, the more revolting it becomes," Sheridan wrote to his commanding officer. "It was no riot, it was an absolute massacre."

Official investigations ultimately tended to ratify Sheridan's initial impressions, amassing evidence, though largely circumstantial, of a plot against the convention. One teenage student told a congressional panel that his class for July 30 was canceled because the teacher worried about police plans for a riot at nearby Mechanics Institute to "kill all" who were "members of the convention or friendly to it." An Army board of inquiry found that city police and the white mob likely followed a "prearranged" program, and conducted "the work of massacre" with a chilling ferocity—shooting, beating, and stabbing to death black men attempting to escape, and "savagely dispatching" wounded victims begging for mercy.[44]

The idea of ex-Confederate police gunning down loyal freedmen in the streets of New Orleans angered a Northern public already riled by Black Codes and the white South's project of restoring a form of slavery. The incident followed a similar police-led massacre of freedmen in Memphis, Tennessee, about twelve weeks earlier. Northerners were losing patience with President Johnson's lenient treatment of unrepentant former Rebels, and some were repulsed by his apparent endorsement of the Southern view that black men daring to seek voting rights had brought this slaughter upon themselves.

Northern voters, if only to preserve the fruits of their costly Civil War victory, decided more had to be done to protect black Southerners. In the elections of 1866, Northerners bolstered Republican power in Washington, awarding the party big, veto-proof majorities in both houses of Congress. In the face of such lopsided results, Johnson's obliging treatment of the former Rebels could no longer set the tone for federal policy. "Congress, and not the executive, is to name the conditions" for fully restoring Southern states to the Union, the *Nation* magazine proclaimed.[45]

L. C. Roudanez's *Tribune* had helped to focus Northern fury on the so-called New Orleans riot long before federal investigators compiled their reports on the event. Houzeau was an eyewitness. The *Tribune's* editor had been present at the Mechanics Institute on that day to cover the convention but soon found himself interviewing victims of police assaults and dodging showers of glass after rampaging officers shot out the Great Hall's high windows.

Later that evening, and for weeks thereafter, sometimes with a squad of U.S. Colored Troops guarding the newsroom amid threats of violence to *Tribune* staff, the nation's first black daily newspaper published accounts of the New Orleans Massacre to enlighten Northern readers about "the true character of this day," and to "arouse the moral sense of the country," Houzeau recalled in his memoir. Many Northern papers ran these articles, welcoming a source of information on the episode that was independent of Southern apologists. An issue of the Philadelphia *Evening Telegraph* carried on its front page alone four items about the riot credited to the *New Orleans Tribune*.[46]

Houzeau saw the New Orleans Massacre as a brazen attempt to "snuff out" the idea of voting rights for black men. But he believed that these enemies of black suffrage actually midwifed what they sought to terminate by awakening Northern wrath, thereby forcing federal lawmakers to confront the issue.

In March 1867, following the previous autumn's blowout elections, congressional Republicans raced to address the Southern crisis. Over Johnson's veto, they passed a series of Reconstruction acts, placing all former Confederate states under military occupation except Tennessee, which had rejoined the Union the previous year after ratifying the Fourteenth Amendment. Under this Congressional Reconstruction program, each of the occupied Southern states would be required to write a new constitution awarding voting rights to black men, and to ratify the Fourteenth Amendment, before it could resume normal relations with the Union. In addition, some officials who had served the Confederacy would be disqualified from voting or holding office.[47]

As the Gulf District's military commander, General Sheridan supervised Congressional Reconstruction in Louisiana, tossing ineligible former Confederates from voter rolls and adding newly eligible black men. He also dismissed many officeholders found to be obstructing the program, earning the lasting enmity of white Louisianians. President Andrew Johnson labeled Sheridan's reign as district commander an "absolute tyranny" and removed him from the post in August 1867. That move likely contributed to Johnson's impeachment by the Republican-controlled House of Representatives early the following year, although he was acquitted in a Senate trial.[48]

For the election of delegates to the new Louisiana constitutional convention, 44,732 white men and 82,907 black men were registered to vote. The state's voting-age population encompassed only slightly more black men than white men, but the sharply lower number of white registered voters might have reflected apathy as much as the zeal of Sheridan's registrars.

Louisiana voters chose fifty black delegates and forty-eight white delegates to represent them at the convention. Many of the black delegates assumed leadership roles fashioning the new state constitution, probably the most progressive of the remarkably progressive batch of state charters created to comply with the Reconstruction Acts. Louisiana's new constitution embraced virtually everything L. C. Roudanez and his allies at *L'Union* and the *Tribune* had been demanding to secure racial justice, including equal access to common carriers and places of business; universal public education; integrated schools; and most importantly, voting rights for black men.

Many of these advances would prove ephemeral, or exist mostly on paper, but it was an exhilarating moment for black Louisianians and their allies, particularly in the *Tribune* community. "Our hearts rejoiced," Houzeau recalled; "all that we could have conceived and asked for in the legal sphere had been accomplished."[49]

Roudanez's *Tribune* was riding high. Leading the fight for equal rights as the official journal of the state Republican Party, the paper had also won lucrative printing contracts from the Republican-controlled Congress in Washington, helping to stave off the fate of its financially busted predecessor. But in spite of these advantages, the fall came swiftly.

In letters home, Houzeau bragged that *Tribune* radicals and their allies had "won all the battles" for equal rights at the constitutional convention. But they were soon outflanked in the scramble for power in Louisiana. While black radicals had been busy embedding integrated schools and other egalitarian policies into the state's fundamental law, transplanted white Northerners at the constitutional convention were engineering the removal of age requirements for serving as governor, permitting their fellow carpetbagger, Henry Clay Warmoth, a charismatic twenty-five-year-old former Union Army colonel from Illinois, to seek the state's highest office.

Roudanez and the *Tribune* strongly preferred another candidate for governor: Francis E. Dumas, a wealthy, highly respected free-black businessman who had shown exceptional valor as an officer in the Louisiana Native Guard during the Civil War. At the state Republican convention in January, Dumas led Warmoth 41 to 37 after the first ballot. But Warmoth rallied on the second ballot to win the party's nomination 45 to 43.

The *Tribune* accused Warmoth of illegally purchasing votes to secure his slim victory margin. But other factors could have accounted for the young carpetbagger's triumph, including the freedmen's affection for Union Army veterans, whom they tended to regard as liberators; or the warnings of prominent free-black leader P. B. S. Pinchback, who believed that nominating a black man for governor was premature and could prompt a white backlash.

The valiant Dumas also carried significant political baggage, especially the inconvenient fact that he was a former slaveholder, like other wealthy creoles of color. Dumas had inherited his slaves and had been forbidden by Louisiana law to liberate them—authorities feared such manumissions undermined the institution of slavery. But Dumas finally freed his slaves when Union armies occupied New Orleans, and in a testament to his vaunted benevolence as a "master," many of them voluntarily enlisted in his Native Guard regiment, for service under his command, to help crush the Confederacy and destroy the scourge of bondage.[50]

Roudanez scorned Warmoth's bid for governor as naked opportunism, believing the young carpetbagger had scant regard for the black Louisianians whose ballots he would blithely harvest. Roudanez quickly assembled an alternative ticket, led by James G. Taliaferro, a white former slaveholder and staunch Unionist who had spent time in a Confederate jail and lately served as president of the state constitutional convention. Roudanez also convinced Dumas to shun the proffered second spot on Warmoth's ticket and run instead to be Taliaferro's lieutenant governor.

Roudanez's creation of a breakaway slate to sink his party's nominee infuriated fellow Republicans. The day after Taliaferro's candidacy for governor was announced, the Louisiana Republican Party struck back, declaring that the *New Orleans Tribune* would no longer serve as its official organ. Republicans in Washington withdrew the *Tribune*'s federal printing contracts. But perhaps the hardest blow was dealt by Houzeau. Distressed by Roudanez's "war cry against the Yankees," Houzeau resigned from the *Tribune*, convinced that challenging the Republican ticket at such a historically pivotal moment was "neither wise, nor logical, nor liberal."[51]

Warmoth won the April 1868 election in a rout. With Oscar James Dunn, a black former house painter and music teacher, as his running mate, the young carpetbagger amassed 64,941 votes to 38,046 for Taliaferro. Freedmen voted overwhelmingly for Warmoth. Louisiana's dispirited Democrats didn't field a candidate, but many backed Taliaferro. Although he was handpicked by the owner of the South's first black daily newspaper, Democrats saw Taliaferro as the best hope on offer for sustaining white supremacy.

Houzeau had recently written to his parents that among black Louisianians, "the influence of the *Tribune* is naturally lost forever." Roudanez seemed to agree. About a week after the election results were tabulated, he shut down his battered newspaper. Apart from a short-lived *Tribune* relaunch the following year, Roudanez mostly withdrew from public life.

Roudanez's rejection of the Republican ticket has been viewed as his most damaging blunder of the period. But in the same election, the new Louisiana state constitution was ratified by a vote of 51,737 to 39,076. Despite his setbacks, Roudanez would reflect with sublime satisfaction on the accomplishments enshrined in that document.

Meanwhile, more Republicans were coming to share Roudanez's harsh appraisal of Governor Warmoth, finding him slow to implement the egalitarian principles of the new state constitution. Warmoth vetoed some civil rights bills, failed to enforce equal public accommodations, and routinely passed over black candidates for government jobs, while awarding appointments to conservative white Republicans and many Democrats. Warmoth and Conway began the process of desegregating New Orleans public schools, probably to quiet the vocal free men of color there, but the governor made no such effort in rural public schools, acceding to the wishes of influential white conservatives. Warmoth also shunned calls by Roudanez and other radicals to award appointive offices to black candidates commensurate with black voting strength, describing them as part of a campaign to "Africanize the state."[52]

Warmoth's courtship of Democrats fueled bitter divisions among Louisiana Republicans and many of them turned against him. Instead of seeking another term as governor in 1872, Warmoth backed a third-party "Fusion" candidate endorsed by the Democrats, thereby siding against the Republican nominee, Vermont-born carpetbagger William Pitt Kellogg.[53]

Some Louisiana Democrats had been downcast about their chances against Republicans in the 1872 election and eagerly embraced the cunning Warmoth as an ally. His control of election administration as governor was said to be worth twenty thousand votes to them. The state's election law, enacted by Republicans to neutralize vote tampering by violent white vigilantes, established a Returning Board with vast powers to disqualify ballots from areas it found to be affected by violence. Warmoth, as governor, was an ex officio member of the five-person Returning Board, and after the election, he engineered the removal of another such member, a Kellogg supporter, and the appointment of three Fusionist-friendly members to fill vacancies. Despite the stout Republican loyalties of the Louisiana electorate's black majority, this Warmoth-built Returning Board produced a vote tally that awarded the governorship to Fusion candidate John McEnery, described by a local newspaper as one of the "negro-hating, schoolhouse burning" class of Bourbonist conservatives. Warmoth's board also put Fusionists in control of both houses of the legislature. Along the way, bushels of Republican ballots were likely suppressed or discarded.

Louisiana Republicans sued, and Republican judges in both state and federal courts ruled in their favor, finding that Warmoth had unlawfully removed the member of the original Returning Board and voiding the governor's subsequent personnel moves. The state court judge likened Warmoth's Returning Board gambit to a "coup d'etat."

Both the state and federal courts recognized a different Returning Board as the legitimate election tribunal. This "legal" Returning Board, formed with the participation of the member Warmoth removed, anointed Kellogg as the governor-elect and awarded Republicans enough victories to control both houses of the state legislature.

Deploying a few more wily maneuvers, Warmoth wriggled out from under the state court judgment. But the December 6 ruling by Judge Edward H. Durrell of the Federal District Court in Louisiana was backed by President Grant with the full power of the federal government, despite doubts among Democrats, and many Republicans, about the judge's authority to intervene in this state matter.[54]

Soon after the federal court ruled against Warmoth, the Republican-controlled Louisiana House of Representatives impeached him, and he was suspended from office while the legislature debated his fate. P. B. S. Pinchback, who had recently become lieutenant governor following the death of Oscar Dunn, served as acting governor during the suspension, which lasted the remainder of Warmoth's term.

While Warmoth had a knack for dubious maneuvers, both sides relied on them to some extent. The "legal" Returning Board, validated by judges in both state and federal courts, pronounced Kellogg the next governor and ratified Republican control of both houses of the state legislature without ever examining any actual election returns—

Warmoth had defied a court order to hand the returns over for inspection. Recent histories of Reconstruction in Louisiana conclude that the state's 1872 election was so fouled with fraud that, to this day, no one knows who actually won.

William Pitt Kellogg took the oath of office as governor in a statehouse ceremony on January 13, 1873. That same day, across town on a platform erected in Lafayette Square, John McEnery also took the oath of office as governor, before "large and enthusiastic crowds," according to the *Daily Picayune*, which hailed him as the leader of the state's "legal government." Besides dueling claimants to the governorship, there were also two bodies of men purporting to be the legitimate state legislature, and pairs of rival claimants to public office in municipalities up and down the state.

When Congress was asked to help sort out the mess in Louisiana, the majority Republicans of a Senate investigating committee issued stern critiques of both sides but basically threw up their hands on the question of who won. They suggested that the federal government could run a do-over election in the state, but the idea was abandoned amid doubts about congressional authority to impose such a remedy. President Grant announced that in the absence of directions from Congress, he would recognize Kellogg and the Republicans as victors in the electoral contest, believing they had stronger claims to legitimacy. Many in his party agreed, especially considering the solid support for Republicans among Louisiana's majority-black electorate.[55]

But Fusionists and Democrats were not inclined to concede. They opted for outrage instead, hurling cries of "usurpation" and pushing matters to a violent confrontation. McEnery organized a militia, and on March 5, 1873, his followers clashed with Metropolitan Police in a failed attempt to occupy several police stations in New Orleans. Supported by federal troops, the Metropolitan Police put down the rebellion quickly, arresting sixty-five attackers. The following day, police dispersed the Fusionist legislature and took possession of its meeting hall.[56]

While the uprising in New Orleans was squelched with dispatch, violent collisions between Fusionist and Republican claimants to office spread across the Louisiana countryside. The deadliest of these by far erupted in the Red River town of Colfax on the afternoon of April 13, 1873—Easter Sunday. A makeshift militia of about 150 freedmen had assembled there, in and around a converted plantation stable functioning as a courthouse, to protect the local Republican government from an approaching posse of hundreds of heavily armed white men.[57]

Colfax was the seat of Grant Parish, a political subdivision named after President Grant that was created by Republicans to house a small black majority, thereby bolstering their control of the state government while creating new patronage jobs. Bitter struggles over office-holding were nothing new there. The parish had been riven by partisan and racial resentments throughout its brief history. But the apocalyptic intensity of the current struggle would separate it from the rest.

The trouble at Colfax began around noon as freedmen, mostly armed with shotguns, sought to fend off attacking white militiamen armed, in the main, with rifles, along with a cannon borrowed from a nearby riverboat. The combatants exchanged volleys for about two hours before the white militia, with its superior numbers and firepower, thoroughly routed their foes. But victory, it seemed, was not the only objective. White militiamen gunned down freedmen running for their lives toward the Red River or through the nearby woods. "The hunt for fleeing freedmen was almost frenzied," according to one recent student of the incident. Several dozen freedmen sought refuge inside the courthouse, returning fire through shattered windows until their attackers set the structure ablaze. A group of freedmen inside the burning courthouse hoisted improvised white flags and surrendered, amid shouted assurances of safe passage from white militiamen. But many of these freedmen were shot dead as they emerged from the inferno, while others perished in the flames.

Around forty freedmen were taken prisoner, and their captors promised to release them in the morning if they agreed to return home in peace. But after nightfall, a group of younger white militiamen led the black captives away in pairs to be executed, often with a bullet to the head. Few of the imprisoned freedmen survived.

White paramilitaries killed about seventy black men on that Easter Sunday in Colfax. While such estimates vary widely, accounts tend to agree that the incident amounted to a massacre of singular savagery. Three white men also lost their lives, two of them apparently felled by wayward gunfire from their own side.[58]

Kellogg appointees, backed by state militia troops and U.S. bluecoats, were soon restored to office in Grant Parish. Meanwhile, newspaper accounts of the "Colfax Massacre" spread across the nation, detailing the "horror" of freedmen "butchered without mercy." Some compared the grisly scene to the notorious Civil War battle of Fort Pillow, in Tennessee, where Confederate troops slaughtered hundreds of mostly black Union soldiers who were attempting to surrender.

The North deplored the Colfax Massacre, but its response was not nearly as powerful as the backlash against the New Orleans Massacre of 1866, possibly reflecting public weariness with Reconstruction. But the Colfax Massacre's most consequential effects nationally would emerge in the U.S. legal system, arguably inflicting more grievous injuries to the freedmen's cause than the rampaging paramilitaries of Grant Parish.[59]

The Colfax Massacre also exerted a baleful sway in Louisiana itself, becoming a model for white vigilante operations across the state. But in New Orleans, a starkly different response took hold, which was evident even from far-off Ohio. Editors of the *Cleveland Leader* noticed in late June that the Colfax Massacre had "produced a reaction" in New Orleans, in the form of a surprising new movement to "bury the antagonisms of the past and unite men upon the broad ground of equal rights." This movement was known to some as "the Beauregard party," after the celebrated ex-Confederate general at its forefront, and the editors were certain that it would soon spread to other Southern states if it prevailed in Louisiana.[60]

I f General Beauregard's mysterious nonappearance at the mass
meeting in Exposition Hall was a sign of second thoughts among
prominent white advocates of the Unification movement, it was hardly
the only sign.

Misgivings among self-proclaimed Unification backers had been a
quiet undercurrent in the New Orleans press for weeks, often in anonymous letters to the editor. One such letter appeared in the *Picayune* a
few days before the Exposition Hall meeting. The writer, identified as
"One of the One Hundred" leaders of the movement, suggested that
black people stood to reap the benefits of Unification, while white
people were making all the concessions.

White leaders had pledged to back the fulfillment of black rights
that had been written into the Constitution and laws but remained
largely a dead letter. What pledges, the anonymous writer asked, "will
our colored fellow-citizens give" to reassure the white population? He
had some suggestions. Many white Southerners feared that impover-
ished former slaves were bent on using their votes and control of government offices to redistribute the wealth of former slaveholders. The
anonymous writer called on black Unification leaders to pledge that
state taxes would not exceed 0.5 percent, and that "useless" state offices
and "exorbitant" compensation for state employees would be abolished.
Other white Unification supporters sought pledges from black leaders
to vote carpetbaggers out of office.

Roudanez had responded angrily weeks earlier to signs of second
thoughts among white Unification leaders, even before the movement's
groundbreaking resolutions were officially adopted. At a conference
of Unification's one hundred "representative men" of both races, one
white leader called for holding a mass meeting to demonstrate broad
support for the just-unveiled resolutions, to "guarantee to the colored
man every public right."

This seemingly modest suggestion "brought Dr. Roudanez to the
floor," and he was furious. If Unification's white leaders were "afraid of

the step they were taking" and felt obliged to first stage a show of public support, maybe black leaders would boycott the mass meeting and
wait until their colleagues made up their minds, Roudanez warned.

Roudanez's outburst recalled the time he led Republican "bolters"
to challenge their party's ticket in 1868, with sobering consequences.
But after the Committee of One Hundred voted unanimously to
adopt Unification's groundbreaking resolutions, Roudanez abruptly
changed course, winning approval for a motion to start planning a mass
meeting in New Orleans, despite his earlier threat to boycott such an
event.

This more modulated Roudanez, evidently determined to give
Unification every chance to succeed, was also a factor at the July 15
Exposition Hall mass meeting. One of the black speakers at the meeting, James Lewis, administrator of public improvements in New Orleans, read to the audience from a document, signed by Roudanez and
other black leaders, intended to allay concerns that white people were
making all the concessions for Unification. The document's vows were
bounteous: "we pledge ourselves to unite all our influence and our en-
ergies with those of our fellow citizens in a common movement to
reduce taxation to a rate corresponding to the resources of the country;
to investigate and correct the public debt; to suppress unnecessary offices; to diminish largely the high salaries and exorbitant emoluments
attached to public office, the useless multiplicity and extravagant compensation of office being among the principal causes of the public de-
moralization and disorder; and, in a word, to secure in Louisiana, as
soon as possible, the establishment of an honest, economic and patri-
otic government. This pledge we publicly make and engage our honor
to maintain."

But while these promises were extended to strike a conciliatory
tone, they were overshadowed by a welter of conditions preceding
them in the text. In sum, the black leaders rather awkwardly proclaimed that they would fulfill their solemn pledges to foster honest

and frugal government just as soon as "existing opposition against the enjoyment of our rights" ended—but presumably not before.

After Lewis finished reading the pledges signed by Roudanez and other black leaders, the Exposition Hall program lurched to an abrupt end. No benedictory remarks issued from the speakers platform. Shouts from the crowd creased the silence, calling for General Beauregard and others to mount the stage, but no one materialized and the meeting was adjourned.[61]

The Exposition Hall event was seen as a make-or-break moment, and a consensus soon formed that the meeting had indeed broken the movement. White conservatives were quick to assign blame. The *Picayune* lamented that as white leaders braved "shafts of disapproval" for supporting racial cooperation, their black counterparts "wantonly and effectively killed the unification movement." The *Picayune* singled out "Dr. Roudanez" and other signers of the pledge document for particular scorn, asserting that these black leaders would not budge "one iota" from their misalliance with carpetbaggers until white Louisianians were "humiliated" and "degraded."

While the *Picayune* exalted white Unification leaders for their courage, the *New Orleans Republican* noted that many of these brave souls "failed to turn up" at Exposition Hall to deliver scheduled remarks, despite their vows to "advocate by speech, and pen, and deed" for the Unification resolutions. Their absence at this crucial meeting suggested that white Unification advocates were "not prepared to carry out their part of the contract." Such wariness was understandable. White Louisianians, especially in the countryside, remained decidedly averse to the Unification resolutions, viewing them as a sure path to a dreaded racial equality.[62]

The demise of Unification registered across the state and beyond. "General Beauregard's attempt to miscegenize the people of Louisiana has failed," the *American Citizen* in Canton, Mississippi, reported. When the movement fell short as a means to break up the alliance of black voters and so-called carpetbaggers, Louisianians who were determined to reestablish white control of the state reassessed their options. Another method for neutralizing black electoral power returned to the fore: armed vigilantes, cloaked in the trappings of law, using violence to unseat officials and intimidate black voters. Disgust with such methods following the Colfax Massacre had fueled the Unification movement's rise, but by mid-1874 white vigilantes were back in the saddle.[63]

CHAPTER 2

"THE SWING OF OLD SOLDIERS"

A group of freedmen in Shreveport, Louisiana, a Red River cotton town in the northwest corner of the state, had an urgent message for President Ulysses S. Grant.

The freedmen were a resourceful and resilient bunch, members of a secret organization called, simply, "the Committee." They drafted a petition to President Grant, dated September 5, 1874, informing him that "these white people" who once held them as slaves had now "disfranchised" them of all their rights of citizenship. They pleaded with Grant to either protect their rights, guaranteed by the recently adopted Fourteenth and Fifteenth Amendments to the Constitution, or find them a U.S. territory where they could live in peace and freedom. "We had as soon to be sunk in the Bottom of the red Sea [than] to live here in the Southern States in the condition that we have been in."[1]

The lives of freedmen had changed considerably in the nearly ten years since the Civil War ended. Black men now voted, held elective office, served on police forces, and sent their children to public schools created by politicians catering to their pent-up demand for education. But Southern whites fiercely resisted these advances, ex-

ploiting freedmen with meager wages, which kept them from accru-
ing much wealth or independence, and using threats and violence to
keep blacks from voting for Republicans—the party of Lincoln and
freeing the slaves.

Committee members, like freedmen across the South, saw Grant as
a potential savior. "Mr President we ask you to look at us as Moses did
the children of Isreal [*sic*]as Abraham Lincoln was called a President
that looked at all men as the Same, and Mr Lincoln is dead and you
have taken his place, as Joshua did Moses in the days of old."[2]

Such voices—unpolished, ungrammatical, but endowed with a raw
eloquence—were seldom represented in newspapers, although the
New York Herald ran an item on the Committee's plea for territorial
sanctuary under the sarcastic headline "Looking for a Paradise."[3]

But the Committee, formed in 1870, was hardly a collective of uto-
pian dreamers. Most of its members had served in the U.S. Army's
famous all-black regiments during the Civil War, so they had seen
something of the world beyond the plantation and knew the security
of a regular paycheck. Their call for territory spoke to the concerns of
freedmen across the South who were never compensated for years of
toil stolen by slavery. Many freedmen now felt trapped in Southern
plantation labor at miserable wages, with little hope of ever being able
to afford a plot of land or a home of their own.[4]

The Committee functioned as a sort of freedmen's intelligence
agency. Its field operatives, numbering up to 150 at any given time,
fanned out across the former Confederacy, working undercover as
plantation hands to learn how black workers were treated and where
they might find the best wages and working conditions. A Committee
member named Henry Adams testified years later that some employers
"would try to pay what they promised from time to time," while others
"didn't pay near what they promised." A bale of cotton sold for about
$125 back then. Adams recalled that some sharecropper families would
produce 100 bales of cotton in a year, but after paying rent to the plantation owner for land, equipment, and lodging, would come away with

perhaps $100 or less in profit, while other families "would not get one dollar."[5]

Committee operatives would report back to headquarters in Shreveport about working and living conditions they found on their travels. The organization's long-term goal was to determine whether freedmen "could remain in the South amongst the people who had held us as slaves, or not," Adams said.[6]

The Committee was forced to confront that issue head-on in the summer of 1874. Freedmen had suffered every type of abuse at the hands of their former masters since emancipation, from random beatings and whippings to outright murder. But freedmen had also enjoyed significant gains over the period, including adoption of the Fourteenth and Fifteenth Amendments, which nourished hopes for better days ahead. But in 1874, resentful Southern whites began arming and drilling insurgent militias, made up mostly of former Confederate soldiers, to systematically remove black officials from power, along with their white Republican allies, by whatever means necessary. A militia calling itself the White League operated in Louisiana, spreading terror to the Committee's home base in Caddo Parish.

"The white people of this state have drawn off from us into white Legues," the petition told Grant. They "will not let us enjoy the rights of a citizenship and they says in this state that none shall hold an office but an honest white man."[7]

The White League pressured employers not to retain freedmen who voted Republican, as most freedmen did, including Adams. A "big, stout, broad-shouldered man," Adams seldom lacked for work. He was managing a string of plantations outside Shreveport when the White League fever spread. His employer, under enormous pressure, reluctantly sacked him, despite the fact that "he thought a heap of me," Adams said.[8]

Robbing freedmen of their wages or barring their employment was hardly the worst of it. Southern whites also murdered freedmen on the slightest provocation and raped black women with impunity, the

Committee's petition said. If Grant couldn't find a way to guarantee the freedmen's rights, or secure a safe homestead for them in some unsettled U.S. territory, "our idea was to appeal to other governments outside the United States," Adams later recalled, "and go there and live under their flag."[9]

Grant had foreseen such a moment a few years earlier when he proposed the annexation of Santo Domingo, the Caribbean nation known today as the Dominican Republic. He believed that former slaves in need of sanctuary might flock to Santo Domingo if it became part of the United States, and that having the option to go there would at least have given them more leverage in bargaining with white planters for better wages. But his annexation plan ended in disaster, rejected by the Senate, though not before it sharply divided the Republican Party.[10]

While the Committee appealed to Grant as their president, the former soldiers in its ranks also played to his sympathies as their wartime commander. "Mr. President you know we are True men and we are law abiding men. Mr. President you have experienced that yourself. [O]ur hearts have ached long enough all over the entire Southern States. [A]ll of this has Sprang from the white Legues. You have led us, and we are willing to be led by you."[11]

The petition, signed by one thousand freedmen, would soon land in Grant's mailbag. It is unclear if he ever personally read its ominous tidings of terror along the Red River. But in a matter of days he would receive a blunt message directly from the White League itself.[12]

On September 14, 1874, thousands of irate white men assembled on Canal Street in downtown New Orleans, its cobblestones slick from a passing shower. A statue of Henry Clay, the Great Compromiser, loomed nearby, extending a conciliatory hand, but the crowd was in no mood for compromise. Many were waving rifles. The Civil War had been over for nearly ten years, but today it was getting a second wind.

General James Longstreet surveyed the ruckus from atop his horse at about 3:30 p.m. Tall and burly, in a businesslike frock coat, his shaggy beard streaked with gray, the former top lieutenant of Confederate hero Robert E. Lee was still a commanding presence at fifty-three years old. Longstreet now led the Louisiana State Militia, a police force comprised largely of former slaves who had served in the Union Army, his old sworn enemy. Some of the men in the rowdy white multitudes spilling down Canal Street had probably served under Longstreet during the war. Now they were on opposite sides.[13]

Longstreet, a close friend of Grant's since their years together at West Point, settled in New Orleans after the war and became Louisiana's most eminent "scalawag." When the Republican Congress enacted its Reconstruction plan in 1867, he implored his fellow Southerners to acknowledge that they were "a conquered people," and to accept "the terms that are offered us by the conquerors." Although he assured Southerners that such cooperation involved no disgrace or humiliation on their part, many could not forgive the man they had known affectionately as "Old Pete" and "Lee's Warhorse."[14]

On Canal Street, Longstreet was flanked by hundreds of officers from the militia's Metropolitan brigade. The many freedmen on this force, in their plain blue uniforms adorned by a simple badge, epitomized the postwar reality that most infuriated white Southerners: former slaves now had political power. A revolt against that idea had driven most of the violence in the South against freedmen and their white Republican allies.

The freedmen had gained civil and political rights largely through federal action. But federal firepower to protect the exercise of those rights was allowed to diminish steadily, from 187,000 U.S. troops stationed in the South in 1865 to 6,000 by 1876, half of them on the Texas border. About two dozen federal troops were in New Orleans that day.[15]

State militias were natural candidates to pick up the slack, but it was difficult to recruit white Southerners for such roles; Longstreet, with his Confederate credentials, had been more successful at it than most.

Whites and blacks served in segregated units in the Louisiana militia, as in the U.S. military back then, but by 1874, white units were melting away in the state's increasingly polarized political climate. Southern Republicans deployed black units more reluctantly, haunted by fear of a race war. The sight of armed black men erased moral boundaries for some white Southerners; the slaughter of black militiamen at Colfax was only the most recent case in point.[16]

Ninety-seven white men were indicted in New Orleans federal court for crimes related to the Colfax Massacre under the Enforcement Act—also known as the "Ku-Klux" law since it was aimed at smashing the Klan. Federal authorities, amid budgetary constraints, decided to bring only nine leaders of the Colfax vigilantes to trial, and only three were convicted by the jury of nine whites and three men of color. In the South at that time, it was extremely difficult to convict white men for crimes against black men. But on June 27, 1874, U.S. Supreme Court justice Joseph Bradley threw out all three Colfax convictions in a circuit court appeal, ruling that most of the crimes were matters within the state's jurisdiction and beyond the reach of federal authority under the Fourteenth Amendment. Other convictions, for violations of civil and voting rights, were nullified because racist intent was not explicitly alleged in the indictment.[17]

Bradley's decision was not the final word. The federal district judge disagreed with his ruling, so the case moved on to the full Supreme Court. But many white Louisianians viewed Bradley's circuit opinion as a preview of what his colleagues on the high court would do, and greeted it "with the wildest demonstrations of approval," Governor Kellogg recalled. Bradley's opinion "was regarded as establishing the principle that hereafter no white man could be punished for killing a negro," Kellogg claimed. White League operations against freedmen and their Republican allies surged across the state that summer.[18]

Bradley's opinion rocked the foundations of Reconstruction Era law enforcement. On September 14, the lawyer for the Colfax defendants, Robert Hardin Marr, whose arguments Justice Bradley had found so persuasive, was again taking aim at those foundations, but not with legal briefs. He was exhorting the angry crowd at the Clay Statue to take up arms for a revolution.

The trouble on Canal Street had been brewing for hours before Longstreet showed up. Marr had stepped onto the wrought-iron balcony of the Crescent Billiard Saloon, overlooking the Clay Statue, at 11:30 a.m. to address the raucous crowd. Newspaper ads and signs pasted to buildings had summoned the "Citizens of New Orleans" to the statue that morning to voice their outrage at Governor Kellogg, one of many white Republicans from the North who moved to the South after the Civil War and won political office with strong support from freedmen, who were a majority of voters in Louisiana then. Many freedmen believed that putting such so-called carpetbaggers in office could help them in their struggles with their former white masters. The crowd by the statue wanted Southern white people back in charge.[19]

Marr, gangly and jug-eared, was a loyal Democrat, and the crowd booed on cue as he repeated familiar partisan attacks. He charged that in the previous election for governor, the Democratic candidate, John McEnery, had actually beaten Kellogg "by a majority of nearly ten thousand," before crooked vote counters cooked up a tally showing the Republican on top. Marr failed to mention that a U.S. Senate committee found that McEnery's allies had themselves stolen twenty thousand votes.[20]

But Kellogg was much more than illegitimate, Marr brayed. He was also supremely insolent, daring to deny the Constitution's solemn guarantee that "the right of the people to bear arms shall never be infringed." Marr was alluding to recent police seizures of large weapons shipments meant for his allies in the White League.

The police were responding to stepped-up White League activity that summer. The paramilitary group had been terrorizing black and white Republican elected officials in the state's outer parishes. Armed bands would ride into town to confront the officials with trumped-up "charges" of wrongdoing and demand their immediate resignation, with the clearly implied threat of violence—a hangman's noose draped over a saddle—if they failed to comply. Such threats were generally sufficient to persuade the officials to flee, but many were murdered.[21]

When Marr finished reading his "charges" against Kellogg, he demanded the governor's "immediate abdication." He then led a small delegation across town to the governor's office to communicate this demand in person. But Kellogg refused to meet with them, citing reports of armed men seen all over the city. The delegation told Kellogg's spokesman that there were no armed men on Canal Street, then returned to the waiting crowd at the rally.

Marr mounted the balcony again to address the swarm of shopkeepers and clerks. He faced the Clay Statue's serene bronze back, and beyond it the muddy Mississippi River several blocks away at the base of Canal Street, where steamboats were boarding spectators for a regatta that afternoon. He left the next step up to the crowd: Will we endure this "usurpation," or rise up and drive Kellogg from power?

"Fight!" shouted many voices. "Hang Kellogg!"

Marr instructed the men to go home, grab a weapon, and return to the statue at 2:30 p.m., ready for battle.[22]

As Longstreet approached the melee by the statue, he planned to confront and gradually disperse the crowd, while spreading out his forces to prevent the demonstrators from regrouping. He had also stationed some five hundred militia troops several blocks behind him to protect the statehouse and armory. But splitting his forces this way made him uneasy.[23]

Longstreet apparently didn't realize that White League operatives dressed in suits and bowler hats, most of them former Confederate soldiers, had been making preparations all day. About a dozen of them had seized City Hall in midafternoon, slashing its telegraph lines to keep reports of their deployments from reaching police stations around the city. Others had built barricades at key intersections on Poydras Street, a block south of Canal, with iron grates torn from the pavement, crates packed with dirt, overturned mattresses, and streetcars rolled off their tracks. By the time Longstreet and his men came along, hundreds of White Leaguers with repeating rifles quietly manned the ramparts. Any approaching Metropolitans would meet a screen of lead.

In offices and meeting halls, other armed White League companies crouched in wait for the signal from their leader, Frederick Nash Ogden, a former Confederate infantry commander and chief of the McEnery militia after the disputed election of 1872. The White Leaguers had been drilling for months, often at night, in out-of-theway courtyards.[24]

One of their objectives was to seize a shipment of weapons aboard a steamboat docked on the Mississippi River several blocks north of Poydras, which authorities had placed under guard. The police had expected such a move, but were more focused on the rowdy Clay Statue gathering, which the White Leaguers had staged in part to divert their attention. "They had reason to believe our forces were small," said Frank Richardson, a former Confederate colonel whose White League battalion mustered at his Camp Street law office that morning. The police seemed to believe they were facing "a mere mob who responded to the public call," he said.

Around 4 p.m., Longstreet ordered a cavalry patrol to disperse the swelling crowd on Canal Street approaching the statue. Onlookers craning from windows and balconies and jamming sidewalks cheered the heroic protesters and jeered the police. The mounted patrol could scarcely be heard amid the hollering clamor as riders beseeched all those "peaceably disposed" to return home. Meanwhile, Longstreet's second in command, Algernon Sydney Badger, a Boston native who moved south after the war, headed to the Clay Statue to disband the armed organization behind this would-be uprising. But, curiously, he found no organized forces whatsoever in the vicinity, just a gaggle of hectoring malcontents.

Out of nowhere, a sniper fired at the cavalry patrol loping up Canal Street, striking a Metropolitan in the arm. The gun's crackling report briefly stilled the scene. The shot might have come from any of the numerous open windows wedged with screaming spectators on both sides of Canal, or even from down on the truculent street.[25]

Confusion swept the Metropolitans' ranks. Then riders brought Longstreet more troubling news. Armed "insurgents" were on the march, advancing down Poydras toward the levee in large numbers. They moved "with the swing of old soldiers." Longstreet knew they would find an open lane to the dock several blocks north where the steamboat packed with weapons was tied. He ordered Badger to hurry his men several blocks east to establish a line of defense along the levee at the base of Canal Street, in hopes of cutting off what now seemed like an invading army. About 8,300 White League troops were involved in the operation, compared with less than half that number of fighters available to the state of Louisiana that day.

Badger deployed his men as ordered and quickly opened fire on the advancing White League forces with a Gatling gun and a pair of Napoleon cannons. But the Metropolitans were in a perilously exposed spot, smack in the middle of a large intersection of several streets.

A company of White League riflemen popped up from behind bales of cotton freight by the waterfront and opened fire, surprising the exposed Metropolitans. A freight train crept slowly up the levee with White Leaguers jogging beside it for cover and shooting at Badger's men. Snipers also fired at the militia troops from windows and rooftops of several surrounding buildings. The Metropolitans fell in clusters.[26]

Then their luck changed—for the worse. A company of white Metropolitans, including former Confederates recruited by Longstreet himself, abruptly formed a huddle and, on a signal from their captain, marched across the levee to join forces with the White League insurgents.

This event exerted "a very demoralizing influence" on the mostly black infantry left behind to man the Metropolitans' besieged position on the levee, Longstreet later said. Perhaps visions of Colfax flashed before their eyes, or of numerous similar episodes of manic excess by Southern whites both during and after the war. In any case, many of the Metropolitans took this opportunity to flee, some seeking refuge in the U.S. Custom House a few blocks to the west, others heading uptown to the statehouse, where the remainder of the militia's forces were stationed in a defensive cordon.[27]

The pounding cannons and other sounds of battle confused regatta spectators in steamboats chugging along the river. Was this another summer storm? Badger, peering between clouds of gun smoke near the waterfront, saw his artillery pieces had been left unguarded by the disintegrating front lines. But before he could address the breach, his horse was blasted out from under him and he crashed onto the cobblestones, hit by multiple shots and severely wounded.

Several companies of White Leaguers now charged down the levee screeching the famous Rebel Yell of the old Confederate Army, a sound like the yipping of coyotes that was queasily familiar to the many former Union soldiers among the Metropolitans. Longstreet watched the raiders advance. A whistling shard of shrapnel struck him and he tumbled off his horse, seriously aggravating an old arm injury. As Metropolitans carted their dazed commander to safety, more of them broke formation and fled.[28]

The invaders continued to stream down the levee, basically unopposed now. Some stopped to seize the arms shipment aboard the unguarded steamboat docked on the river. Others raided the now-undefended state militia armory, making off with stockpiled weapons and ammunition.

White Southerners would come to celebrate the fighting on this day as the Battle of Liberty Place. When it was over, the White League forces had suffered 21 killed and 19 wounded, while 11 state militia officers were killed and 60 wounded. But those tallies understated the lopsided outcome. Before daybreak Tuesday, White League negotiators had convinced police and militia holdouts in the Custom House to surrender in exchange for safe passage. Meanwhile, Kellogg, the state's Republican governor, was nowhere to be found. The White League controlled New Orleans, and with it the state government—at least for the moment.[29]

The coup's organizers took pains to signal that their quarrel was not with the U.S. government, unlike rebellious Confederates of yore. Democrat D. B. Penn, McEnery's running mate in the disputed governor's election of 1872, declared himself acting governor, but also sent a telegram to Grant insisting that Louisiana remained faithful to the Stars and Stripes. Penn assured the president that "the people of this State" declare their "unswerving loyalty and respect" for the U.S. government and its officers, and "only ask of you to withhold any aid or protection from our enemies," the Kellogg government.[30]

By claiming to speak for "the people of this State," Penn apparently meant the *white* people. He also found it necessary to send a separate public message to "the Colored People of Louisiana," promising that "no harm is meant toward you, your property or your rights," and advising black Louisianians: "Pursue your usual avocations, and you will not be molested."[31]

The White League insurrection spoke to discontented white Southerners across the region, appearing to accomplish, in a single, bold stroke, the dearest desires of so many, including the termination of so-called Negro rule and the banishment of a hated carpetbag governor, even if such results were only temporary. Ethelbert Barksdale, editor of the *Weekly Clarion* of Jackson, Mississippi, proclaimed that the September 14 White League coup "taught a wronged people what it is possible for them to do, if they but dare."[32]

CHAPTER 3

YANKEE PANKY

Marshall Harvey Twitchell stepped off the train in occupied New Orleans the morning after the coup on an urgent errand. Emerging from the station at the base of Canal Street, he strode past cotton bales and other makeshift barricades still strewn on the levee, and the carcasses of a few dead horses. Knots of people were gaping at bloodstains left from the battle. Twitchell avoided eye contact with the White League troops patrolling the area, but one or two of them might have recognized him. He stared straight ahead and kept moving.

A Vermont native, Twitchell was a somewhat notorious "carpetbag" Republican official from Red River Parish in the northwest corner of the state. His habit of arching one eyebrow gave his high-cheekboned face an air of Yankee hauteur. The enemy might consider him a prize catch, but he had to risk it. The White League fever sweeping Louisiana had recently cost him dearly. Three family members had been killed and he was now a marked man, frantic to protect what was left of his once-prosperous life in the postwar South.

At his first stop, a bank on Camp Street, Twitchell scooped a stack of securities out of his safe-deposit box, fearing they would be confiscated by White League operatives now clearly moving to crush the state Republican Party. Then he rushed several blocks back to Canal Street and the massive Custom House, where U.S. soldiers guarding the locked gate let him pass.

A crowd of onlookers stood vigil across the street, a mixture of jovial whites and edgy freedmen. Squinting in the bright sun, they scanned the four-story granite fortress, which was pocked with bullet holes from the previous day's fight. They searched the windows for signs of life, or surrender, from the Kellogg regime. The lanky governor himself was said to be inside, lying low. Wounded generals Longstreet and Badger had reportedly been carted there during the battle. But Longstreet had gone home hours earlier; his physical injuries weren't as severe as the injury to his reputation inflicted by the previous day's lopsided loss. Badger, meanwhile, had been moved to Charity Hospital, where he clung to life, though surgeons couldn't save his shattered right leg.

Twitchell prowled the dusky Custom House corridors, where dazed or fitfully sleeping militia troops spent a restless night before their leaders grudgingly surrendered around daybreak. Finding his destination, he tucked his securities into an office safe overseen by U.S. troops. His tasks completed, he recalled the flickering looks of recognition near the train station.[1]

Twitchell had been on the run for weeks. Around midafternoon on July 27, 1874, as he rode a Red River steamboat bound for New Orleans, he learned from passengers boarding at Campti about the White League invasion of nearby Natchitoches. Hundreds of armed men on horseback had swept through the town earlier that day demanding the resignations of Republican officials, black and white, and promising bitter consequences if their targets failed to pack up and leave. The officials cleared out in a hurry.

The White League movement had previously consisted of little more than angry editorials and speeches at loud rallies demanding the restoration of white rule. But Twitchell had been warned that the group was drilling armed recruits, mostly former Confederate soldiers, and would soon be mounting an offensive against Republicans. Until that day aboard the steamboat he couldn't bring himself to believe such things would actually happen. His thoughts quickly turned to the group's likely next targets: himself and his family![2]

Some white Louisianians saw Twitchell, a former Union soldier, as the incarnation of their "carpetbagger" nightmares: a white Northerner who settled in the South after the war and prospered magnificently under the new order of things. The Vermonter had married a Southern belle, acquired a 620-acre cotton plantation on some of the best bottomland in the Red River Valley, and held a seat in the state Senate owing to overwhelming support from newly enfranchised black voters. His father-in-law, also a plantation owner, tutored him in the fine points of cotton husbandry. And many members of the Twitchell clan had moved from Vermont to live in Marshall's new community, including his three sisters, a brother, their spouses, and his widowed mother. Twitchell also used his political clout to help his brother and two brothers-in-law land jobs as Red River Parish officials.

For a while, Twitchell enjoyed substantial support from local merchants, including Democrats who benefited from his access to the new Republican levers of power in the state. But as the White League began issuing threats to discourage whites from associating with Republicans, Twitchell's business allies drifted away. Nervous friends advised him to raise a militia to go after White League leaders, but he was unruffled, confident that U.S. Army bluecoats would step in before things got out of hand. He simply "did not believe the federal government would stand quietly by and see a re-organized Confederate army crush out the loyal elements of this country."[3]

With his square jaw, wavy chestnut hair, and scar along his left cheek from a war wound, the ruggedly handsome Twitchell was a commanding figure in the Red River Valley. At five feet seven inches tall he was not an imposing physical specimen. But his upright military bearing, combined with an easy manner and wry sense of humor, created the winning impression that he was both projecting authority and subverting it at the same time.

For the past several months, however, a new gravity tugged at Twitchell. His wife, Adele, had died of tuberculosis in February, and his sickly infant son, Daniel, passed away a few weeks later. After some soul-searching, Twitchell had decided to quit politics and focus on his surviving son, Marshall, and on business. But Republican friends ultimately managed to change his mind, insisting that his strong leadership was essential if they were to stave off the White League.[4]

An episode in Twitchell's adolescence helped to prepare him in some measure to confront powerful factions bent on his destruction. He was born on February 29, 1840, in Townshend, Vermont, home to one of the state's best secondary schools, the Leland Seminary, where he enrolled at age thirteen to study Greek, Latin, mathematics, mineralogy, and English literature. After his sixteenth birthday, he attended class only in the fall term, a normal course for a farmer's son like him. In spring he helped with planting. But during his free winters, Twitchell began teaching school himself, for twelve dollars a month. He once taught a high school class in a rugged mountain hamlet west of Townshend. He was seventeen at the time, and many of his students were older and bigger than him, and had a reputation for scaring off teachers. Convinced that he "could not rule the school by force" and not wanting to slink away in defeat, Twitchell adopted a divide-and-conquer strategy. He managed to win the allegiance of some of the rougher boys, whose influence helped to keep the others in line. "This forced study of human nature proved of more value to me in after life than any other term of equal length," he recalled decades later.[5]

Twitchell had set his sights beyond the family farm by the time he graduated from high school. He began reading law with a Townshend attorney to pursue a career as a lawyer. But the Civil War shelved his plans. He joined the Union Army to lend a hand following its loss at Bull Run in July 1861, but expected to resume his legal studies soon, after the rebellion was swiftly crushed. In the meantime, he hoped his military service would give him the opportunity for some mind-broadening travel "at the expense of the government" to places he longed to see, like New York, Philadelphia, Washington, and Richmond.[6]

Twitchell rose to the rank of first sergeant, then in 1864 he applied for an officer's commission in the newly formed United States Colored Troops. The Emancipation Proclamation had been issued about a year earlier, and Congress granted former slaves permission to serve in the U.S. Army, although at much less than normal pay and only under the supervision of white officers.

Twitchell performed well on USCT officer-candidate exams in April 1864 and was offered a captain's commission, but months would pass before his new orders were issued. In the meantime, he returned to his unit, the Vermont Brigade, which had rolled up a distinguished combat reputation, seeing action in most of the biggest battles of the war's Eastern Theater. Twitchell had escaped injury so far, but on May 4, 1864, near Fredericksburg, Virginia, during the Battle of the Wilderness, he was shot in the face. The bullet grazed his left eye socket and skimmed his skull before popping out behind his ear.

When Twitchell awoke hours later, he was flat on his back, corpses sprawled on either side. His bruised and horribly swollen face, caked with dried blood and bandages, made him monstrous to behold. He asked an orderly when he would be moved to a hospital and received a chilling reply: "There are no ambulances for dead men."

If not for the intervention of an old schoolmate who happened upon the wounded sergeant and somehow recognized him, Twitchell might have been left for dead. His wounds were cleaned and rebandaged, and he was carted to a field hospital in a Fredericksburg church; he would soon be shipped north, where his convalescence lasted months. Eventually he was pronounced fit for duty again, but his vision and hearing were permanently impaired.[7]

Twitchell finally took command of H Company in the 109th Regiment, United States Colored Troops, in late September 1864. His unit consisted of ninety-four mostly illiterate former slaves who had been given no consistent leadership so far, and it showed in their loose discipline. "It was rightfully considered the fag end of the regiment," Twitchell recalled. But as he sized up his troops, he knew his fellow officers were whispering doubts about him, the twenty-four-year-old "boy captain" who seemed to be in over his head.

Twitchell spent a couple of relaxed days getting acquainted with his men, while announcing that big changes were coming. Beginning on the third day, he made a list of "delinquents," whom he ordered to assemble that evening fully armed and outfitted with heavy knapsacks for a long march and drilling. These rigorous outings lasted until about 9 p.m. Soon the number of derelicts fell sharply to at most one or two a night, and they would be forced to march back and forth near Twitchell's tent.

When the 109th was ordered east to join the main body of Union forces laying siege to Richmond, Twitchell could see how far his unit had progressed. "The splendid and perfect soldiers which these men were making, excelling even the best white troops I had ever seen, caused me to look forward with intense interest to their first battle."

Twitchell continued to be impressed by his men's performance, though they saw little combat for the remainder of the war beyond a few defensive skirmishes. The new commander of the Army near Richmond, General Edward O. C. Ord, disdained black troops and rarely used them. During the fall of Richmond in April 1865, Ord halted two units of approaching black troops in the suburbs and sent white soldiers to occupy the city center.[8]

After the war ended, Twitchell's unit was dispatched to Indianola, Texas, as part of General Philip H. Sheridan's troop buildup along the border to scare the French out of Mexico. It was a dreary posting, but Twitchell got a reprieve in August when he complained of a severe toothache. The post surgeon, lacking the right tools, sent his patient to New Orleans for treatment, and a chance to see the city for the first time.

Twitchell pounced on the opportunity to fashion a permanent escape from Texas. The Freedmen's Bureau, created by Congress to help former slaves adjust to the postwar world, was looking for agents, and USCT officers were ideal candidates. Twitchell visited the bureau's New Orleans storefront during his dental leave and was hired on the spot. The Freedmen's Bureau was part of the War Department, so the move amounted to a military transfer. Twitchell would be posted at his current rank to Bienville Parish in northwest Louisiana, part of the notoriously stubborn trans-Mississippi South, the last region of the Confederacy to surrender.[9]

Twitchell and nine black soldiers set up Bienville Parish's first Freedmen's Bureau outpost at the end of October 1865 in the isolated town of Sparta, three days' ride from New Orleans and twenty-five miles through dense woods from the nearest military base, with no telegraph. "I was surrounded by a community in which there were at least one thousand disbanded Confederate soldiers, all having no love for the government which had just vanquished them and of which I was the representative," Twitchell later wrote. "There was an intense bitterness against the colored soldiers, once their slaves but now, under my direction, their masters."

Twitchell's job was to explain that whites and blacks should now regard one another as "employer and employee." The U.S. government wanted work to go on as in old times, but Twitchell would decide how much an ex-slave would be paid, "in case he and his former master did not agree." Crowds gathered to hear Twitchell deliver this message on tours of the countryside.

Much of a bureau agent's time was spent resolving disputes between planters and their former bondsmen. Twitchell tried to protect the freedmen's interests and guard them against physical abuse, but the bureau's emphasis on maintaining production, and its strange premise that former slaves were strangers to hard work, produced retrograde policies. For instance, assigning black children to lengthy unpaid "apprenticeships" with planters who taught no marketable skills beyond "field hand" seemed like slavery renamed.[10]

In early January 1866, Adele Coleman, a slim and very pretty twenty-year-old who recently graduated from finishing school, was hired to teach music at the Sparta Academy. She lodged at the Mays Hotel, where Twitchell often took his supper. Soon the handsome Yankee captain and the vivacious young belle were inseparable, often meeting for meals or long, arm-in-arm promenades around town. Naturally, this was scandalous fraternizing with the enemy, and the relationship quickly veered into Shakespearean territory, including hostile relatives and a cross-dressing heroine.

A vindictive former suitor informed Adele's parents that she was keeping company with a Yankee. They instantly sent her brother Gus to fetch her home to the family plantation in Brush Valley, about twenty miles away, where she was cloistered and prayed over. Days later, Gus surged forth with a pistol and some notion of drawing the Yankee scoundrel into a duel. Fate seemed to frown on the couple. But Adele was a spirited girl, and dashing young men were thin on the ground in the wasted postwar South. She had a plan.

While Gus was on the warpath, Twitchell was summoned one night by an orderly to greet a peculiar visitor, a skittish young man seated atop a horse who insisted on keeping to the shadows. Twitchell cocked his pistol and held it under his coat as he stepped outside to confront the rider. "What do you want?" he demanded.

"Marshall," a female voice replied, "don't you know me?" It was Adele! She had borrowed a boy's clothes so she could travel inconspicuously and warn Twitchell of her brother's designs. Twitchell put her in a carriage for a romantic all-night ride back to Brush Valley, where her parents were sick with worry over their missing daughter.

Such episodes gradually convinced the Colemans that Adele wouldn't relinquish her Yankee beau and they found a way to embrace him. The couple was married in a twilight ceremony at Brush Valley on July 24, 1866. Twitchell wore his blue Army uniform at Adele's request. But they soon met new obstacles. When Twitchell announced he would carry his bride back to Vermont to settle down once his imminent discharge from the Army was complete, he met fierce resistance from Adele's family. But he didn't budge. Adele's mother then revealed that her daughter had a sore spot on one lung, which doctors feared was consumption. A move to frigid Vermont would likely kill her. Of course, that was that. Twitchell well knew that consumption ravaged his state. They would remain in Louisiana.

White propagandists contorted Twitchell's experience to fit a cartoonish stereotype of Yankee "carpetbaggers" plotting to overrun the prostrate South and leech it dry. The truth was less colorful, involving a man alert to opportunities and adjusting to unforeseen factors like Adele's illness.

The always thrifty Twitchell tapped his savings for a down payment on a cotton plantation in Bienville Parish. His new father-in-law, Isaac Coleman, bought the plantation next door and they ran their holdings as a joint concern.

As Twitchell adjusted to his new domestic life, the nation's political plates shifted to create additional opportunities for people like him. The federal Reconstruction Acts of 1867 required rebellious Southern states to write new constitutions disenfranchising many former Confederates and granting black suffrage. Twitchell was recruited as Bienville Parish's delegate to the state constitutional convention. His service in the USCT and the Freedmen's Bureau gave him standing with black voters, and his acceptance into a prominent Southern white family won him significant white backing.

In 1868, Twitchell stood for election as parish judge. He lost but was awarded the office when the winner was disqualified as an ex-Confederate. Then Twitchell won election to the state Senate in 1870. That same year he sold his Bienville plantation and bought a larger one on the Red River across from Coushatta. His plan to create a new Red River Parish, with Coushatta as the seat, was adopted by the legislature the following year.

The Red River Parish law and related measures created a slew of new offices, including sheriff, justices of the peace, tax collector, and police jurors, to be appointed by the Republican governor, who always relied on Twitchell to choose the nominees. Twitchell himself became president of the school board and the police jury, which was similar to a county court, and he was an active speculator in local real estate. He also helped his brother and three brothers-in-law land jobs as Red River Parish officials.[11]

Twitchell consistently advocated for the interests of his black constituents, who made up about two-thirds of the parish's population. While he chose more whites for official posts, probably because there were fewer educated blacks in Red River Parish than elsewhere in the state, he recruited many black allies for such jobs as coroner, justice of the peace, and police juror. And he boasted that freedmen felt "secure in that parish," safe from the white thugs who preyed on blacks during Reconstruction, usually without legal consequences. "Whenever there was a murder, we would either arrest the party or force him out of the parish," Twitchell said.

Twitchell also strongly supported education for freedmen, which he believed was their only path to political parity with whites. But he recognized that "the white people disliked to see the negro educated." He pushed a plan for two new schools in each ward, one for blacks and one for whites. When he learned of threats by "the wild young men" to destroy the freedmen's schools, he announced that "the day the colored school in any neighborhood was broken up, that day I would withdraw the money from the white school in that district." The black schools weren't disturbed while Republicans ruled the state.[12]

Twitchell had arguably proved that Reconstruction could succeed with a centrist strategy, advancing black rights while promoting economic opportunity for all. But perhaps he can be faulted for underestimating, as he and his allies prospered, the potential for a backlash, which seemed to take him by surprise as it gathered strength in the summer of 1874.

On the steamboat docked at Campti, as Twitchell listened to the boarding passengers recounting scenes from Natchitoches, he was unsure what to do next. Despite his many encouraging words to friends, he was hardly confident of Washington's military intentions. Would U.S. troops be sent to Louisiana now that the White League had moved beyond mere threats? Twitchell's base of operations in the Red River town of Coushatta was less than a day's ride from Natchitoches. His first impulse was to leap off the boat and rush back there to help fend off an invasion. But could he hope to assemble enough defenders? And how would he get there? Was it smarter to continue on as planned and attend the state Republican convention in New Orleans, using the opportunity to alert U.S. authorities there of the danger, and persuade them to send the cavalry to Coushatta?

As Twitchell's thoughts churned, he didn't notice that the steamboat had left the dock at Campti and resumed chugging toward New Orleans. The decision was now out of his hands. But it would never again be far from his thoughts. For the rest of his life, he would return to those hectic, hesitant moments on the Red River.

Several days after Twitchell arrived in New Orleans, on August 3, 1874, he received a pair of letters from Coushatta. The news was grim. White Leaguers there were openly talking of copying the Natchitoches uprising, in words too strong to leave any doubt about their intentions. "It is simply extermination" of Republicans, wrote Coushatta sheriff Frank Edgerton, Twitchell's brother-in-law. "It is generally believed that you have gone after troops," he told Twitchell. "It is my firm belief that you can live here only on horseback in the woods if you do not get them."

Twitchell wrote back immediately, telling Edgerton he had met with the governor and the U.S. marshal in New Orleans. "[A]s soon as some overt act is committed" by the White Leaguers, a marshal could be dispatched to Coushatta who "will doubtless take United States troops with him," he told Edgerton. In the meantime, if White Leaguers demanded Edgerton's resignation under threat of violence, Twitchell told him he must step down to save his life.

It wasn't an altogether reassuring message, but that hardly mattered.

White League agents stole Twitchell's letter en route and his brother-in-law never saw it.

In late August, while Twitchell was still in New Orleans, as many as one thousand White League operatives swept into Coushatta from the countryside near Shreveport, Minden, and Natchitoches, and the Piney Woods of East Texas. They roamed the streets in rowdy gangs shouting threats outside the homes of Republican officials.

Coushatta's White League leaders, backed by squads of these rural gunmen, tracked down and "arrested" Sheriff Edgerton, along with Twitchell's brother Homer and another brother-in-law. They also hauled in three other white Republican officials and twenty prominent black party members. It was an unsubtle assault on Republican governance in Coushatta, jewel of the party's Reconstruction experiment in the state.

The raiders dragged their six white prisoners before a shabby kangaroo court on trumped-up charges of plotting a violent "negro uprising"—a lurid fantasy invoked across the region in this era to excuse white vigilante violence. The six prisoners agreed to resign for safe passage out of town. But as their caravan of captives neared the parish border, its guards skulked away on cue when another armed mob galloped into view with guns blazing, killing Homer Twitchell, Sheriff Edgerton, and a third prisoner on the spot. The mob then took the other three prisoners into custody, but soon shot them dead as well. Other squads back in Coushatta hanged two black captives, and broke the arms and legs of a third before roasting him to death over a fire.

News of this "Coushatta Massacre" staggered Louisiana Republicans and spread swiftly across the nation. While reports of Southern atrocities against freedmen were regrettably routine at this point, the number and rank of the white victims got people's attention.

Twitchell was visiting a friend in Pass Christian, Mississippi, when he learned of the murders by telegram days later. He took the first train to New Orleans to confer with Governor Kellogg, and wired Washington to request a deployment of U.S. troops to Coushatta. Then he went to the federal courthouse and obtained an appointment as a U.S.

commissioner, which gave him authority to investigate the murders of his loved ones and bring their killers to justice.

Twitchell's profound grief fueled his rage at the killers' utter lack of honor and humanity. They disarmed their prey not for the sake of public peace, as they piously proclaimed, but so their victims "could offer no dangerous resistance to their own murder," he later wrote. Such treachery became, for Twitchell, the true substance of "so-called Southern chivalry."[13]

O n the day after the New Orleans coup, having locked his securities in the safe, Twitchell departed the Custom House "to the surprise of everybody" still finding sanctuary there. Outside he again dodged White League patrols, but instead of returning to the Canal Street station, he crossed town and caught the train at the Clairborne Street depot, eluding an operative posted at the other station to capture him.

Twitchell was still wrestling with his grief, but he couldn't afford to let down his guard. White League operatives were keen to find him and conclude their deadly business with the head of the Twitchell clan. For the moment, he was safe and still at liberty to seek some measure of vengeance for his family. But Louisiana Republicans might have been forgiven just then for feeling abandoned by their allies in Washington.[14]

CHAPTER 4

SYMPATHY FOR THE JUNTA

President Grant convened his cabinet two days after the New Orleans coup to weigh the federal response. Among the group of bewhiskered gentlemen seated around the stout walnut table in the White House Treaty Room, Grant was easily the most recognizable, although compared with his glory days as the lean and relentless commander of Union forces, the jowly former general "looked older—much older."

Grant asked his advisors if he should summon lawmakers back to Washington for a special session of Congress to deal with the Louisiana uprising—the biggest military clash on U.S. soil since the Civil War. All opposed the idea, preferring to let their fellow Republicans stay home campaigning for the fast-approaching elections.

The discussion then ranged over alarming terrain, including big shipments of arms flowing to the White League and similar groups mobilizing across the South, and the sorry state of U.S. Army forts in the region. But despite the white militants' evident mission to nullify the rights of former slaves, a strain of sympathy for the Louisiana insurgents threaded the conversation. Postmaster General Marshall Jewell read a telegram from a subordinate in New Orleans reporting that the "wealth, intelligence and business interest of the place" applauded the coup. The morning newspapers said that white U.S. soldiers in the city "cheered" the insurgents, confirming suspicions that many Northern enlisted men commiserated with the White League.

But Grant had already set the tone of the official federal response the previous afternoon, issuing a proclamation ordering the "turbulent and disorderly persons" who had overthrown Louisiana's government "to disperse and retire peaceably to their respective abodes." Jewell and Secretary of the Treasury Benjamin Bristow, both recent additions to the cabinet, had been surprised that Grant would issue such a proclamation without first consulting his advisors. "They are new members, otherwise they [would] not be surprised," Secretary of State Hamilton Fish noted wryly.[1]

Grant had operated this way for years, bypassing advisors, following his own impulses. Even when he was a young Army commander, he often slipped the leash of his superior officers, quick-marching his troops through Southern forests to catch opposing armies off balance before telegraph messengers could find him with the latest cautious orders from Washington.

Downstairs at the White House in the soaring Green Room, an immense portrait of a young General Grant on horseback watched over the premises. Such images of Grant—trim and ruggedly handsome, with chestnut hair and whiskers, and soulful eyes that evoked a kindly melancholy—were a powerful motif of the Civil War era. When delegates at the 1872 Republican National Convention in Philadelphia nominated Grant for a second term as president, he was unable to accept in person. But a giant portrait of his younger self on horseback was unfurled onstage and the crowd erupted in whooping and dancing, and belted out a delirious version of "John Brown's Body."[2]

Grant had decided to use his enormous stature after the Civil War to seek the presidency largely out of a sense of duty, to protect the so-called fruits of victory, especially the rights of freedmen, which would be lost, he feared, if left in the care of "mere trading politicians." He took office in 1869 as the youngest president in U.S. history at forty-six. But the White House years had not been kind. Scandals tainted his administration, mostly involving subordinates, although charges of cronyism and nepotism clung to him personally—he named his father U.S. postmaster in Covington, Kentucky, and gave minor posts to many other relatives.

Such lapses were gifts to Democratic editors, who liked to portray the quiet, unassuming Grant as a coarse and ruthless old warhorse with a bent for corruption. If he sent troops to the South to protect freedmen, Democrats accused him of behaving like a "Caesar" to help his carpetbagger henchmen loot the region's treasuries. One editor called him "a mean, grasping, stupid tyrant, devoid of all noble impulses."[3]

The Green Room portrait of Grant was a gift from an admirer in Louisiana, but Republican policies in that state had few admirers. While Republicans in Washington had engineered voting rights for freedmen, they generally didn't provide military protection from Southern whites intent on erasing freedmen's votes through violence and fraud. Louisiana Republicans had created a Returning Board to neutralize such tactics, empowering it to toss out ballots in areas tainted by voter intimidation or other tampering. The Returning Board helped Republicans win elections, but its vast power to discard ballots made even their Washington allies uncomfortable, and lent an air of moral righteousness to their opponents' objections. It didn't help that Grant had appointed his sister-in-law's husband, James F. Casey, as collector of customs in New Orleans, stirring nepotism into the unsavory mix.

Even after Warmoth sought to wield the Returning Board against Republicans in 1872, Democrats denounced Kellogg as a usurper. While Republicans found the state's election process hard to defend, many shuddered at the alternative: former slave drivers seizing power by stealing or suppressing the votes of former slaves.[4]

Republicans remained on the wrong foot politically when Grant's cabinet deliberated after the New Orleans coup. Everyone eventually agreed that recognizing the White League junta was out of the question because that would invite "the violent overthrow" of other Republican state governments reliant on freedmen's votes, including North and South Carolina, Alabama, and Mississippi. So Grant approved Kellogg's formal request for federal intervention—the first wave of U.S. troops had already arrived in New Orleans, and many more would follow. But the president refused "very emphatically" to impose martial law, citing lingering doubts about Kellogg's legitimacy.

U.S. Army General William H. Emory met with Penn, Marr, and John McEnery, the Democratic candidate for governor in the disputed 1872 election, on September 17. The Southerners quickly agreed to surrender state offices and seized weapons. They said they had no quarrel with the federal government. But some weapons stolen from state arsenals by White League forces were not surrendered, and none of the coup leaders was arrested, much less prosecuted.[5]

U.S. officials restored Kellogg to power around 10 a.m. on September 19 in the governor's office at the sprawling St. Louis Hotel. A quiet crowd of about five hundred freedmen had gathered across the street to mark the event. Soon shopkeepers complained that the commotion was disrupting business and White League patrols broke up the crowd. They would remain on duty until arrangements were made to replace the shattered Metropolitan Police.[6]

In the meantime, more U.S. military reinforcements flowed into Louisiana over the next few weeks. The Army dispatched three regiments of infantry and a battery of artillery. The Navy docked a small fleet of gunboats in the Mississippi River near New Orleans, manned by U.S. Marines. The Seventh Cavalry galloped into the outer parishes to patrol trouble spots like the Red River Valley.[7]

The solicitude shown to the White Leaguers might have owed something to General Emory's warm feelings for the coup leaders. He pushed for them to be "pardoned and exempted from prosecution" because of their prompt cooperation with federal authorities, "even when laboring under the most maddening impulses," he said in a letter to Grant.[8]

The White League militants also found pockets of sympathy in the Northern press. "We must say frankly that we know of no case of armed resistance to an established government in modern times in which the insurgents had more plainly the right on their side," said the *Nation* magazine. The *New-York Tribune* was harsher:

> Gen. Grant has vanquished the people of Louisiana again. He has telegraphed to his generals and his admirals; he has set the army and navy in motion. . . . The outrage stands out henceforth in all its naked deformity, an unpardonable crime against popular suffrage and the sovereignty of a State.[9]

Grant was indeed determined to roll back the coup. The president "means business in this thing" and "grows a little black in the face when talking about it," Jewell wrote to a friend. Grant's response to the crisis boosted his party's morale, especially in the South, and polished his own image. "The loyalty of the republic again looked to the soldier-President to meet the emergency," the *National Republican* reported on the day after the cabinet meeting.[10]

But soon the fall elections stunned Republicans everywhere. Democrats won control of the U.S. House of Representatives for the first time since before the Civil War, adding 90 seats for a 69-vote majority. A deepening economic depression partly drove the Republican debacle, but Grant's Louisiana policy might have hurt his party amid warming Northern feelings for the white South.

Adelbert Ames, the Republican governor of Mississippi, which had a sizable black majority, couldn't fathom what Northern voters were thinking when they handed power back to the party of the white South, especially since the Civil War was "not yet over!" Ames wrote to his wife that darker days lay ahead: "The old rebel spirit . . . will roam over our land, thirsty for revenge."[11]

CHAPTER 5

INVADERS

A ragtag army of black men approached the hilltop city of Vicksburg, Mississippi, around 9 a.m. on December 7, 1874, after hiking much of the night. The lookout posted in the soaring cupola of the Warren County courthouse—the city's highest point—had an unobstructed view for miles in every direction on this crisp, cloudless morning. Scanning the horizon with his telescope, he saw hundreds of "colored men" advancing in ragged brigades near the outskirts of town. He sounded the alarm.[1]

Volunteers for a white citizens militia, responding to an earlier warning, were already massing in the courthouse square as the big tower bell began clanging. Anxious onlookers filled the streets "like driving hogs or cattle," said William Wood, a black carpenter who was trying to steer clear of the excitable white people.[2]

H. H. Miller, a forty-eight-year-old lawyer who had served in the Confederate Army, was deputized to lead the city's defense. He picked about seventy-five well-armed men from the cluster of volunteers and set out. Near the city limits, they found the "invaders" spread along the crest of a hill overlooking a ravine spanned by a narrow bridge.

Miller sent scouts to cover approaches to the bridge, then rode up toward the men spread across the hill. There were about 125 of them, armed at most with a pistol shoved in a waistband, or a shotgun suitable for bird hunting. Perhaps half of them bore no weapons.

Miller spoke to a mixed-race man with rather long, straight hair who identified himself as Andrew Owen, the group's leader. In a voice loud enough for many of the others to hear, Miller warned Owen that it was illegal for armed bands to enter the city limits, and that they should disperse now and return to their homes, or else face the consequences.

Owen waved away any talk of consequences. He and his men were here on important business for the Warren County sheriff, Peter Crosby. Then he stared at Miller and made a demand of his own: "Where is Crosby?"[3]

I t was a fair question. Several months before this so-called Negro invasion, the city's white people had staged an invasion of their own. They were frustrated that former slaves, or "freedmen," who made up a majority of the city's population, used their newly awarded voting rights to elect black officials, some of whom faced credible charges of corruption. Black officials and their Republican allies were also charged with collectively robbing productive whites with ruinously high taxes to fund unprecedented luxuries like public schools. Whites decided they were justified in restoring themselves to power by whatever means necessary, including the deployment of armed gangs threatening violence to keep blacks from the polls.[4]

Such methods helped whites win city elections in August 1874. Then they began plotting to retake the county government. County Sheriff Peter Crosby's office was their primary target. Crosby, a mixed-race former slave who served in the Union Army during the Civil War, had won his previous election handily, with overwhelming support from blacks. But whites didn't challenge Crosby at the ballot box.

County sheriffs in Mississippi collected taxes and had to be bonded, or insured against potential losses of taxpayer funds. A white "taxpayer's league" claimed that the underwriters of Sheriff Crosby's bond possessed insufficient means to make good on possible claims. The group could have taken the matter to court and let a judge decide if the sheriff should be disqualified to serve. But it chose a different path. About five hundred armed men surrounded Crosby's office, demanded his resignation over the bond issue, and threatened to settle things with a rope if he refused. Crosby, believing his life was in danger, reluctantly agreed to step down.[5]

O wen and his men had answered the call for a posse to help Crosby retake the sheriff's office. But Crosby was in the militia's custody now. Miller had ordered him seized soon after the posse was spotted outside town.

Owen asked for safe passage to speak with Crosby and was escorted to "the farthest room, in the farthest corner" of the courthouse, where the prisoner was housed. Their meeting was brief. Crosby told Owen to "disband your men" and send them on their way. He wanted no confrontation. In view of the white militia's far superior firepower, it was perhaps a simple concession to reality.

Owen returned to his men waiting on the hillside and told them to "go right back home," that their business was finished. The freedmen started to withdraw, but after they had hiked several hundred yards, a group of white militiamen on horseback began firing at them. Soon other militiamen joined the shooting.

A group of Owen's men fell back and pleaded with him to lead them in a counterattack against the militia. "You shall not do it if I can prevent it," Owen said. But seeing that the men still intended to fight, he shouted: "If you do it you will have to put a bullet in *me*. Everything is settled. Let us go home."

As the militia continued firing, a few of Owen's men ignored his warning and formed up in a line to shoot back. Owen pulled out his revolver and held it high. "If you return the fire *I* will give you the next volley," he shouted. His men reluctantly stood down.

With bullets whistling all around, Owen dove into a ditch to take cover and the retreating freedmen scattered. Despite Owen's warnings, some of his men stopped to return fire, though at that distance their pistols and bird guns were no match for the militia's high-powered rifles. Eight or nine freedmen were killed in this skirmish, while the white militiamen emerged from it unscathed.

The freedmen had been "firing at long range with short range guns," one militia member recalled. Given the disparities in weaponry, the militia's attack "didn't require any valor," he said.

"It was no battle; it was a simple massacre," Republicans on a congressional investigating committee later concluded. "The killing of these men, thus retiring in good faith, was murder, willful, cowardly, and in violation of all laws of peace or of war."

Miller apparently rescued many freedmen from the melee by sending them under guard to the courthouse as prisoners. Owen was among those rounded up.[6]

But the white militia was far from finished. Mounted patrols clattered down Vicksburg's sloping streets into lower-lying neighborhoods, where many freedmen leased former slave cabins on plantation land. Perhaps the whites sought revenge for two militiamen slain in later skirmishes with Owen's fleeing troops, though they might have been felled by wayward militia fire. Perhaps the whites simply wanted to dispense a bracing reminder to the servile population that even abortive rebellions have consequences.

Around midmorning on December 7, five armed white men on horseback stopped a couple of miles outside town at the home of Robert Banks, a middle-aged freedman. Banks was standing near his front door, perhaps curious about the ruckus in the streets. Two of the white men told him to hold the reins of their beasts, then barged into his house, where they found his teenage son, Robert, and several frightened women, including his wife, Louisa. The men grabbed the boy and ordered him to turn over any weapons in the house. He showed them a pistol stashed in the rafters, then sprinted out the back door. The men gave chase and one of them raised his rifle and shot young Robert in the back, killing him instantly.

Amid the women's anguished wailing, the two white men walked out the front door and asked the elder Robert Banks to tie their horses and step into the road. He quietly obeyed, and one of the white men shot him through the neck. He was dead before his wife reached his side.[7]

Such reprisal attacks went on for days. On the evening of December 8, Buck Wonell, a freedman who leased a small house on the Edwards plantation several miles outside of Vicksburg, tried to evade a large group of white men approaching on horseback "that was going to kill all the black people," said his wife, Peggy. "There was a whole army coming. I could not tell how many; they were the same as blackbirds."

Buck was apparently seeking a white authority figure to vouch for him. He ran to the Edwards house, about fifteen yards from his own, "for them to friend him," Peggy said. Buck had worked for the family, but when the white horsemen rode up and consulted Miss Martha, Mr. Edwards's only daughter, she gave no quarter. According to Peggy's testimony, Miss Martha told the white horsemen: "Don't shoot him here. But take him out of the yard and I don't care what you do with him."

The white horsemen did as Miss Martha requested. "They brought him outside of the back gate and shot him right down." The bullet pierced Buck's upper jaw and "he just fell and died right off," Peggy said. His body lay there "for two nights and two days, and the dogs ate his face and head all off before we women could bury him."[8]

William Wood said he saw the abandoned bodies of four dead black men "lying on the road" as he walked to work in the countryside two days after the violence began. He had avoided traveling for a while to keep out of trouble. "I don't care to be hunted from one part of the world to the other, nor to have them come along and shoot me down just like I was a rabbit."[9]

There is broad agreement that two whites were killed during the Vicksburg "troubles," and historians generally put the number of freedmen killed at about twenty-five. But some argue that white planters fed the press deliberate undercounts of black casualties to preserve calm labor relations, and that as many as three hundred freedmen were killed. Wood said some of the dead were found only much later, when buzzards roosting in the trees signaled the presence of abandoned corpses.[10]

Press reports from Vicksburg reflected whites' hyperactive paranoia about "negro uprisings" dating back to slavery times, and their desire to be seen as victims. On December 8, the New Orleans *Picayune* reported that "8,000 Negroes" had invaded Vicksburg and "refused" to disperse. Another false report said freedmen were "burning dwellings and gin houses."[11]

White Vicksburg's apparent distress prompted offers of help from its Southern neighbors. On the night of December 7, about 160 armed white men arrived in Vicksburg from Louisiana. On December 12, George W. Walton, a freedman who was president of the Warren County Board of Supervisors, received a telegram from Texas, addressed to his office, clearly sent by someone expecting a white person to be on the receiving end:

TRINITY, TEX., December 12, 1874
To the President of the Board of Supervisors:

Do you want any men? Can raise good crowd within twenty-four hours to kill out your negroes.
J. G. Gates and A. H. Mason.[12]

Not all news dispatches from Vicksburg followed the white party line. The *Cincinnati Commercial* reported on December 11 that the nation had been misled. A "slaughter of colored men" had taken place in Vicksburg, set in motion by "hot headed and irresponsible" men intent on ousting Sheriff Crosby. Freedmen who tried to aid the sheriff were "chased through the woods and the fields and shot down like dogs," the report said. "Many were shot after they gave up, and some were shot on their knees while begging for mercy."

Congressional investigators concluded that "White Line" vigilantes behind the violence in Vicksburg were "unquestionably an extension into Mississippi" of the Louisiana White League. Journalists had published similar theories, but these judgments seemed to overshoot the evidence. Even if white vigilantes in Mississippi drew inspiration from the Louisiana White League, the Mississippi militants were likely motivated by local grievances, and influence appeared to flow in both directions.

Historian Mark Grimsley explains the organized resistance to Radical Reconstruction mounted by white Southerners as an example of a "complex insurgency," one with "no single directing brain but rather a functional relationship among several groups with common attitudes, enemies and objectives." Such broadly sympathetic relations might even include ad hoc assistance, as when armed white Louisianians rushed to Vicksburg following reports of "troubles" with the black population there.

White conservatives in Mississippi had been impressed by a sense of Reconstruction's fragility even before the September 1874 White League coup in New Orleans. When the Grant administration balked at sending troops to corral Mississippi White Line militants who were using intimidation tactics prior to the August 1874 municipal elections in Vicksburg, conservatives saw a path to the ultimate "recovery of white rule," according to historian John S. McNeily. Conservative victories in those municipal elections meanwhile "promoted the success of the White League" in neighboring Louisiana, historian Joe Gray Taylor reports.[13]

Mississippi White Liners drew further encouragement from the White League insurrection in New Orleans the following month, and from Democrats' smashing victory over Republicans in the fall 1874 national elections, when public "meetings to express the common rejoicing were held all over the South." The *Cincinnati Commercial* noted the effect of those elections on the men behind the "massacre" in Vicksburg, reporting that they were "animated by the conviction that there has been a political revolution in the North, and that their time is come."[14]

CHAPTER 6

FEAR OF A BLACK STATE

The king of the Sandwich Islands, a famously affable fellow known as the "Merrie Monarch," arrived at the White House for a state dinner in his honor on December 22, 1874. His visit promised a break from the crisis vexing President Ulysses S. Grant, who, in a matter of hours, would launch a secret plan to rescue former slaves under siege in the South. But the visiting monarch in some ways embodied the crisis.

The king was a beefy thirty-eight-year-old Polynesian named David Kalakaua, with large, tranquil eyes, coal-black hair, and plump cheeks framed by shaggy side whiskers. As sovereigns go, he maintained a modest profile: the azure sash under his dinner jacket was his only display of rank. But he navigated Washington society with regal ease, charming the satin-gowned wives of cabinet secretaries in the oval-shaped Blue Room; narrating cliff-diving escapades with rapt reporters in his hotel drawing room. "I think nothing of making a leap into the water from a precipice five hundred feet high," he explained, demonstrating a pre-dive posture. Where he grew up, "even little girls jump from heights three and four hundred feet from the water."

Kalakaua had attended his nation's finest schools. Although English was not his native tongue, one observer said that he spoke it "with the greatest ease and purity," exhibiting "a strength and character which mark him as no ordinary man." An accomplished poet and musician, the king would revive many native cultural traditions in his balmy realm—which was also known as Hawaii—including hula dancing, ukulele music, and surfing. A song he wrote would become his country's national anthem.[1]

But by far the most fascinating things about Kalakaua to U.S. observers were his relatively dark skin, full lips, and other features that suggested he had an African ancestor. Newspapers north and south belittled him with labels like "Saddle Colored Royalty" and "copper-colored potentate," comparing his appearance to such things as "a newly-polished mahogany table." One reporter declared that the king "would pass" for a mixed-race gentleman "with a good tailor."

The press mostly presented Kalakaua's weeks-long tour, with its military escorts and marching bands, as a diverting spectacle, much the way American media would swoon over royalty in later years—he was the first reigning monarch ever to visit the United States. But editors routinely folded demeaning episodes into the pageantry. A young woman maneuvering to sit at the king's table during the state dinner withdrew her request after learning of his "complexion." An old black man waiting in the crowd at the Washington train depot to view the royal arrival blurted out in astonishment upon sighting Kalakaua: "'Foe God! The king is a negro!" (Southern editors substituted the most offensive slurs.) When Kalakaua's tour reached New York City, a drunken alderman in the official greeting party referred to him as a "damn'd nagur."[2]

Kalakaua never responded publicly to these insults, but they echoed the recent experiences of African American former slaves. When their rights were expanded in the years after the Civil War to include voting, many freedmen were elected or appointed to public office in Southern states, especially in areas with large populations of former slaves. But no matter how high they climbed, they couldn't escape the lash of respectable white opinion. A freedman who became a successful attorney and was elected speaker of the South Carolina House of Representatives was described as "a very good specimen of the typical steamboat barber" by a Midwestern newspaper, which also referred to a group of black state senators as "lusty looking" and better suited for "the corn field."[3]

Frederick Douglass defined this slimy press tactic as "writing the negro down." Reporters working in this mode sought to undermine freedmen in public office, mocking the "dusky tide" of former slaves flooding Southern capitals, some of whose nongenteel manners signaled to their press critics nothing short of "a descent into barbarism." Douglass claimed that some anti-freedmen propaganda in newspapers had an even darker purpose: "to fire the negro-hating heart to deeds of violence against the black race."[4]

Freedmen and their allies were clearly under siege in the final weeks of 1874. Although Grant had responded to the September coup in New Orleans with a huge deployment of U.S. troops and firepower, White League militants were still menacing the state's Republican government. Over the past several days, they had issued threats of violence against officials counting ballots from the state legislative elections in November, and were believed to be plotting an attack on the legislature when it reconvened on January 4.[5]

Grant dispatched troops to restore order in Vicksburg, Mississippi, and a congressional committee would investigate the recent explosion of murderous violence against freedmen there. Former slaves in Alabama sent Grant a petition in early December seeking protection from violent white vigilantes, who had helped to restore conservative white Democrats to power in their state in the recent elections. The petition, written by Philip Joseph, a freeborn black newspaper editor, said the "colored people" of Alabama faced a campaign of "secret assassinations, lynching" and threats to "deprive us of employment and the renting of lands" for voting the wrong way. Echoing the Louisiana freedmen who petitioned Grant in September, the Alabama freedmen suggested they might seek refuge outside the United States if Grant couldn't protect their rights. "Shall we be compelled to repeat the history of the Israelites and go into exile?"[6]

A few hours before Kalakaua came to dinner, Grant forwarded the Alabama freedmen's petition to the House of Representatives, where several investigations of Southern outrages were underway. As Grant sat in the White House dining room across the table from the Hawaiian king, perhaps he recalled the fiascoes that ensued the last time he rolled out a secret plan to rescue the former slaves.

L ong before the royal food tasters blessed all twenty courses plated on Limoges china at the White House dinner, long before the champagne began to flow and the Cuban cigars were puffed, it was clear that Washington wished to be more than just friends with Kalakaua's tropical archipelago.[7]

Weeks earlier, Grant had dispatched the sloop USS *Benicia* to carry the king and his keepers across the heaving Pacific 2,400 miles to San Francisco, where they boarded the recently completed Transcontinental Railroad. The secretaries of state, of the Navy, and of war greeted Kalakaua at the Washington train depot, flanked by U.S. troops presenting arms and the red-jacketed Marine Band blowing brassy anthems. The king rode downtown in Grant's personal carriage as cheering crowds filled rooftops and spilled into the streets. A block of thirteen rooms awaited him at the posh Arlington Hotel, including an opulent grand parlor and a bedroom suite with lace curtains and blue silk upholstery. His chambers were studded with "a profusion of spittoons," the *Washington Evening Star* noted, because "[m]ost kings do expectorate, and let fly right and left."[8]

Kalakaua's American tour, underwritten by U.S. taxpayers, cost about $25,000, or half a million in today's dollars. U.S. officials said it was an opportunity for the two nations to strike a "reciprocity" trade deal. But in secret dispatches U.S. diplomats had long been pressing the case for eventual annexation of the islands, mostly on strategic grounds, an outcome dearly desired by Hawaii's sugar barons, many of whom were descendants of American missionaries. It was hoped that until annexation could be arranged, a trade deal would bind the islands to the United States "by the chains of self-interest, never to be severed," as one diplomat phrased it in a secret State Department dispatch.[9]

The Hawaii annexation plan was among Washington's worst-kept secrets. It popped up everywhere in unattributed news reports as the real reason behind Kalakaua's visit. Grant hadn't taken a position on it yet. He was still smarting from the failure of his own annexation proposal a few years earlier, a debacle so damaging he promised the American people never to recommend another new acquisition of territory without first securing their support. But as Grant's options for helping the freedmen dwindled, he remained convinced that his 1870 proposal to annex Santo Domingo would have leveled the playing field for freedmen in the South, and his inability to enact it would eat at him for the rest of his life.[10]

In a memo Grant wrote early in his first term under the heading "Reasons Why San Domingo Should Be Annexed to the United States," he named economic and security benefits from the Caribbean nation's loamy soil and strategic natural harbors. But he also cataloged game-changing effects on Reconstruction and race relations.

"The present difficulty in bringing all parts of the United States to a happy unity and love of country grows out of the prejudice to color," Grant wrote in the memo. "The prejudice is a senseless one, but it exists."

Grant hoped that making Santo Domingo part of the United States would neutralize the effects of that prejudice by giving freedmen a possible sanctuary. He believed that the Caribbean nation, whose sparse population was largely black and mixed-race, was rich enough in land and natural resources to accommodate all U.S. freedmen who might wish to emigrate there. But he also believed that simply having that option would make life easier for the former slaves, giving them leverage in bargaining with white planters for better wages and working conditions. And if freedmen still couldn't get a better deal in the South after annexation, they could exercise their new rights securely, as full American citizens, in Santo Domingo.

Others were also optimistic about the policy, even believing that Santo Domingo would be admitted to the union as a state where freedmen could flourish. One such believer wrote to Secretary of State Hamilton Fish that Santo Domingo "would not only be made a state of great importance, but an asylum for our negro population & the solution to the Negro Problem."[11]

Grant shied away from making such points publicly, and generally confined his sales pitch to annexation's economic and security benefits, like cheaper coffee and sugar, and a new Caribbean U.S. Navy base. Possibly he felt that the public wouldn't be receptive to a new federal effort on behalf of freedmen. The Fifteenth Amendment had recently been adopted, prohibiting the denial of voting rights on account of race. A feeling was abroad in the land that the United States had already done quite enough for "the Negro," after waging a bloody civil war to end slavery and enshrining the rights of freedmen in the national charter.[12]

But while Grant emphasized economics and natural resources, annexation opponents focused on Santo Domingo's mixed-race population. The entire episode, much like the press treatment of Kalakaua, demonstrated that the "prejudice to color" wasn't confined to Southern whites or the Democratic Party. A pair of Republican senators were annexation's most vocal foes: Massachusetts senator Charles Sumner and Missouri senator Carl Schurz. Both men were staunch friends of the freedmen, and they cast their opposition as support for the native black residents of Santo Domingo and neighboring Haiti, who, they insisted, were entitled to rule in those places without U.S. interference.

But neither man was fond of Grant, and they were not above stoking racial anxieties to undermine his plan.

When the Senate began debating annexation in 1870, Sumner, the great antislavery orator, was nearly sixty, sallow and slope-shouldered. But he still preened like a dandy with his flopping mane, walking stick, and stylish cravats, and could still hold galleries with his booming, sonorous voice. He thundered that the annexation plan sought "the incorporation within our political system and family of States of part of an island now held by a semi-barbarous race, the descendants of African slaves, whose attempts at self-governance, continued for upward of half a century, have been but a series of blood-stained failures."[13]

Schurz was equally harsh. The forty-one-year-old German immigrant was another antislavery hero. Tall and spindly, with thick brown hair issuing in wayward ringlets, he peered intensely from rimless spectacles and stalked the Senate floor like a mantis. If the United States annexed Santo Domingo, he insisted, it would invoke Manifest Destiny to devour the entire Caribbean region. What then would be done with the "millions" of new mixed-race U.S. citizens this would create? "You cannot exterminate them all," Schurz declared rather chillingly. These new territories must be admitted as states "upon an equal footing with the states you represent," Schurz told his Senate colleagues, asking them to envision the motley characters who would then be "sitting in the Halls of Congress, throwing the weight of their intelligence, their morality, their political notions and habits, their prejudices and passions, into the scale of destinies of this Republic." In case his scorn wasn't clear, he added: "Does not your imagination recoil from the picture?"[14]

The annexation proposal was soundly defeated. Suspicion of financial improprieties by White House aides who negotiated the Santo Domingo treaty didn't help its prospects. But the London *Spectator* saw another vulnerability, noting that "the dread of the negro is on all politicians."[15]

Recriminations over the annexation debacle split the Republican Party into warring factions, weakening federal efforts to help the former slaves. Grant's secret plan to create a freedmen's sanctuary had backfired, leaving him more reliant on military force to protect freedmen and their allies in the South.[16]

CHAPTER 7

"A TRIP SOUTH MIGHT BE AGREEABLE"

John C. Winsmith, a former Confederate officer from Spartan-burg, South Carolina, who became a Republican after the Civil War, wrote to Grant in October 1874 warning that "bad men" were planning "another butchery of the white and colored Republicans" in his state. These men, unwilling to accept "the results" of the Civil War, had organized "white leagues, rifle clubs and a secret police" to accomplish their brutal work. But they could still be stopped, Winsmith said, if the president took one simple step: send General Sheridan!

"His presence here—the power of his great name and of his military renown—will cause the traitors to tremble," Winsmith said. "I believe if General Sheridan comes soon the bloody plans of the Traitors and murderers will be thwarted."[1]

Winsmith was far from alone in thinking that U.S. Army General Philip H. Sheridan could alter the course of events with his mere presence. Grant's mailbags contained many such pleas, and Grant himself held a similar view of Sheridan's prowess. Ever since the Civil War, Sheridan had been Grant's go-to commander for particularly gnarly missions, like whipping the sluggish U.S. Cavalry into shape, or cornering Lee's army near Appomattox, Virginia, to hasten the conflict's end. Sheridan was currently running the Army's brutal war against the Plains Indians.

Sheridan vaulted to national fame in 1864 by leading his troops to a miraculous come-from-behind victory in the Battle of Cedar Creek, inspiring the popular poem "Sheridan's Ride." About five feet, five inches tall, "Little Phil" Sheridan was described by one breathless journalist as a wiry "miracle of war," known for streaking ahead of his troops, saber drawn, gray eyes flashing rage, screaming insults at Confederate "fiends."

A hero in the North, Sheridan was loathed in the South for his harsh tactics. Under orders to smash the breadbasket of Lee's army, Virginia's Shenandoah Valley, Sheridan confiscated crops and livestock and put the torch to barns and mills across the region in a campaign that became known as "the burning." Sheridan later said of his methods, "The people must be left nothing but their eyes to weep with over the war."[2]

Sheridan came to be identified with such "hard war" tactics, but he was carrying out a policy articulated by the commanding general himself. To dismantle Confederate support networks among Virginia's civilian population, Grant had ordered his armies to leave the Shenandoah Valley so bereft of nourishment "that crows flying over it for the balance of this season will have to carry their provender with them."

Grant developed a close working relationship with Sheridan despite the fact that their temperaments could have hardly been more different. Sheridan was known for his volatility and bluster, while the famously unassuming, self-effacing Grant was described as "a man who could remain silent in several languages."

But beneath these stark contrasts lurked the common weaves in their experiences. Both men grew up in Ohio in solidly middle-class homes, both attended West Point, and along the way to storied military accomplishments, each was tripped up by a career-derailing setback.

After Grant graduated from West Point he saw extensive action in the Mexican War and earned a number of battlefield promotions. For him, the peacetime Army proved more hazardous. Assigned to an isolated post in the Pacific Northwest, far from his wife and young children, a lonely, brooding Captain Grant was apparently found to be mildly under the influence of alcohol while on duty by a fastidious superior officer, who presented him with an awful choice: face charges or resign from the military. Grant struggled with alcohol for much of his life but generally managed to keep it under control with help from family and friends. Confronted with possible charges, he opted to resign from the military and fell into a years-long scramble for income to support his family, failing at various vocations and occasionally selling firewood on street corners to get by. Eventually, and most reluctantly, Grant went to work at his father's tannery in Galena, Illinois. But his ultimate rescue from the perils of civilian work arrived in 1861 with the onset of the Civil War. Following Lincoln's call for volunteers to put down the Southern rebellion, Grant's valuable military experience shone through and his official reenlistment in the Army and rise in its ranks was swift. By August 1861, he had been promoted to general and placed in command of the Union Army on the Mississippi River.

Sheridan also endured a period of exile linked to a character quirk—his volcanic temper. About a year short of graduation at West Point, during a field drill, he took offense at an order from a higher-ranking fellow cadet. An enraged Sheridan lowered his rifle, to which a bayonet was affixed, and charged at the cadet, screaming: "God damn you, sir! I will run you through!" Fortunately, Sheridan stopped short of carrying out this threat, but the other cadet reported the incident to academy authorities. The following day, as the cadet sat on the front porch of his barracks, Sheridan appeared and punched him on the side of the head. Sheridan might well have been expelled for his actions, but the academy supervisor recommended just a one-year suspension, which was approved by the War Department. Sheridan went back to his former job in a dry goods store, stewing over the unfairness of it all, but returned to West Point the following year and graduated.

Grant won a string of impressive early victories in the Civil War's Western Theater and quickly became known as an extraordinarily aggressive commander who took the fight to the enemy. Displaying a kindred ethos, Sheridan also rose rapidly in the ranks, becoming a brigadier general in 1862. At the Battle of Chattanooga in 1863, Grant took note of his fiery subordinate's gifts. After Union forces had secured their victory, Sheridan led his men in pursuit of Confederate General Braxton Bragg's retreating armies, capturing scores of enemy prisoners and a bounteous haul of weapons in the process. If the Union commander on the field had not refused to send more troops to assist Sheridan's brigades, they might have done significantly more damage to the enemy. Grant clearly thought so. With "the instinct of military genius," Grant later recalled, Sheridan had pushed ahead. "If others had followed his example, we should have had Bragg's army," Grant concluded.[3]

Soon after Lincoln tapped Grant to lead the entire Union war effort, Grant summoned Sheridan back east to lend a hand, ultimately deploying him in the pivotal Shenandoah Valley campaign. It was not only Sheridan's soldierly instincts that Grant admired. "I believe General Sheridan has no superior as a general, either living or dead, and perhaps not an equal," Grant said years later. "People think he is only capable of leading an army in battle, or to do a particular thing he is told to do. But I mean, all the qualities of a commander which enable him to direct over as large a territory as any two nations can cover in war. He has judgment, prudence, foresight and power to deal with the dispositions needed in a great war. I entertained this opinion of him before he became generally known in the late war."[4]

As Kalakaua boarded the train out of Washington on December 23, a delegation of Louisiana Republicans visited the White House to discuss worrisome developments: White League terrorists were promising to overthrow their state's government again, even though U.S. forces had maintained a robust presence in New Orleans since the September 14 uprising; bluecoat cavalry patrolled the city's cobblestone streets; Navy warships commanded the harbor; squads of infantry polished their boots in barracks along the perimeter. But the commander of these estimable forces, the paunchy, pale, and graying General William Emory, known for his cordial relations with Southern white leaders, seemed out of step with the mission. Grant's visitors wanted Emory replaced with a more assertive officer. Grant heard them out, stroking his beard, but made no commitment beyond some hopeful generalities. He promised to "decide in a few days what should be done to further assure the people of the South that they would be fully protected hereafter against the lawless acts of the White Leaguers in Louisiana, Alabama and Mississippi," according to the *New York Herald*.

But when the Louisiana delegation left the White House, Grant summoned Secretary of War William Belknap and directed him to send an urgent, confidential telegram:

War Department
Washington, D.C., December 24, 1874
Gen. P. H. Sheridan,
Chicago, Ill.:

GENERAL: The president sent for me this morning, and desires me to say to you that he wishes you to visit the States of Louisiana and Mississippi, and especially New Orleans, La., and Vicksburg and Jackson, Miss., and ascertain for yourself, and for his information, the general condition of matters in those localities. You need not confine your visit to the States of Louisiana and Mississippi, and may extend your trip to other States, Alabama, etc., if you see proper, nor need you confine your visit in the States of Louisiana and Mississippi to the places named. What the President desires is the true condition of affairs, and to receive such suggestions from you as you may deem advisable and judicious. Inclosed herewith is an order authorizing you to assume command of the Military Division of the South, or any portion of that division, should you see proper to do so. It may be possible that circumstances may arise which would render this a proper course to pursue. You can, if you desire it, see General McDowell in Louisville, and make known to him confidentially the object of your trip, but this is not required of you. Communication with him by you is left entirely to your own judgment. Of course, you can take with you such gentlemen of your staff as you wish, and it is best that the trip should appear to be one as much of pleasure as of business, for the fact of your mere presence in the localities referred to will have, it is presumed, a beneficial effect. The President thinks, and so do I, that a trip South might be agreeable to you, and that you might be able to obtain a good deal of information on the subject about which we desire to learn. You can make your return by Washington, and make a verbal report, and also inform me from time to time of your views and conclusions.

Yours, truly, etc.,
W. W. Belknap, Secretary of War.

Under orders to make his excursion "appear to be" a vacation, Sheridan was accompanied by a rather large traveling party, including Army Quartermaster General Daniel H. Rucker and his twenty-two-year-old daughter, Irene. Turbulent Louisiana would be the first stop on their undercover tour.[5]

On December 28, as Sheridan's train chugged toward New Orleans, Postmaster General Marshall Jewell wrote that Grant seemed "plucky and serene," and was determined "to protect the colored voter in his rights to the extent of his power under the law, and if we cannot protect them we shall lose most of the fruits of this terrible war."[6]

Grant shared details of Sheridan's new mission with those who needed to know, including Belknap, keeping most of his advisors in the dark, even Secretary of State Hamilton Fish, whose opinions he valued highly on most matters. During a December 29 cabinet meeting, Grant didn't mention the plan even when the discussion turned to Louisiana. Grant also signaled another change of heart, announcing to the cabinet that if there was trouble in New Orleans when the legislature reconvened, he might need to impose martial law. But Attorney General George H. Williams did not endorse the idea. "[T]here is some doubt in the law as to the president's authority," Fish noted in his diary.[7]

CHAPTER 8

A LOCAL CLUB

Frederick Nash Ogden, the redheaded, barrel-chested "Chief of the White League," testified before a visiting subcommittee of the U.S. House of Representatives on New Year's Eve 1874. Spectators crowded the New Orleans courtroom. Newspapers across the nation also paid heed.

President Grant, in his recent annual message to Congress, had lamented reports from the fall election campaign of efforts by "White Leagues and other societies" to suppress the votes of black Southerners through "acts of violence and intimidation." He vowed to send U.S. troops if necessary to help defeat these threats, but also acknowledged "complaints" about the propriety of such federal interference, inviting Congress to investigate "whether the alleged wrongs to colored citizens" were "real" or "manufactured" for partisan purposes.

Congress was quick to take up Grant's request. Since his annual message devoted considerable attention to troubles in Louisiana, the House created a special committee to investigate the 1874 election there, and the subcommittee's New Orleans visit was part of that effort. But while two of the panel's three members were Republicans, if Grant hoped they would ensure a penetrating examination of "White

Leagues" and political violence against black citizens he would be sorely disappointed.[1]

White Leagues had emerged across Louisiana in recent months. Ogden's New Orleans branch of the burgeoning movement, the Crescent City White League, was established in June 1874 and quickly struck a major blow, overthrowing the carpetbagger regime of Republican governor William Pitt Kellogg on September 14 of that year in the biggest armed clash on U.S. soil since the Civil War. The conservative New Orleans press hailed Ogden on that occasion as a conquering hero.

Despite Ogden's role in a violent coup, the visiting subcommittee did little to challenge his portrayal of the Crescent City White League as a benign society of public-spirited citizens. Ogden testified that his heavily armed, highly trained militia of over 2,500 men was really just "a club," whose members were organized "purely for defensive purposes" having "nothing at all" to do with politics. An additional ten thousand armed and trained White Leaguers operated in parishes across the state, but Ogden testified that they were under the command of local officers, although he conceded that they might unite their forces with his "if I gave the order."

Asked about possible White League involvement in reprisals against black citizens who voted Republican in the recent elections, Ogden denied it, claiming that the group's only role in the elections was guarding polling stations. He also denied that his organization's name was meant to suggest only white men should hold office. In a show of transparency, Ogden submitted a copy of the Crescent City White League's constitution to the subcommittee. "Our constitution says that we will defend the rights of all classes of people," he testified.

Despite Ogden's insistence that his organization shunned politics, its constitution plainly stated that one of the Crescent City White League's primary objectives was "to drive incompetent and corrupt men from office" to restore "an honest and intelligent" state government. Many Louisiana Republicans, black and white, had indeed been driven from office in recent months, both before and especially after the New Orleans coup that ousted Governor Kellogg, temporarily as it turned out. The subcommittee did not press Ogden to explain the contradiction.

While Ogden submitted a copy of his group's constitution for the record, the Crescent City White League was also governed by a "platform," which he apparently did not surrender to the visiting congressmen, although its text had stained the pages of the local conservative press. Perhaps Ogden judged it unsuitable for the Northern audience he wished to address through the subcommittee's megaphone. The platform's scalding language conveyed a far clearer idea of the White League's viciously racist aims, couched in a febrile plea to rescue "civilization" from the mortal danger posed by an alleged black "barbarism."

The threat was rapidly escalating, the platform declared, as black Louisianians grew more assertive with their "incessant demands for office from the state, city and federal government." Their mounting "arrogance" foretold the emergence of an even greater danger, the platform warned: an "oath bound and blindly obedient league of the blacks," commanded by "the most cunning and unscrupulous negroes in the state," which could plunge Louisiana into "a war of races." Somehow the best way to stave off this racial apocalypse was for white men to form a "league of the whites." The platform called upon the white men of New Orleans to set aside past party differences and join the Crescent City White League "in an earnest effort to re-establish a white man's government in the city and the State."[2]

In the days leading up to the Crescent City White League's debut, the *Picayune* published, apparently with Ogden's connivance, a series of fictitious articles presented as truthful news revealing the existence of a supposed "Black League" plotting a murderous attack against white Louisianians. One such fictitious article exposed a Black League plan to stage "a grand parade of the colored militia" on the Fourth of July. As platoons of armed black men marched through the city, they would "enter all saloons, soda water stands and other places of public resort and demand eatables and drinkables." If their demands were refused, they would take what they wanted and smash "everything in the establishment," the *Picayune* reported. If the militiamen met physical resistance, they would commence firing "at once" to "kill the proprietor and as many white men as possible." At that point, other black people present "would rally to their support," and the black militiamen would "kill all the men and keep all the women."[3]

The *Picayune's* lurid Black League hoax fit the mold of antebellum slave revolt fantasies, which were rolled out periodically to justify violence against black people by casting it as a response to an outrageous provocation. The day after the *Picayune* revealed the horrifying soda shop plot, its front page announced the debut of the Crescent City White League. But in the same issue, responding to skepticism about the Black League plot, the *Picayune* all but confessed that its coverage of the matter had been an invention: "if there never was such a plot, our article will only have the effect of promoting on the part of the whites, an organization which all must admit to be imminently necessary." In other words, the reporting was justified even if false, as long as it motivated recruits to join the White League.

The visiting subcommittee gave Ogden an opportunity to address the matter for the record. "Had there been any such organization as a Black League before your White League was organized," asked one of the panel's two Republicans, William Walter Phelps of New Jersey.

"I have heard that there was such an organization, but I do not know," Ogden replied rather wanly, vacillating about an entity that his platform stamped as a threat to civilization itself. The subcommittee did not press him to elaborate.[4]

New Orleans conservatives likely were not shocked to find the subcommittee extending the benefit of the doubt to its star witness, despite the fact that two of the panel's three members were Republicans. While past congressional investigations led by Republicans had seriously damaged the white South's political standing, such as the select committee that examined the 1866 Mechanics Institute massacre, the current panel gave the *Picayune* "no reason to fear" the results of this inquiry.

The Louisiana subcommittee reflected deepening divisions among Republicans following the Santo Domingo debacle a few years earlier, particularly after a breakaway faction led by Missouri senator Carl Schurz and others launched the Liberal Republican Party in 1872 to oppose Grant's reelection. The party nominated *New-York Tribune* founder and editor Horace Greeley for president and mounted a blistering critique of Grant, alleging that his Reconstruction policies abused Southern whites by deploying military force to prop up unqualified black officeholders and rapacious carpetbaggers. Since the Liberal Republican indictment dovetailed with grievances of Southern whites, the national Democratic Party backed Greeley for president in 1872, the only time in U.S. history that one of the two major parties endorsed the candidate of a third party. Greeley, formerly a prominent abolitionist and strong supporter of black rights, had lately soured on the freedmen, echoing Democrats' complaints about the alleged fecklessness of the former slaves.

Grant trounced Greeley to win reelection in 1872. But discontent with Grant's leadership festered among many Republicans and erupted anew following the party's catastrophic losses in the congressional elections of 1874, for which some blame fell on the president's messy Louisiana interventions.

The two Republicans on the Louisiana subcommittee belonged to this discontented "reform" wing of the party. The *Picayune* praised one of them, Charles Foster of Ohio, for his "fairness," and it positively exalted Phelps of New Jersey, the panel's other Republican, for his "perfect integrity." Republican Speaker of the House James J. Blaine might have appointed these particular Republicans to the investigation as a conciliatory gesture to Southern conservatives, to ease tensions in hopes of keeping the Louisiana eyesore off the nation's front pages. Blaine also nursed presidential ambitions and the risk of embarrass-

ing Grant might not have troubled him, since the president had yet
to scuttle speculation that he might seek a third term in the White
House. But whatever the motives behind their appointments, Foster
and Phelps clearly charmed Southern conservatives. The *New Orleans
Times* ranked them among "the best class of Republicans."[5]

Even as New Orleans conservatives embraced the subcommittee's
Republicans, Grant's allies complained that the panel's investigation
seemed halfhearted, and possibly biased against the president. The
staunchly Republican Chicago *Inter-Ocean* reported that the subcommittee seemed "too anxious to leave," declining to call important witnesses lest they disturb "opinions already formed."

Since the subcommittee's inquiry was limited to the 1874 campaign, it also never explored Ogden's extensive prior involvement in
Louisiana's explosion of political violence after the Civil War.

When the war began, Frederick Nash Ogden was a husky, twenty-
six-year-old cotton clerk sharing a room in a New Orleans boarding-
house. He was easily the least distinguished member of the wealthy
and powerful Nash-Ogden clan, which was replete with influential
lawyers and government officials. But Fred enlisted in the Confederate Army and showed a knack for war, becoming the commander of a
mounted infantry division.

Ogden's talent for organized violence paved his way into politics after
the war, when violence seemed inseparable from public affairs in New
Orleans. As president of the Crescent City Democratic Club, he led
street-level resistance to Republican rule, busting up rallies with clubs
and fists, or harassing rivals with images of coffins emblazoned with
the word "Carpetbagger." But family connections still counted. Fred's
cousin Horatio Nash Ogden, a lawyer, sued to abolish the Metropolitan
Police, a Republican rampart that employed many black officers; cousin
Robert Nash Ogden, a state senator, cajoled conservative officers in the
U.S. Army to overlook the Democratic Club's violent forays.

The Crescent City Democratic Club was one of several violent
paramilitary groups in the state that sought to engineer Democratic

victories "by whatever means necessary," according to Louisiana Reconstruction historian Joe Gray Taylor. "It should be clearly understood that, basically, all of these were terrorist organizations," Taylor writes.

After White Leagues were organized in Alexandria and Opelousas, Louisiana, during the spring of 1874, the Crescent City Democratic Club changed its name to the Crescent City White League, joining the militant movement as a "vehement protest" against the "political miscegenation" of the recent "Unification scheme," one member later recalled.

Some of the White League's activities proved difficult to dismiss as the harmless avocations of a local club even for the sympathetic Louisiana subcommittee. After Ogden testified that one of his motivations for deploying the White League on election day was to preserve the peace in New Orleans, Republican Charles Foster asked rather snidely: "How did you preserve the peace on the 14th of September?"

Of course, on that famous afternoon the White League had violently overthrown the government of Louisiana, which did not seem like the work of peacekeepers. Yet Ogden now asserted that he and his army had set out that afternoon simply to retrieve a shipment of weapons aboard a docked steamboat, and turned to do battle only when police surprised them on the levee. The ensuing clash just happened to give coup organizers an opportunity to seize control of the state.

Foster seemed incredulous. Was Ogden now asserting that if the White League "did anything to overthrow the Kellogg government it was accidental?"

"Yes sir," Ogden replied, "accidental."

Of course, the September 14 coup was no accident. Its meticulous planning even involved sending a White League spy to tip local authorities about the gun shipment, ensuring that police were massed on the levee when Ogden arrived with his troops, who dispatched them in short order.[6]

The subcommittee's report ultimately embraced Ogden's version of the September 14 coup, portraying it as the largely coincidental result of a collision between police and White League troops out retrieving weapons. As for the allegations cited by Grant that gave impetus to the probe—that white Southerners were employing "acts of violence and intimidation" to discourage black citizens from voting—the subcommittee came up empty, reporting: "No general intimidation of republican voters was established; no colored man was produced who had been threatened or assaulted by any conservative because of political opinion, or discharged from employment or refused employment." But the subcommittee did manage to substantiate conservatives' claims that large numbers of white voters were intimidated when federal troops helped marshals arrest white citizens on charges of intimidating black voters.

In both the hearings and the report, the subcommittee focused the bulk of its attention on the oft-maligned Louisiana Returning Board, finding that its wholesale rejection of ballots, in contests allegedly tainted by violence, was "arbitrary, unjust and illegal," wrongfully preventing conservatives from gaining control of the state House of Representatives. But there was reason to doubt whether the subcommittee had conducted an equally searching probe of political violence and intimidation in the 1874 campaign. The panel had located "no colored man" threatened with loss of employment for voting Republican, although such reprisals were openly discussed in newspapers sympathetic to the White League. The subcommittee also did not detect "general intimidation" of black voters. But the visiting congressmen refused to seek testimony from Major Lewis Merrill, commander of U.S. troops in the violent northwest region of the state, whose views on the intimidation of black voters were decidedly at odds with theirs.

"The condition of these poor people is pitiable," Merrill wrote of the region's black residents in a November 1874 report to headquarters. "They are systematically plundered of their crops and driven away from their homes—at best, when they even escape personal violence or death—in such numbers that it is not exaggeration to say that the entire black population of this section is absolutely terror-struck; and if remaining at their homes at all, doing so in almost hourly apprehension of the visits of White-Leaguers."

A few years earlier in South Carolina, Merrill's investigations helped federal prosecutors in the newly created Department of Justice build hundreds of successful cases against members of the Ku Klux Klan, in a crackdown that eventually crippled the terrorist organization. Attorney General Amos Akerman praised Merrill as both "bold" and "prudent, with a good legal head," in short "just the man for the work." The Louisiana subcommittee took testimony from ninety-five witnesses in eight days, but had "no time to wait" for Merrill and many other witnesses whose testimony was sought by local Republicans, the *Inter-Ocean* reported.[7]

Just as the subcommittee seemed eager to leave town, the panel decided to rush the publication of its principal findings to meet "the exigency that now exists" in Louisiana affairs. Its voluminous full report would follow later, but withholding a summary of its findings for a "delay of weeks" while testimony and documentary evidence— including Merrill's letters—was laboriously transcribed and printed simply would not do.

The proximate cause of the new "exigency" in Louisiana affairs was General Philip H. Sheridan, who had checked into a suite at the St. Charles Hotel mere hours before the subcommittee's hearings commenced. Ostensibly on a "pleasure trip," Sheridan would soon expose to the nation a decidedly darker portrait of the White League than the one on view in the subcommittee's chambers, while igniting perhaps the most destructive political conflagration of the Grant era.[8]

CHAPTER 9

KANGAROO QUORUM

Around 1,800 U.S. bluecoats crowded the narrow streets of New Orleans's French Quarter to guard the St. Louis Hotel, where the state House of Representatives was about to convene amid threats of new White League trouble on January 4, 1875. The sprawling hotel, with its shaded archways framed by rococo grillwork, echoed the old quarter's elegant European endowment. But on this clear, chilly morning it looked like a garrison.

A few blocks to the east, U.S. artillery companies armed with Gatling guns and Napoleon cannons surveilled the levee. To the south, cavalry squads stood ready, their anxious horses pawing the cobblestone streets behind the Custom House. A rooftop sentry there scanned the horizon, poised to signal warships on the river in case of attack. Another infantry company remained in reserve across town, ready to rush the assembly hall at the sound of the bugle.

In December, the Louisiana Returning Board had tossed out thousands of ballots from the fall election that it found to be tainted by fraud and violence, which helped Republicans. White Leaguers then began issuing threats like those that had preceded their September 14 coup in New Orleans. Federal authorities had been caught flat-footed by that uprising. They were ready this time.

Thousands of onlookers had also been collecting in strident or pensive clusters near the hotel. It is likely that few among them noticed the most valuable U.S. military asset on the premises that day: General Philip H. Sheridan. Dressed in civilian clothes and still pretending to be on vacation, he looked like just another stumpy, middle-aged man with a walrus mustache as he strolled the quarter about 10 a.m. to cast a hard eye on the arrangement of U.S. forces.[1]

Finding no holes in the security cordon, Sheridan withdrew to monitor developments at the U.S. Custom House with the regional commander, General William H. Emory. "A very weak old man, entirely unfitted for this place," Sheridan would soon report to Washington about his stolid, sixty-three-year-old host.

Rumors plagued the capitol as the hour drew near for the House to convene. Some black Republicans had reportedly been abducted to smooth the Democrats' path to a majority. Other lawmakers feared they would be murdered if they ventured to the city to claim their seats. Democrats boasted that they would depose Kellogg by week's end, if he wasn't assassinated in the meantime. Since the White League had staged one violent revolution already on September 14, it was difficult to dismiss talk of another.[2]

But some believed Sheridan's presence radically altered the equation. The Chicago *Inter-Ocean* was among the nation's staunchest Republican newspapers and took a booster's pride in Sheridan, a Chicago resident and hometown hero. The paper's editors had long called for "decisive measures" against the White League and their ilk. "[M]agnanimity is lost on the graceless scoundrels who are overturning the law and committing deeds of violence and bloodshed in the South. They appreciate but one argument, and that, force."

The *Inter-Ocean* conceded that Grant's freedom to send soldiers to the South was constrained by a disapproving Northern public, which had grown "callous to massacres" of freedmen amid disinformation from the Democratic press. But the *Inter-Ocean*'s editors sensed a new mood rising, partly thanks to their own efforts to "awaken in the hearts

of the people that love of the right for right's own sake which appeared
to lie dormant."

The editors now believed Sheridan's trip to New Orleans could produce a timely remedy. Perhaps they had obtained "leaked" information
about the actual agenda behind Sheridan's trip, since they suggested
that more than a vacation was in store for him. "Treason, revolution, rebellion have grown budded, and are ready to blossom; but if we do not
mistake, the little army of men directed by Sheridan will come upon
these noxious plants like frost upon an opening flower, and will wither
them in a day."[3]

K ellogg had ordered police to step up security at the St. Louis
  Hotel. Entry was barred to anyone but elected representatives
and credentialed journalists. Thick boards and props barricaded doors
and windows. Some Republican members had been camping in the
building for days to avoid kidnapping, or worse.

All seemed calm as the House convened about midday in its roomy
converted ballroom, sunlight spilling from floor-to-ceiling windows.
When the clerk called the roll of recently elected members, 52 Republicans, including 29 blacks, and 50 Democrats, all of them white, answered to their names. But just after noon, events began unfolding on
the House floor that wouldn't have been out of place in a dime novel.[4]

As the clerk was announcing the roll call results, a Democrat shot
up from his chair. Shouting to make himself heard in every corner of
the hall, he nominated a fellow Democrat, Louis Wiltz, former mayor
of New Orleans, to be Speaker of the House. Democrats from wall
to wall erupted in deafening hoots and cheers. But the clerk, staring
crossly at the member who had interrupted him, barked that the nomination was "out of order." No members had been sworn in yet. Clearly
it was premature to take up other business.

Ignoring the clerk, a Democrat stood and loudly called for "the
yeas and nays" on the nomination. Democrats in unison vigorously

shouted "aye," then commenced another round of raucous cheers, in the midst of which Wiltz leapt onto the rostrum. Tall and angular, with a sprucely trimmed brown beard, the forty-year-old's practiced air of authority lent a sense of normalcy to the confusion as he proceeded to nudge the clerk aside, seize the gavel, and assume command of the hall, as if he were the duly elected Speaker.

Republicans jumped out of their seats shouting furious objections. Many demanded a roll call vote on the speakership, so each member could be polled individually on such a crucial matter. Under normal rules, requests by only two members were sufficient to trigger such a vote. But Wiltz ignored their pleas and charged on, quickly declaring that a new clerk and a new sergeant at arms had also been elected in voice votes. These men now stepped forward into a chorus of Republican catcalls and jeers.

The turmoil intensified when about three dozen men emerged from the shadows and turned down their lapels to reveal blue-ribbon badges bearing the words "Assistant Sergeant At Arms" in gold letters. They weren't members of the House, and it wasn't clear how they had gotten past the security checkpoints. Republicans alleged that they were known White League operatives.[5]

Amid an earsplitting storm of dissent from outraged Republicans, the new clerk proceeded to the chamber's first order of business. In a rapid series of voice votes absent any debate, the Democrats resolved five election races that the Returning Board had found too close to call. A Democrat was declared the winner in each and sworn in, apparently cementing that party's control of the House, which had been in Republican hands when the day began.

Wiltz, in brief remarks before the hopelessly chaotic assembly, promised fair treatment for all members—Republican and Democrat, black and white. But when a black House member stood and openly accused him of seizing the Speaker's chair illegally, hearing such a charge from "a colored member" was "too much for the Democrats

and they clamored for his arrest and expulsion," an *Inter-Ocean* correspondent reported.

Wiltz then called for a vote pitting himself against his opponents'
nominee for Speaker. But Republicans objected. They said that allowing the five newest Democratic members to vote in the Speaker election, after they had been admitted to the House in sham proceedings
only moments ago, would guarantee an unfair victory for Wiltz. When
Republicans tried to stage a formal protest during the roll call vote,
tensions mounted rapidly. According to the *Inter-Ocean*:

> Republicans were advised not to answer to their names. One
> colored member pressed a question of privilege. When told to
> sit down by Wiltz, he declined, and this so enraged Wiltz that his
> hand flew to the neighborhood of his coat tail, where revolvers
> are usually kept. The members accused Wiltz of putting his
> hand in his pocket as though to draw his pistol, and this Wiltz
> did not deny.[6]

Republicans could see that another coup was in progress, to seize
control of the legislature this time. They soon decided to exit the hall
and deny the Democrats a quorum—the legal minimum head count
for doing legislative business. But when the Republicans neared the
foyer, a group of the new deputy sergeants at arms blocked their path.

The sergeants drew pistols and knives; so did some Republicans.
Shouts and threats rapidly devolved into bedlam. Some Republicans
formed a phalanx and made a dash for the lobby, where city police
pleaded for calm. Other Republicans dove behind chairs or under ta-
bles, as did some journalists. "The pressure of a finger upon a trigger
would have precipitated a fight, and it appalls one to think of the result," an *Inter-Ocean* reporter wrote. Bloodshed was narrowly avoided.

The Democrats then made a move that was decidedly at odds with
their antifederal convictions: they asked U.S. troops stationed nearby

to restore order in the building. Soon the squad's commander, Colonel Régis de Trobriand, an aristocratic French émigré who wore his cap at a jaunty angle, arrived in the House chamber. As he walked down the center aisle, sword clanking against his thigh, the Democratic lawmakers cheered.[7]

Louisiana Democrats routinely mocked Kellogg's government for being unable to survive without "U.S. bayonets" on call to bail him out, which seemed accurate enough following the September 14 coup. So the Democrats who took over the House chamber must have expected that Kellogg would also seek help from the U.S. troops surrounding the statehouse, and had probably prepared for that possibility in an operation that seemed meticulously planned.

After some Republicans escaped the House chamber and alerted Kellogg about the upheaval there, he sent a note to U.S. military officials a few blocks away, telling them an "illegal assembly" had seized the hall, and asking for the removal of anyone not approved by the Returning Board. General Emory quickly consulted the visiting Sheridan. "Were I the Department commander," replied the iron-willed hero of Cedar Creek, "I would not hesitate to comply with the requisition of the governor."[8]

Colonel de Trobriand soon returned to the House chamber, but on a far different mission. Democrats didn't cheer his arrival this time, but kept on conducting legislative business, despite the absence of most Republicans. De Trobriand told the Democrats that unauthorized persons had to be removed from the chamber. Would they comply voluntarily or require him to use force?[9]

Southern Democrats and White Leaguers showed a subtle appreciation for what are now called optics—how their actions were seen by the broader public, especially in the North. After the September 14 coup, Louisiana Democrats publicly deferred to federal authority, insisted freedmen's rights must be protected, and adopted the pose of

idealistic citizen activists in the tradition of America's founding revolutionaries. This deceptive, self-serving narrative gave Democratic
editors in the North something to rally around that was more pal-
atable than raw white supremacy. It also grabbed hold in Southern
lore and was refined over time, though it was potent from the start. A
New Orleans tourist guide published only a year after the September
14 White League uprising was already comparing it to the Boston
Tea Party.[10]

Democrats weren't above outright censorship to limit the play of
some stories in the North. An *Inter-Ocean* correspondent recalled
that after the September 14 uprising, Southern telegraph operators
"altered, omitted and even suppressed" journalistic dispatches and private letters "not in harmony" with their political views. He reported
that "Marr, one of the leaders of the White League," was overheard
ordering "the manager of the Western Union office to submit to him
all dispatches referring to the troubles before they were sent." Republicans also mistrusted Southern employees of the Associated Press, a
Western Union business ally, because they were "all White Leaguers,"
according to the *Inter-Ocean* correspondent.[11]

As House Democrats confronted Colonel de Trobriand during his
return visit, they clearly attempted to shape how the encounter would
be viewed by the country at large. Wiltz stagily warned the officer
against interfering with the "legally organized" legislature of a sover-
eign state, over which U.S. forces had no authority. He declared that to
evict its members, de Trobriand must employ force.

De Trobriand approached the five ineligible members one at a
time. Each acknowledged not being approved by the Returning Board.
"Now will you be satisfied that force enough has been used, if I put
my hand on your shoulder," the officer asked, "or do you want me to
employ an armed soldier before you will leave the Hall?" Four of the
five requested a soldier and were separately escorted out by a single in-
fantryman shouldering a rifle with fixed bayonet. Before exiting, each
recited a stock speech: "I do most solemnly protest against such violent

proceedings and I respectfully request that my protest be spread on the records."[12]

Soon Wiltz drafted an indignant telegram to President Grant, which he distributed to the press, associating his rump legislature with the highest principles of American government. "The house is the representation of the sovereignty of the State," Wiltz's telegram concluded, "and I know of no law which warrants either the executive of the State or the United States Army to interfere with its organization or proceedings."[13]

The journalist covering this drama for the *Inter-Ocean* reported that the takeover of the House chamber was done "to compel the use of troops" and make Democrats "martyrs to military interference." His page-one story published the following morning said Democrats had admitted to staging the entire episode for "political effect," and could be heard boasting about their success later that evening in the buzzing rotunda of the St. Charles Hotel.[14]

If the story ended there, Louisiana Democrats possibly would have reaped the political benefits they sought, assuming the reporter's account was accurate. But the fact that they had initially invited Colonel de Trobriand into the House chamber and requested that he restore order tended to undercut their message of U.S. military "interference." What they really needed was a prominent symbol of federal power, preferably shaking a fist in their direction.

Enter General Philip H. Sheridan, nursing a righteous fury as he returned to his room at the St. Charles, perhaps passing groups of White League revelers in the rotunda. His superiors in Washington had ordered him to inform them "from time to time of your views and conclusions" as his confidential mission progressed. Tonight would be one of those times. Writing never came easy for Sheridan, but he sat at the small desk in his hotel room to compose a very important telegram.[15]

CHAPTER 10

"THE GENIUS OF SMALLNESS"

The manhandling of Louisiana lawmakers by federal troops was Grant's "Crowning Outrage" against a long-suffering state, wailed the *Memphis Daily Appeal*. The *Richmond Whig* warned that Sheridan would "shoot and hang citizens of Louisiana as if they were dogs."

Addressing a mass-protest meeting at New York's Cooper Union, the white-whiskered poet and journalist William Cullen Bryant recalled his shock upon learning that federal bluecoats had tossed conservative Louisiana lawmakers "into the street." Such shabby methods for changing governments might suit a rickety republic like Spain, "but it will not *do* for this country," the eighty-year-old bard scolded.

Amid the surging tide of indignation following the Louisiana incident and Sheridan's arrogant "banditti dispatches," spectators packed U.S. Senate galleries on January 11, 1875, to hear the latest jeremiad from Missouri senator Carl Schurz, President Grant's "high-stepping" nemesis.

Schurz's opposition to annexing Santo Domingo years earlier was only the beginning of his battles with the president. Soon after the annexation fight, he mounted a frontal assault on Reconstruction itself, condemning the use of federal troops to enforce freedmen's rights in Southern states as a danger to foundational American liberties. Schurz and his allies also championed the restoration of voting rights to ex-Confederates, so "the better class" could resume management of Southern affairs.

Ultimately Schurz led other dissident Republicans in the formation of a new party, the Liberal Republicans, to oppose Grant's reelection in 1872. While the party's presidential candidate, Horace Greeley, lost badly to Grant, attacks on Reconstruction by Schurz and other Liberal Republicans soured public perceptions of federal efforts to sustain the rights of former slaves.[1]

Campaigning for Greeley in 1872, Schurz acknowledged the "uncommonly perplexing" challenges Grant faced upon assuming the presidency a few years earlier, above all the task of reconciling "the Southern people" to a postwar reality without slavery. But Schurz claimed that Grant was also blessed with "the confidence of the country," and the sheer inspirational power of the moment's possibilities. "A success great enough to be the envy of the world was within reach," Schurz averred. "It did not require very great men to see and appreciate such opportunities, but it required what I might call the genius of smallness to lose them all."

According to Schurz, Grant squandered a historic opportunity to heal the nation by declining to extend a generous hand of friendship to Southerners, "to lift them up from their prostration, to guide them out of their errors." Grant and his Republican allies instead chose "the bayonet law, the Ku-Klux law," sending federal troops to protect black Republican voters from Southern terrorists. Schurz insisted that white Southerners would have moved to safeguard black rights on their own, if they had been approached on friendlier terms. The federal deployment of troops in the South protected "the rights of some," but imperiled "the rights of all," Schurz alleged, shunning "constitutional limitations of power" to prop up Grant's rapacious carpetbag-Republican allies. [2]

With federal bayonets flashing in the Louisiana legislature, the Grant administration's latest New Orleans escapade might have seemed like a stark illustration of Schurz's warnings over the years. Schurz told the packed U.S. Senate chamber that he was "profoundly alarmed" by the recent news from Louisiana, as it appeared that federal troops had run roughshod over both legislative freedom from executive interference and limits on federal power to intrude on state government affairs.

"Before laying their hands upon things so important and sacred, the authorities should have well assured themselves that they have the clearest, most obvious and most unequivocal warrant of law," Schurz admonished. He found no such warrant. "Where is the law," Schurz demanded, that permits the national government to "invade a legislative body by armed force to drag out persons seated as members of a state legislature that others may take their places?"

As for Sheridan's proposal to haul White Leaguers before military tribunals to reap swift justice, Schurz dismissed it as not just illegal but downright "appalling."

The cascade of press reports about recent events in New Orleans accurately reflected the public's alarm, Schurz declared. "On all sides we hear the question asked: If this can be done in Louisiana, if such things be sustained by Congress, how long will it be before it can be done in Massachusetts and Ohio? How long before the constitutional rights of all the states, the self government of all the people, will be trampled under foot?"

Schurz conceded that his fellow lawmakers had acted with good intentions when they enabled Grant's extraordinary use of the military during Reconstruction. Southern society was "disturbed by violent tendencies and grave disorders," he acknowledged. "I have never denied it, and nobody has more earnestly condemned and denounced the acts of violence." But Schurz maintained that the postwar South's violent disorders were temporary, the "offspring of circumstances," and would naturally dissipate, while the use of federal "brute force" to combat these disorders gravely imperiled the nation. Without a course correction, he warned, abuses of power such as those recently on display in the Louisiana legislature gradually would be established as precedents, and the constitutional principles sustaining American liberty would be "obliterated."[3]

S churz hadn't always opposed the deployment of troops to enforce Radical Reconstruction in the South. He had even been a darling of Republican Radicals during the early postwar period, and his formative political experiences were those of a full-blown revolutionary.

Schurz was born in 1829 in the German town of Liblar, then part of the Kingdom of Prussia. Enrolled at the University of Bonn when the revolutions of 1848 swept Europe, he pushed for democratic reforms with other student activists, discovering his considerable skills as an orator and polemicist in the process. As Prussia moved to crush the rebellion, Schurz joined the armed resistance, then fled the country to avoid execution when the revolutionaries were defeated, escaping through a sewage tunnel to find refuge in Switzerland. But Schurz soon returned to engineer a daring jailbreak, freeing his former teacher and revolutionary comrade, the poet Gottfried Kinkel, from Berlin's Spandau prison and helping the fugitive escape to Scotland.

Schurz decamped to England, married a fellow German expatriate, Margarethe Meyer, and the couple emigrated to America, settling in Watertown, Wisconsin. Meyer established the first U.S. kindergarten there in 1856. Meanwhile the legend of Schurz's revolutionary exploits made the handsome young swashbuckler something of a hero among the wave of idealistic Germans who resettled in the United States after the Prussian crackdown. These German "Forty-Eighters" were a prized voting bloc. When Schurz's own idealism drew him to the fledgling Republican Party, he became an emissary to the German immigrant community, most notably while stumping for Abraham Lincoln during the 1860 presidential campaign. Lincoln rewarded his young German friend by making him the U.S. ambassador to Spain, and later a general in the Union Army. Schurz saw action at Gettysburg and other critical engagements of the Civil War.

Schurz emerged as one of the most prominent Radical voices in the nation after the war ended. During a visit with Lincoln's successor, Andrew Johnson, at the White House, Schurz was alarmed to learn that the new president's Reconstruction plan might allow only white men to vote in elections to reestablish Southern state governments. Schurz warned Johnson that this policy would embolden former Confederates and leave freedmen in peril, with their former masters writing all the laws. He asked Johnson to allow freedmen to vote so they could exert a loyal influence on the new governments of the rebel states. Schurz also encouraged the president to send a trusted envoy to the South, to inform himself of current facts on the ground as he devised Reconstruction policies.

Johnson had no interest in empowering freedmen. His aim was to restore the South much as it was before the war—minus formal slavery—with white people in charge and black people in subservient roles. But in the months immediately following Lincoln's assassination, as Johnson settled into his new job, he seemed content to allow Radicals like Schurz to believe his mind remained open about black suffrage and other controversies. So while Johnson implemented his Reconstruction plan based on white suffrage, with no provision for giving freedmen any voice in government, despite the warnings of Schurz and other Radicals that this would surely put former Confederates back in control, the president also asked Schurz to visit the South as his envoy, to gather facts and report back with recommendations, as if he had not already decided on a firm policy.

Johnson would soon regret it.

Schurz's Southern tour took him to five of the eleven former Confederate states. He did not detect any appetite among white Southerners for a renewal of their armed insurrection, but he soon discovered that acts of violence against freedmen were routine, amid scant white acceptance of the new free-labor system. Since former slaves no longer represented a "pecuniary value" on the ledgers of ex-slaveholders, "the maiming and killing" of freedmen "seems to be looked upon by many as one of those venial offenses which must be forgiven," Schurz observed.

Some mistreatment of freedmen reflected strategies to retain control of their labor. An Army colonel stationed in Mississippi told Schurz that white people refused "to sell or lease lands to black men," believing that if freedmen were held propertyless and could not raise their own crops, they would be forced to resume plantation labor at barely subsistence wages, and that "this kind of slavery will be better than none at all."[4]

Schurz sent regular updates about his findings to the White House. Johnson mostly ignored them. But the president grew increasingly annoyed by Schurz's output, especially his articles about the South for the *Boston Advertiser*, which buttressed Radical critiques of Johnson's Reconstruction policies.

The relationship finally ruptured after Schurz opposed a plan by Mississippi's governor to create a state militia composed of former Confederate soldiers. The idea of reactivating part of the Confederate Army struck Schurz as "glaringly absurd," especially at a moment of such peril for freedmen and white Union loyalists in the South. But Johnson sided with the governor, brusquely instructing his envoy to do the same. When Schurz wrote back to continue the argument, Johnson did not respond. Rumors appeared in the press that Schurz would be recalled by the president. Schurz protested to the White House. Johnson ignored him.

When Schurz returned to Washington after his Southern tour, Johnson kept him waiting before granting a grudging audience. The president's manner was aloof, barely civil. He asked not a single question about his envoy's months-long mission. Schurz said he was writing up an "elaborate report" for the president. Johnson replied that he needn't bother.

Determined not to let Johnson "suppress" his testimony, Schurz sat down to work on his report. Meanwhile, Johnson moved to eclipse it with the testimony of a far brighter star. He asked General Grant to make a fact-finding tour of the South and submit a report to the president.

After a whirlwind five-day trip, Grant produced a report of just over two pages, declaring that "the mass of thinking men of the south" accepted the war's outcome "in good faith" as a settlement of questions that divided the nation. While Grant also discussed continuing challenges, including the need to keep federal troops in the South until "civil authority is fully established," Johnson framed the revered general's report as a complete endorsement of administration policy.[5]

Despite Johnson's best efforts to obscure it, Schurz's report "created an immediate sensation." The forty-six-page document, with an additional sixty pages of supporting material, amounted to an indictment of Johnson's Reconstruction policy and a warning that the former Confederate states were far from ready to resume self-government.

Johnson claimed that white Southerners had shown "a laudable desire to renew their allegiance to the government and to repair the devastations of war by a prompt and cheerful return to peaceful pursuits." The graphic accounts of "maimed, mutilated and murdered freedmen" in Schurz's report sharply rebuked such happy talk.

Schurz's report concluded that if Reconstruction's success required white Southerners to "accommodate themselves to the results of the war," especially free labor, their behavior was falling "far short of what must be insisted upon." He called for keeping U.S. troops in the former Confederate states until free labor was "firmly established." He also advocated giving freedmen the right to vote, to bring their loyal influence to bear on Southern governments and help them fend off oppressive laws like the Black Codes. Schurz went even further than many Radicals by suggesting that freedmen should also be "endowed with the ownership of land," to afford them both the means to make a living and a "moral" interest in the community. This policy would do more to combat the problem of vagrancy among freedmen "than the severest penal laws," Schurz contended.

Not only did Schurz's proposals clash with Johnson's white-supremacist vision, but his report also pinned the blame for Southern intransigence on the president's lenient Reconstruction plan. Schurz revealed that immediately after the war, the "public mind" in the former Confederate states "was so despondent" that Southerners were prepared to accept "whatever conditions" the North might impose for readmission to the Union. But white Southerners abruptly hardened their attitudes after President Johnson issued his proclamation on Reconstruction involving white voters only, which "substituted new hopes for them," Schurz reported.

After Johnson issued his Reconstruction plan, white Southerners began expecting to "recover the preponderating influence" they had enjoyed in former times, according to Major General Quincy Gillmore of the U.S. Army, stationed in Hilton Head, South Carolina. Freedmen regarded this turn of events "with growing suspicion" and "the most lively apprehensions," Gillmore told Schurz.

The *New-York Tribune* published the entire Schurz report, minus supporting documents, and amplified its message that an opportunity had been tragically squandered when Johnson's policy, making no allowance for black suffrage, reawakened Southern recalcitrance. "The mistake has been our failure to impose suffrage on the South in the hour of our triumph," the *Tribune* concluded.[6]

Although Grant's report was also well received by the press, he soon had second thoughts about his work. Apparently surprised by the level of violence against freedmen documented by Schurz, Grant ordered his Southern commanders to inform him of all "outrages committed by white people against the blacks, and the reverse." It was soon clear that freedmen were in desperate need of protection, and that Union soldiers and veterans in the South were also at risk. A mortified Grant acknowledged to Schurz: "you were right and I was wrong."[7]

By the time Schurz was denouncing Grant before packed Senate galleries on January 11, 1875, the two men had accomplished something of a role reversal. Now it was Grant declaring that federal troops should protect the rights of freedmen for as long as those rights were under siege in the South, while Schurz struck a conciliatory tone toward white Southerners, portraying them as the victims of rapacious Northern adventurers who were maintained in power by federal bayonets.

S churz had announced his intention to speak on Louisiana matters days in advance, and Senate visitors' galleries began filling at "an early hour" on January 11; the overflowing audience spilled into lobbies "crowded with ladies." Many foreign diplomats attended with their families, and three of the seven members of Grant's cabinet were seen lounging on sofas reserved for special guests on the Senate floor.

The blistering Louisiana controversy likely drove some of this turnout, as did Schurz's reputation for riveting oratory. An ardent journalist described one Schurz speech, against the annexation of Santo Domingo, as an effort "which, for eloquence, clearness of statement, wit, sarcasm, and readiness of repartee, has never been surpassed in any legislative assembly of the world."[8]

Not everyone was mesmerized by the lanky senator's rhetorical flights. Grant shared his opinion of Schurz during a candid post-presidential interview with the *New York Herald*, declaring: "he is a humbug."

Frederick Douglass had arrived at a similar appraisal of Schurz, whom he once revered as a political hero. After Schurz was elected to the U.S. Senate from Missouri in 1868, he abandoned his Radical allies on Reconstruction, possibly influenced by lukewarm feelings about black suffrage among German immigrants, his base of support. When Schurz led the Liberal Republican revolt and joined forces with

Southern Democrats, Douglass reassessed his hero as one of the "shallow demagogues" of that movement, guilty of "treason" against the Republican Party's noble cause of equal rights. Historian Eric Foner does not question the sincerity of Schurz's claim that "black rights would be more secure" in the South after federal intervention ceased and "local self-government" was restored. But Foner suggests there was an element of self-delusion in such views, and that whether Schurz "quite appreciated it or not, his program had no other meaning than a return to white supremacy."

As Schurz addressed the Senate on events in Louisiana, he portrayed a Republican Party that had strayed from its ideals. He warned his fellow lawmakers that if Grant's cavalier disregard of constitutional principles was ratified by congressional acquiescence, the machinery of government could become "a mere instrument of ring rule, a tool to manufacture majorities and to organize plunder." In the age of the corrupt Tweed Ring, Schurz conjured future Sheridans routinely fixing elections to keep crooked officials in power.[9]

While Schurz claimed to approach these matters "in no partisan spirit," his remarks were scrupulously one-sided, agreeing at virtually every point with the positions of Louisiana Democrats. Many Republicans insisted that Democrats had actually been the ones manhandling the Louisiana legislature when they illegally seized control of the lower house. Schurz's high-minded speech did not weigh any testimony along those lines, and most press coverage also ignored it. But the *National Republican*, known as Grant's mouthpiece, described Schurz's speech as a "Defense of Mob Law."

Schurz's remarks, fair or not, captured the moment, echoing protests against the "Louisiana Outrage" staged in several cities, often by local Democratic Party organizations. *New York Herald* editors boiled down the message of an anti-Grant "indignation meeting" in their city: "America Not Yet Ready for the Reign of Caesar or Cromwell."

Schurz was something of a keynote speaker in this cyclone of dissent, even attracting personal attention from Grant's cabinet. He returned the favor. As Schurz cataloged the administration's outrages for his colleagues, he recalled a telegram sent to Sheridan during the "banditti" episode by Secretary of War William Belknap, one of the three cabinet members then seated in the Senate chamber. "Be assured," Belknap had wired to Sheridan, in dulcet phrases soon to be displayed in newspapers across the nation, "that the President and Cabinet confide in your wisdom, and rest in the belief that all acts of yours have been and will be judicious."

Schurz could not contain his scorn. "The whole government have full confidence in his judgment and wisdom," he mocked. Meanwhile, as the citizens of a nervous nation learned of Sheridan's plan to round up white Louisianians "by the wholesale" for "drum-head court martial," they rightly feared for "the safety of republican institutions and the rights of every man in the land," Schurz keened.[10]

As Schurz and others flogged the administration, Grant was mostly silent. The Senate had officially asked him to explain whether any members of the U.S. Army had interfered in the organization of the Louisiana legislature, and if so, "by what authority." Press reports suggested that Grant's pending reply to the Senate had been delayed by wrangling among his advisors, some pushing him to take a hard line toward Southern ruffians, while others favored an acknowledgment of error and overreach.

Administration allies sought clues to Grant's state of mind. Would he be willing to check his aggressive proclivities? How would he respond to Sheridan's audacious plan for dismantling the White League? Would the president back his plucky general, or would Grant "back down"?[11]

CHAPTER 11

WAR IN PEACETIME

Two days after Sheridan's "banditti" telegram detonated on the nation's front pages, Grant and his cabinet took stock of the scorching political crisis in a meeting described as "one of the stormiest the White House had ever seen."

The federal troops stationed in New Orleans were part of the forces Grant deployed to Louisiana the previous September, responding to a request by Governor Kellogg under Article IV, Section 4, of the U.S. Constitution, which guarantees to every state a Republican form of government and pledges protection against domestic violence upon the petition of the state legislature or the governor, if the legislature cannot be convened.

Attorney General George Williams justified the behavior of federal troops in the Louisiana legislature as an exercise in peacekeeping, conducted at the governor's request and consistent with the Army's mission following the September 1874 White League insurrection. Secretary of the Navy George Robeson agreed, describing the Democrats' attempt to overthrow the legislature as "an outrage" that the governor was duty bound to thwart.

Grant signaled his approval of the emerging consensus. But Hamilton Fish moved quickly to rescue the president from himself yet again.

The secretary of state declared that Louisiana's governor had no business meddling in the affairs of the legislature, unless there was "violent interference" with the lower chamber as it organized itself following the election. Fish claimed that no one had alleged such interference, and therefore sending soldiers to eject members from the chamber was "inexcusable."

Fish also condemned the notorious telegrams that ricocheted between Sheridan and Secretary of War William Belknap during the Louisiana episode, finding them offensive, misleading, and "unwise." It was bad enough that Sheridan characterized a sizable share of Louisiana citizens as "banditti," proposing a lawless procedure suggestive of lynching for dealing with them. Belknap then made things worse in his reply to Sheridan, blessing the general's recklessness: "The president and all of us have full confidence, and thoroughly approve your course," Belknap told Sheridan.

Fish pronounced himself "unwilling to appear before the public as having such confidence or as approving Sheridan's course." He counseled Grant to put some distance between the administration and the misbegotten episode in Louisiana.

"I think it is the duty of the administration to disclaim and denounce" those who brought troops into the Louisiana legislature, and to "withdraw" from Belknap's expressions of "confidence" in Sheridan on behalf of the cabinet, Fish proclaimed.

A former governor of New York and U.S. senator, Fish was Grant's longest-serving cabinet secretary. Grant had been a political novice when he became president, and often tapped the older man's wealth of experience to avoid greenhorn errors. Somewhat restless in this role, Fish periodically threatened to resign, only to be talked out of it by an anxious Grant, who viewed him as irreplaceable. After Grant left office, he told an interviewer that for sound judgment in the White House, he had relied "above all" on Hamilton Fish.[1]

But Fish was not particularly supportive of Reconstruction efforts to defend the rights of freedmen, the core of Sheridan's mission to

New Orleans. An entry in the secretary of state's diary about an 1871 cabinet presentation by then–attorney general Amos Akerman, on the subject of Ku Klux Klan atrocities, offers a glimpse of Fish's mindset:

> Akerman introduces KuKlux; he has it "on the brain"; he tells a number of stories, one of a fellow being castrated, with terribly minute & tedious details of each case. It has got to be a bore to listen twice a week to this same thing.

After Fish called on Grant, before the assembled cabinet, to "disclaim and denounce" the military's behavior in the Louisiana legislature, the president erupted. He would "certainly not denounce it." Nor would he censure Sheridan.

The *New-York Tribune* reported three days later that if Grant persisted in his Louisiana policy, Fish would probably resign, and Treasury Secretary Benjamin H. Bristow might follow the secretary of state out the door. That same day, Schurz delivered his Senate speech condemning the administration's lawlessness in Louisiana.

The *Tribune*'s report suggested that Fish and Bristow were largely in agreement on Louisiana matters. But during the cabinet meeting, Fish asserted that most white Louisianians were "honest, sincere and moral." Bristow, a Kentucky-born Southerner, believed that white Louisianians were mostly disloyal and prepared to justify the murder of black people, along with the persecution of political opponents. Still, he thought that Sheridan used the term *banditti* to describe leaders of the armed White League, not the white population generally.

Bristow agreed with Fish that the administration's Louisiana adventure was a debacle, and that Sheridan's "wild" proposals could not be endorsed. But Bristow agreed more with Sheridan about the nature of the White League, viewing it as a "wicked and inexcusable organization" seeking to "overthrow" the postwar constitutional amendments and "reduce the colored people to actual, if not nominal, slavery."

Critics of Reconstruction warned that federal troops in Louisiana endangered "republican institutions." Bristow cited the threat posed to those same institutions by private armies like the White League. "In a government of laws there can be no such thing as an organized force outside of duly constituted authorities, without immediate danger to the very existence of the government itself," he maintained.

Bristow believed that the White League was all the more dangerous because it assumed "an air of respectability." He observed this process firsthand when the House Louisiana subcommittee returned to Washington and began sharing its findings. The subcommittee had "come back prepared to whitewash the White League and the rebels of Louisiana generally," Bristow wrote to a friend. Fish appeared to embrace this laundered subcommittee narrative, uncritically recording the panel's expected findings in his diary—that "members of the White League were among the most respectable citizens," with "no rowdies, or disorderly persons, among them," and committed "no intimidation" of black voters in the recent Louisiana election.[2]

Bristow was well versed on the threat of Southern white vigilantism. When the Civil War began, he was a young lawyer with strong antislavery and pro-union views. He enlisted in the Union Army, raised two regiments of Kentucky bluecoats, and rose to the rank of colonel, getting seriously wounded in action along the way. After the war, he became his state's U.S. attorney and zealously prosecuted white Kentuckians who violated the civil rights of their emancipated black neighbors. When Congress created the Department of Justice in 1870, largely to combat the well-organized menace of the Ku Klux Klan, Grant appointed Bristow as the nation's first solicitor general, to work with another prominent defender of black civil rights from the South, Amos Akerman, the new attorney general. Both men believed in prosecuting the Klan aggressively. Akerman warned one U.S. attorney that Klansmen interpreted "kindness on the part of the government as evidence of timidity" and were "emboldened to lawlessness by it." Bristow sought to make examples of socially prominent Klan suspects. "The higher the social standing," he told a U.S. attorney, "the more important is a vigorous prosecution."

As Treasury secretary, Bristow was no longer in the front ranks of civil rights enforcement, but he believed the government's "highest and most solemn duty" was to smash the White League and punish its leaders. To accomplish that goal, he would "go to the very verge of constitutional power, upon the most liberal construction of constitutional provisions." Yet he could not endorse Sheridan's "banditti" plan for corralling the White League. "I cannot consent to convert the army into a mob," Bristow explained, also noting that it was illegal to try White Leaguers before military commissions in peacetime when civilian courts were operating.

In January 1875, nearly ten years after the Civil War ended, many saw the federal government's ability to protect the freedmen as more precarious than ever after Supreme Court rulings tightened limits on Washington's civil rights enforcement authority, even as the public wearied of supporting interventions in the Southern states. Bristow did not share this mounting pessimism.

"I am out of all patience with the idea that this Government, after having manumitted four millions of slaves cannot by law protect them from murder and outrage," Bristow wrote to a friend. "If this be true we have perpetrated a cruel outrage in making them free. I do not accept any such lame and impotent conclusion. I believe it is entirely within the power of Congress to furnish protection through the Courts and under the forms of law."[3]

Around the time Bristow left the Department of Justice a few years earlier, federal prosecutors were growing confident in their ability to put down white vigilante violence in the South. Their success reflected the efforts of congressional Republicans to inscribe the results of the Civil War in the law of the land. Many of these Republicans had understood their handiwork, in the Civil Rights Act of 1866 and the Thirteenth, Fourteenth, and Fifteenth Amendments to the U.S. Constitution, as endowing the national government with authority to protect the rights of all U.S. citizens.

With these enactments on the books, freedmen could seek help in federal court if states failed to protect their rights, and their tormentors could be indicted by U.S. attorneys when local police turned a blind eye. Although such outcomes were departures from the states' rights view that authority over the protection of such rights rested with the states, courts initially acceded to the new federal framework.

Judges even learned to live with aggressive congressional measures aimed at crushing the Klan. Lawmakers sought to neutralize the group mostly through "ordinary criminal process" in a series of Enforcement Acts. But the heavily armed, tightly drilled paramilitary force was clearly no ordinary criminal gang: "these combinations amount to war, and cannot be crushed under any other theory," Attorney General Akerman famously said of the Klan. To address this outsize threat, Congress authorized the Army to assist prosecutors in rounding up suspects. Lawmakers also gave the president authority to suspend the writ of habeas corpus, so prosecutors could detain Klansmen indefinitely without an arraignment or indictment. But this highly controversial authority, enacted in April 1871, contained an expiration date "at the end of the next regular session of Congress," which fell on June 10, 1872.[4]

Targeting the Klan required agents and attorneys of the fledgling Department of Justice to investigate crimes over vast geographical areas, on lean budgets with no support staff, while individual cases could comprise hundreds of suspects. But by the middle of 1872, overworked federal prosecutors were winning the war against the Klan. Although agents in the field advised Washington to keep the pressure on, in June 1873 the Grant administration suspended most Klan prosecutions and pardoned all remaining prisoners from the organization, hoping to generate goodwill in the South and silence critics of federal intervention.

No one believed that white vigilante terror had been fully eradicated when the administration adopted its conciliatory strategy in 1873. But federal officials seemed confident that the constitutional and statutory arsenal they had built after the war to protect black rights could deal with further episodes of violence if conciliation failed.[5]

The outlook changed abruptly after the U.S. Supreme Court grappled with a big part of that arsenal, the Fourteenth Amendment, for the first time in an 1873 case involving New Orleans butchers. They sought to overturn a law enacted by the Louisiana legislature requiring all of the city's meat merchants to ply their trade in a state-licensed slaughterhouse downstream from the city, to stop animal wastes from leaching into the water supply and causing outbreaks of yellow fever and cholera. The butchers were represented by John Archibald Campbell, a former U.S. Supreme Court justice who quit the bench during the Civil War and served in the Confederate government. Campbell loathed the idea of black men voting and holding seats in the state legislature, and he specialized in using the courts to stymie Louisiana's biracial Republican government. He sought relief for the white butchers by invoking the new Fourteenth Amendment, which had been created principally to protect the rights of Southern freedmen. Campbell argued that when the Louisiana legislature ignored the white butchers' right to pursue their vocation as they saw fit, it abridged their "privileges or immunities" as U.S. citizens, in violation of the Fourteenth Amendment.

The Supreme Court upheld Louisiana's slaughterhouse law in a 5–4 decision written by Justice Samuel Freeman Miller, a Lincoln appointee who disdained Campbell for working with the Confederacy and undermining Reconstruction. But as he knocked down Campbell's arguments one by one, Miller severely circumscribed federal powers to secure the civil rights of freedmen under the Fourteenth Amendment, arguably inflicting vastly more damage on Reconstruction than even his former colleague intended.

Miller held that employment rights claimed by the butchers were not protected by the "privileges or immunities" clause of the Fourteenth

Amendment, because the clause shielded only rights of national citizenship, such as running for federal office, access to ports and navigable waterways, and travel on the high seas. The butchers' employment rights, like civil rights generally, were protected by the states, as they had always been. The privileges or immunities clause had not transferred the "protection of all the civil rights" from the states to the federal government, Miller concluded.

Many critics have argued that Miller got this wrong; that the Fourteenth Amendment's framers, moved by concerns over the freedmen's safety, clearly intended to endow the federal government with the power to protect civil rights under the privileges or immunities clause. If the amendment protects only such rights as access to ports and navigable waters, "it was a vain and idle enactment, which accomplished nothing, and most unnecessarily excited Congress and the people on its passage," Justice Stephen J. Field wrote in dissent.

Slaughterhouse ranks among the Supreme Court's most infamous decisions. Akhil Reed Amar of Yale Law School has accused the *Slaughterhouse* majority of "strangling the privileges or immunities clause in its crib." By leaving the protection of freedmen's civil rights to Southern state governments, *Slaughterhouse* effectively left former slaves at the mercy of their former masters.

Miller's ruling probably reflected waning support among moderate Republicans for the reordering of American federalism embodied in the Fourteenth Amendment, which had been seen as codifying results of the Civil War. The Grant administration's more conciliatory policy on Klan prosecutions in 1873 emerged amid similar political pressures.[6]

Before *Slaughterhouse*, lower federal courts had mostly sustained Washington's authority to protect civil rights as U.S. attorneys rolled up Klan convictions under the Enforcement Acts. How a Supreme Court case involving white butchers would affect the protection of former slaves was not immediately clear to contemporary observers. But in June 1874, when Justice Bradley applied the *Slaughterhouse* majority's reading of the Fourteenth Amendment in his circuit court opinion freeing all three men convicted in the massacre of black Republicans at Colfax, Louisiana, the result landed with the lucidity of a thunderbolt.

Louisiana conservatives hailed the ruling, which also pronounced two sections of the Enforcement Act of 1870 unconstitutional, as the dawn of their deliverance, a signal that "oppressed" white Southerners would be freed from federal harassment. The *New Orleans Bulletin* published Bradley's opinion in full, splaying his opaque paragraphs across the entire front page like a flag of liberation. Bradley's ruling was not quite the last word on these matters. The Colfax prisoners were at liberty pending review of the case by the full Supreme Court, and the Enforcement Act was still law until a majority of the justices said otherwise. But white Louisianians believed Justice Bradley was in touch with the full court's thinking, and that his views on these matters mirrored those of his colleagues. Attorney General Williams halted civil rights prosecutions under the Enforcement Act pending clarification from the high court. Meanwhile, the federal prosecutor in the Colfax case, U.S. Attorney James Beckwith, expected Bradley's ruling to fuel white vigilante violence against Louisiana Republicans of both races, and predicted there would be five hundred murders before the November election.[7]

Even before Justice Bradley issued his circuit court opinion, the White League vigilante movement had begun stirring in Louisiana's country parishes. Within days of Bradley's ruling, a dominant White League branch emerged in New Orleans, soon to join namesake up-country groups in terrorizing black and white Republicans, while maintaining a gallant posture in the press. But the violence was not confined to Louisiana. In the summer and fall of 1874, white vigilante groups assaulted Republicans in Alabama, Mississippi, South Carolina, and elsewhere, as federal authorities struggled to mount an effective response amid doubts about their jurisdiction. Some feared that a brutal new version of the rebellion launched in 1861 was at hand. After Bradley's ruling, the belief was widespread among Democrats that "any man may murder a Republican, for political reasons without the slightest reason to fear that he will be punished," a prominent Alabama Republican attested, "but with every reason to believe he will be applauded for the act."

Grant had been responding to the pleas of nervous Louisiana Republicans when he secretly dispatched Sheridan to New Orleans and other trouble spots on Christmas Eve 1874. Following the incident in the Louisiana legislature, Grant himself was suddenly a principal target of national fury over affairs in the South.

Governor Kellogg arguably initiated the involvement of federal troops in the Louisiana legislature, yet Grant was vilified as chief engineer of the outrage, and likened to that great purger of parliaments Oliver Cromwell. As the Senate awaited Grant's formal reply to its queries about the shocking events in Louisiana, Grant took personal charge of the draft response prepared by Attorney General Williams. The president "wishes to put it in his own way" and "examine carefully the whole of it," Fish recorded in his diary.

Grant had bristled at the idea of denouncing U.S. military personnel involved in the Louisiana incident, but Fish believed that the turbulent cabinet meeting on the matter had ultimately given the president pause. Grant now seemed "somewhat impressed with doubt as to the entire correctness of what had been done," Fish recalled.

But as Grant put the finishing touches on his reply to the Senate, he also sought input on outrages that could not be laid at the feet of federal authorities. He requested a "synopsis" of a report in progress about "the number of political murders in Louisiana" in recent years. The report was the work of General Phil Sheridan, perhaps the only person more vilified than Grant during the Louisiana affair. Among the white citizens of New Orleans, hating Sheridan "appears just now to be a religion," the *New York Times* noted.[8]

CHAPTER 12

MAKING MARTYRS

General Phil Sheridan emerged from his suite dressed in civilian clothes for an evening promenade across the bustling rotunda of the St. Charles Hotel two days after the fracas in the Louisiana legislature. A few doors down in Parlor Q, speakers at a rally of "Northern and Western" merchants had just finished denouncing the general's recent incendiary telegrams. Similar demonstrations were staged downtown at the Chamber of Commerce, the Board of Underwriters, and the New Orleans Cotton Exchange, where Sheridan was charged with spreading falsehoods "to detract from our good name as law-loving and law abiding citizens" and to "injure the commercial interests of our city."

As Sheridan strolled across the rotunda puffing his cigar, he didn't appear to notice the flocks of onlookers marking his movements, or their "murmurs of suppressed rage" and scattered hisses. Gaggles of reporters also kept watch, having established a semipermanent stakeout in the rotunda near Sheridan's temporary headquarters, where they sized up his visitors as sources of intelligence and potential "Extras."

Sheridan's days in New Orleans were a social minefield. At the hotel's restaurant, his party was greeted with audible groans from other customers, some of whom approached his table brandishing newspaper articles that ridiculed "the little general," with choice insults underscored. Shop windows in the city featured Sheridan-themed caricatures, like the figurine depicting a frail elderly gentleman captioned "one of the banditti."

As local and national newspapers feasted on Sheridan's bombast and controversies, he used them as well. In a confidential wire to Belknap explaining the purpose of his "banditti" telegrams, Sheridan wrote: "The object of my dispatches has been to break down the White Leaguers whose influence intimidated the citizens and all the state authorities." Sheridan had evidently leaked the telegrams to the newspapers in an effort to keep the vigilantes at bay. He also challenged the White League during press interviews, as when he told the *New-York Tribune*, "You cannot have good government in any country where secretly armed bodies of men exist without putting them down. I propose to do it."[1]

Sheridan claimed that his "banditti" pronouncements bucked up the local population. But many white residents found even the term offensive. "Whatever else may be said," a *New Orleans Times* reporter scolded Sheridan, "we are not bandits."

Sheridan tried to explain that the word *banditti* had been meant to apply only to leaders of the White League, not the entire population of Louisiana; also that it was a technical term, employed by the U.S. attorney general to designate persons eligible to be tried by military tribunals for violating codes of armed conflict. Sheridan had privately given the same explanation to Belknap. But the reporter was not impressed. He viewed the White League as an association of respectable citizens defending the people's interests. "I do not see why they deserve the epithet of banditti," he told Sheridan.

The nation had heard a great deal about the wounded feelings of white Southerners since the publication of Sheridan's telegrams. The general even detected a strategy in the attacks directed at him, which he judged unlikely to succeed. Prominent people in New Orleans had been "manufacturing sensational protests for northern political consumption," Sheridan wired to Belknap. "They seem to be trying to make martyrs of themselves; it cannot be done at this late day; there have been too many bleeding negroes and ostracized white citizens for their statements to be believed."

Editors of the *New Orleans Bulletin* cited this telegram, also evidently leaked to the press, as proof of Sheridan's "contempt" for public opinion. The *Bulletin*'s editors also seemed troubled that Sheridan had "Held Up to Public View" the topic of "Bleeding Negroes," proclaiming this news in a headline atop the front page.

Grant was expected to steer public discussion of Southern outrages toward the plight of former slaves and their white allies in the region when he submitted his reply to the Senate about the January 4 incident in the Louisiana legislature. Sheridan had already sent the president a detailed report on the events of that day, alleging that several men who stealthily donned "assistant sergeant at arms" badges during the operation were "well known as captains of White League companies in the city."

The Crescent City White League's increasingly famous leader, Frederick Nash Ogden, issued a technical denial that oddly seemed to both confirm Sheridan's basic allegation and salute the Democrats' sly maneuvers in the legislature. "The White League did not assemble on the 4th of January," Ogden told the *New York Herald*, "and took no part as an organization in the action of that day which has stirred so deeply the popular heart in all parts of our country." Ogden did not deny that several White League officers had taken part in the stirring escapade, whatever the group had done "as an organization."[2]

Sheridan also sent the president a synopsis of his promised report on white vigilante "terrorism," addressing its demoralizing effects in Louisiana and elsewhere. Sheridan claimed there was "ample evidence" that "more than twelve hundred persons" had been "killed and wounded" in Louisiana since 1868 "on account of their political sentiments." The victims were overwhelmingly black men, many slain in "frightful massacres," at Colfax and elsewhere, that were already well known to the public. Many others perished in isolated incidents of depravity. "Two White Leaguers rode up to a negro cabin and called for a drink of water," Sheridan reported to Grant about a typical incident of this sort. "When the old colored man turned to draw it, they shot him in the back and killed him." Such murders in the South were seldom investigated in the best of circumstances, and now courts in many districts were "all broken up," their judges driven off by White League threats; meanwhile, killers of freedmen and so-called carpetbaggers were regarded by their neighbors "rather as heroes than as criminals," Sheridan reported.

General George A. Forsyth, one of Sheridan's top aides, drew the assignment of investigating White League terror and its effects in Louisiana for the promised report. Forsyth sought to gather facts from the vigilantes' principal victims, but he soon hit a wall. "I find it quite impossible to get information from the colored people," he wrote to Sheridan from Shreveport. Black Louisianians faced near-certain violent reprisals for cooperating with federal troops against the White League. They were naturally reluctant to be seen consorting with an officer on Sheridan's staff. So Forsyth hired three agents—two black men and one white—to go undercover and persuade witnesses to cooperate. One of the agents was Henry Adams of Shreveport, a cofounder of the Committee, the group established by black former soldiers that surreptitiously examined freedmen's working conditions to protect them from being cheated.

Adams earned fifty dollars per month working as a "scout" for Sheridan. Years later, when it was suggested that this was "a pretty good business," Adams was quick to disagree. "No, sir; a very dangerous business," he replied. "I had ten times rather have been employed splitting rails. We daren't let nobody know what we was up to."[3]

Dangerous conditions were nothing new for Adams. In his own deposition for the Forsyth investigation, Adams testified that when he returned to Shreveport in 1869, following his service in the U.S. Army, "white people commenced talking about killing out" former black soldiers in the area. The white residents worried that "the discharged soldiers was going to spoil the other negroes, so they could not do anything with them," Adams recalled. He and other ex-soldiers were helping freedmen interpret contracts drawn up with white employers, so the former slaves could get all the wages they were owed. But when shortfalls were discovered, the freedmen seldom got their money, though some "got a whipping when they went home," Adams testified.

Adams recalled some abuses inflicted on freedmen that seemed left over from slavery days, like white men riding "with bull whips in their hands" as they supervised black field laborers, "same as they did in 1858." He saw white employers barge into "colored men's houses and drive their wives out to work, curse their wives for damn bitches." Meanwhile, wanton violence was everywhere. Riding the ferry across the Red River, Adams watched a white man "beat a colored man badly, about twenty-five licks as hard as he could drive them." On a sidewalk in New Orleans, he saw six white men club a black man "all but to death" before tossing their victim, limp and bloody, into his own dray and hauling him off to jail—because he had called one of the white men "a damn s—of a b—," Adams testified.

Rampant violence and intimidation also infested politics. Adams heard white men warn former slaves not to vote Republican or else "they would not let them have no more credit." He saw "large bodies of white men" break up black churches on the Sunday night before a Monday election "to scare them out" and keep black men away from the polls the next day.

The situation was no better when Sheridan reported to Washington on the eve of Grant's reply to the Senate. A pair of black men in Shreveport who had recently testified about frauds committed against them had been "compelled to flee for their lives" amid White League threats of reprisals. The pair managed to reach New Orleans hidden "in a cargo of cotton," Sheridan wrote. He also told Grant about a Bossier Parish judge warned by White Leaguers that if he stood for office as a Republican, he would not live to see another election.

Sheridan had been the target of such threats himself. In an earlier telegram to Washington, he reported that some of "the banditti" had promised to assassinate him because he dared to tell the truth. "I am not afraid," Sheridan declared. He vowed that no threat would deter him from informing the government about Southern localities "where the very air has been impregnated with assassination for several years."

When that particular telegram made its way to the newspapers, residents of New Orleans embraced it with glee. Toy shops displayed dolls with stumpy legs and bloated heads above the caption "I am not afraid." Newsboys hawking papers shouted scarifying headlines and proclaimed, "But I am not afraid." Actresses won roaring ovations by interrupting performances to exclaim, "I am not afraid."

Sheridan endured such abuse with equal parts good humor and indifference, eased by his blossoming relationship with Miss Rucker, the quartermaster general's daughter, in whose company he lingered during their group's sojourn in the Crescent City. Before it was over, the grizzled warrior and the beguiling military brat were engaged to be married, and the peculiar backdrop of their courtship in New Orleans became a matter of legend:

> It was there that Phil was thrown in daily contact with Irene. On the streets and in the hotels epithets far from complimentary saluted his ears. The Southern ladies turned their backs upon him and elevated their noses, while the chivalry made manifest to him that his presence was tolerated only through compulsion. It was then he turned to his *inamorata* for consolation and comfort.

New Orleanians enjoyed mocking Sheridan, but they also feared him a little. Newspapers routinely published rumors of his plans to begin arresting White League leaders. Those leaders did not seem too concerned for the moment, as even many Republicans were annoyed by Sheridan's "Vindictive and Silly 'Banditti' Effusion." But one could never be sure what the stormy general might do, especially if Grant were to get behind his proposal.

While Sheridan's plan to summarily round up White League "banditti" was met with widespread scorn, it was arguably not so different from measures employed a few years earlier to cripple the Klan. The Enforcement Act of 1871 incorporated martial law elements similar to Sheridan's approach, empowering the president to suspend the writ of habeas corpus, a temporary grant of authority that expired in 1872. Sheridan himself seemed to recognize a kinship in his approach. When Republican congressman George F. Hoar paid the general a visit in New Orleans, Sheridan told him, "What you want to do, Mr. Hoar, when you get back to Washington, is to suspend the what-do-you-call-it." Hoar understood that Sheridan was referring to the writ of habeas corpus, the suspension of which the general evidently saw as an important tool for dismantling the White League.[4]

If Sheridan's superiors in Washington decided to confront worsening legal and political headwinds to resume aggressive civil rights enforcement in the South, something akin to his plan would likely be necessary. Former attorney general Akerman's dictum about the Klan and its paramilitary character clearly seemed to fit groups like the White League: "these combinations amount to war, and cannot be crushed under any other theory."

Public support for employing such "heroic measures" to confront vigilante violence in the South had long since cooled, but there were pockets of enthusiasm for Sheridan's plan. Editors of the *Cincinnati Gazette* applauded its "justice and moral force" in dealing with "the armed rebel organizations according to their true characters." They feared that downplaying Southern sedition and murder was an invitation to anarchy. If the South organized for war and committed acts of war, the *Gazette*'s editors asked, should it not be dealt with "by the rules of war?"[5]

Many of Sheridan's most zealous backers saw him as the main thing standing between themselves and the apocalypse. This group likely included the roughly one thousand mostly black Republicans who braved high winds and driving rain on the evening of January 11,

1875, to pack the basement of Union Chapel in New Orleans for a "mass meeting" in support of Little Phil and his blistering dispatches.

Charles Lowell, a former speaker of the state House of Representatives, opened the proceedings with a reminder to the audience that Ulysses S. Grant, their great ally in Washington, understood rebellion and "knew how to put it down." Amid roaring applause for these sentiments, Lowell pronounced that "the hero," Phil Sheridan, would see to their security in the meantime, prompting further wild ovations.

Hugh J. Campbell, a handsome young carpetbagger serving in the state militia, addressed the sense of foreboding in the air, acknowledging that as the nation debated recent events in Louisiana, the cause of freedom was "trembling in the balance." But Campbell heaped praise on the little general who stirred up all the controversy. Until Sheridan arrived in New Orleans, a mass meeting like this one "would not have been safe for us," Campbell observed amid affirming shouts from the crowd.

J. Sella Martin, a trim, whiskerless black man who escaped slavery in Alabama and served in the Louisiana legislature, told the gathering that he had previously been taken in by white conservatives promising to honor his rights in exchange for political support, during the 1872 Fusion alliance between Democrats and Liberal Republicans. Martin lamented that Louisiana Democrats betrayed those vows. But he reassured his listeners that the nation at large would not forsake Southern Republicans, insisting that after years of war and sacrifice, the cause of freedom was simply too dear to "the great heart of the American people" for such a thing to happen.[6]

CHAPTER 13

"A REPROACH UPON THE STATE AND COUNTRY"

Louisiana's leading citizens clustered in the rotunda of the St. Charles Hotel on the evening of January 13, 1875, awaiting news of Grant's reply to the U.S. Senate about the actions of federal bluecoats in their state's legislature. Frederick Nash Ogden, the burly, redheaded chief of the White League, was among those present, along with the man he installed as temporary governor in the September 14 coup, D. B. Penn. Steps away from these two, General Philip H. Sheridan, clad in plain evening clothes, leaned against a marble column puffing a cigar.

Sheridan had summoned the nation's attention to Louisiana by calling for "the arrest and trial" of White League "ringleaders." Depending on the contents of Grant's reply to the Senate, the threat that such arrests could commence imminently, with Sheridan issuing orders to his ready flanks of aides and adjutants, hung over the clamorous rotunda. But the local "banditti" seemed untroubled. Penn did not believe that Grant would unleash Little Phil. There "will be no fight," he assured a visiting journalist; "the president is backing down."

That morning's *New-York Tribune* had surprisingly published a similar forecast. Only a day earlier, the paper predicted that the "obstinate" president would sustain an aggressive policy in Louisiana, even though "the whole country is against him." But the *Tribune* now abruptly reversed itself, reporting that Grant would heed the public outcry after all and relinquish his "fanatical" plans to impose a Sheridan-style crackdown in Louisiana and other trouble spots.

The House subcommittee investigating Louisiana affairs had also affected Grant's thinking, the *Tribune* noted. The panel's report was not yet published, but its findings had been seeping into newspapers, including its discovery that the White League was not, in fact, a gang of coldblooded killers, but was instead an alliance of estimable men "who would not countenance lawlessness of any kind." The Louisiana subcommittee had also discovered "no intimidation" of black voters during the state's fall campaign.[1]

House Republicans had created the special Louisiana committee, and its subcommittee offspring, following an explicit suggestion in Grant's annual message the previous month. Grant had hoped such a committee would settle disputes over the authenticity of reports of political violence against black citizens. But even before the subcommittee completed its work, Grant questioned the loyalties of its Republican members and complained to Fish about Speaker Blaine's manner of selecting them. Blaine had first asked Grant to name a preferred candidate for the committee, then declined to appoint the candidate Grant named, which struck the president as "remarkable," Fish noted.

Now as Grant prepared to send his much-anticipated reply to the Senate, the subcommittee, controlled by members of his own party, had all but exonerated the White League, based on a very selective reading of the evidence, and effectively joined the chorus of protest directed at the administration over its actions in Louisiana. Such factors likely fed the ebullient mood of *Picayune* editors sizing up the prospects for loosening the federal grip on their long-suffering state:

It is generally conceded that if we ever had a strong case before
the country, we have it now; that if there has ever been a time
when, secure in their sympathy and intelligent comprehension,
we could confidently leave our affairs to be dealt with by the
people of the United States, that time is the present.[2]

As Grant worked with advisors on his reply to the Senate a few
days earlier, he found himself alone in the room with Secretary
of State Hamilton Fish. Grant took the opportunity to declare, rather
brusquely, that under no circumstances would he apologize for anything that had been done by federal troops in Louisiana.

Encountering Grant "in this mood," Fish delicately suggested that
many of the president's allies had been troubled, as a matter of "fundamental constitutional principle," by the idea of "military interference
with a legislative body." Fish then read aloud from notes he had drafted,
for possible insertion into Grant's reply, to remove any doubt about the
president's opposition to such actions by the military, and blame any
missteps on well-meaning soldiers using their best judgment.

Grant listened closely, offering no comment, and his finished reply
to the Senate indeed clarified the matter, stating: "I am well aware that
any military interference by the officers or troops of the United States
with the organization of the State legislature or its proceedings is . . .
repugnant to our ideas of government."

But before Grant's message to the Senate delivered that reassur-
ance, it addressed a number of other principles and facts that had been
missing in the one-sided discussion of Louisiana matters so far. For
those tempted to blame the actions of federal soldiers for the state's
misfortunes, Grant reminded the senators that "lawlessness, turbu-
lence and bloodshed" had characterized Louisiana politics for years.

Grant cited the 1866 New Orleans massacre of freedmen, which
had horrified much of the nation and helped to spur passage of the
Military Reconstruction Acts the following year. A white backlash

against black enfranchisement fueled even more widespread Louisiana violence in 1868, starkly suppressing Republican participation in the fall election. As Grant swept to a decisive victory nationally in the 1868 presidential race, he lost Louisiana to his Democratic rival by a whopping 41 percent margin, although the Union hero was very popular among the state's majority-black electorate. Louisiana freedmen were so thoroughly terrorized that Grant received not a single vote in St. Landry Parish, although the Republican candidate for governor six months earlier had gotten about 2,500 votes there, while winning the state in a rout with strong support from newly enfranchised black voters.[3]

But Grant referred only glancingly to those bleak, bloody episodes, focusing most of his attention on the bitterly contested 1872 election in Louisiana, which had fueled so many insurrections since, including the September 1874 New Orleans coup against Governor Kellogg. The 1872 election was also cited as partial justification for the Democrats' recent caper in the Louisiana legislature.

Grant reminded the senators that while Louisiana Democrats "bitterly and persistently alleged" that Kellogg did not legitimately win the governorship in 1872, a U.S. Senate committee had concluded that Kellogg himself had been robbed of about twenty thousand votes through "manipulation of the election machinery" by his opponents. Conceding that there were "no reliable returns" of the results, Grant asserted that Kellogg had more right to the office than his Democratic rival, McEnery, whose claim was "undoubtedly based on fraud."

By far the foulest consequence of the misbegotten 1872 election emerged the following spring at Colfax, Louisiana. McEnery supporters, who had been zealously "misinformed" about the election, committed "a butchery" of Kellogg backers at Colfax, Grant told the Senate, describing it as an event "which in blood-thirstiness and barbarity is hardly surpassed by any acts of savage warfare."

Seeking to put the true nature of the crimes "beyond controversy," Grant quoted from the transcript of the accused Colfax killers' federal trial, recounting facts agreed upon by counsel for both sides and read into the record by the judge: As part of a campaign to remove Kellogg officials by force, armed McEnery loyalists attacked black militiamen at Colfax who were guarding a sheriff and a judge appointed by the new governor. After many of the militiamen were killed, the Kellogg forces surrendered. About thirty-seven black militiamen were taken prisoner by the McEnery loyalists. But when night fell, the prisoners "were led out, two by two, and shot," the judge stated for the record. Federal marshals investigating the carnage days later found that the great majority of the approximately seventy black men killed overall at Colfax had suffered pistol shots to the head, "most of them in the back of the head," the judge stated.

To hold the people of Louisiana "generally responsible for these atrocities would not be just," Grant acknowledged. Yet at every turn, obstacles had been thrown in the way of federal efforts to prosecute the killers, while "so-called conservative" newspapers "justified the massacre" and denounced U.S. law enforcement officials as agents of "tyranny" and "despotism," the president recalled.

Grant reminded the senators that while ferocious complaints about supposedly illegitimate officeholders rang across the Louisiana landscape, every one of the Colfax killers had so far escaped justice, "and no way can be found in this boasted land of civilization and Christianity to punish the perpetrators of this bloody and monstrous crime."

The president recounted a number of other unpunished murders of black Republicans and their white allies in Louisiana before arriving at the great crime of which he and his administration stood accused before the nation. Grant told the senators that he first learned of "the late legislative imbroglio in Louisiana" the morning after it occurred, and had given no orders regarding any such actions by federal troops.

"I can conceive of no case, not involving rebellion or insurrection," where federal interference in the proceedings of a state legislature could be justified, Grant explained. But he believed that circumstances on the ground exempted the soldiers from any "intentional wrong" in the matter. Since they had been dispatched to Louisiana the previous September, in the wake of the White League coup, to prevent domestic violence, they likely saw it as their duty to act "when called upon by the governor for that purpose."

Each branch of a legislature is the final judge of its own members' qualifications, but this was not, Grant argued, a case of federal forces substituting their own judgments. Rather, it was a mob preventing a legislature from organizing itself in the first place. It was therefore the governor's duty "to suppress the disturbance" and allow rightfully elected legislators to organize the house. If the governor had summoned the Metropolitan Police for this purpose instead of federal forces, he might well have produced another "bloody conflict with the White League," like the clash on September 14, Grant asserted. In any case, evidence that the presence of federal troops actually preserved order included the fact that each side sought their assistance.

Grant supposed it was debatable whether Kellogg had any business getting involved in the legislature's affairs on January 4. But "there would have been no trouble if those who now complain of illegal interference had allowed the house to be organized in a lawful and regular manner," Grant countered. Even Phelps of the Louisiana subcommittee judged the Democrats' January 4 legislative coup to be "illegal," since they violated a state law requiring the "Clerk of the last House" to preside over the chamber's organization after an election.

As for Sheridan's menacing dispatches, Grant assured the senators that they sprang from no political motives, but expressed an honest assessment of dangerous conditions then prevailing in Louisiana and threats posed by the White League. Sheridan had "suggested summary modes of procedure" against the vigilante group, "which, though they cannot be adopted, would, if legal, soon put an end to the troubles and disorders in that state," Grant explained in a meticulously parsed passage. "General Sheridan was looking at facts, and possibly, not thinking of proceedings which would be the only proper ones to pursue in time of peace, thought more of the utterly lawless condition

of society surrounding him at the time of his dispatch, and of what
would prove a sure remedy."

Sheridan "never proposed to do an illegal act," Grant argued, continuing his defense of the vilified general, "nor expressed determination to proceed beyond what the law in the future might authorize for
the punishment of the atrocities which have been committed." Grant
now adopted the censorious tones of an Old Testament prophet. "It is
a deplorable fact that political crimes and murders have been committed in Louisiana which have gone unpunished, and which have been
justified or apologized for, which must rest as a reproach upon the
State and country long after the present generation has passed away."

Grant reminded the senators that he had long since urged Congress to address Louisiana's political violence and tumult over disputed
elections, and he believed that the lawmakers' inaction had "produced
great evil." He now asked Congress again to address the state's difficulties, and "to take such action as to leave my duties perfectly clear in
dealing with the affairs of Louisiana."

President Grant insisted that he "deplored the necessity" of sending
troops to interfere in the domestic concerns of any state. But he vowed
that, to the extent Congress had empowered him to enforce it, "neither
Ku-Klux-Klans, White Leagues, nor any other association using arms
and violence to execute their unlawful purposes" would be "permitted
in that way to govern any part of this country."[4]

William Hepworth Dixon, a moderately famous British author
with bushy chin whiskers, a tousled mane, and a penetrating
eye, mingled with the crowd awaiting news of Grant's message in the
rotunda of the St. Charles Hotel. The prolific Dixon had turned out
popular volumes on numerous subjects, including English prisons, the
Holy Land, and eminent detainees of the Tower of London. His current project wrestled with a timelier topic: "The great conflict of races
on the American soil as seen in 1875."

Dixon's sympathies in this conflict would be evident throughout his book, beginning with the title: "White Conquest."

In Dixon's telling, a climactic scene in the great struggle between races would unfold this very evening in the St. Charles rotunda, which he describes as a palatial setting "where merchants buy and sell, where gamblers square accounts, where duellists look for seconds, and where everyone devours the news."

From "every corner of the earth," news arrived by wire in the rotunda, Dixon reported, and amid the convivial roar of conversation under the soaring dome, "all ears are strained" toward the telegraph clerks, who read aloud from bulletins as they landed.

Scanning the rotunda crowd, Dixon noticed young Irene Rucker peering down "wistfully" from a high gallery "into the sea of dark and bearded faces" below, an assemblage that included her traveling companion General Phil Sheridan. "Poor girl!" Dixon observed. "She has reason to suppose that every man is armed. She knows that all these people hate her lover with a fury not to be appeased by blood. Who can assure her that the evening will not close in massacre."

At last, a clerk announced that news had arrived from Washington. Dixon describes the scene:

> "Read, read!" scream a hundred voices. One of the clerks jumps on a bench, the printed telegraph slip in his hand, and waving it before his audience, cries out lustily: "Gentlemen, the President backs down!"
>
> "Backs down?" each wild and pallid auditor asks his neighbor; "Yes, backs down!"

Tensions in the rotunda dissipated "at once," Dixon reports. Some in the crowd slipped away "to spread the news," while others scoured the wires for details. In Dixon's telling, as far as the rotunda was concerned, the core meaning of Grant's nuanced communiqué was clear: "Sheridan is not sustained."

The rotunda telegraph clerk was likely reading a bulletin from the next day's *New-York Tribune*. But the Grant-friendly *National Republican* denied that the president had "backed down" in the slightest, and blasted the *Tribune*'s claims to the contrary as "the thinnest kind of subterfuge."

While some viewed Grant's message to the Senate as a retreat from Sheridan's bold program, the president's defense of administration actions, and righteous condemnation of vigilante murderers and their enablers, boosted morale among scandal-weary Republicans, even moderates. But the moderates remained disillusioned with federal Reconstruction policy overall. Many proved unwilling to back Grant's attempt, following the embarrassing Louisiana episode, to consolidate his administration's enforcement authority.

Grant had acknowledged, after consulting with his advisors, that Sheridan's banditti plan did not conform with then-current law. In keeping with his pledge to stymie "White Leagues" and other violent groups, Grant endorsed a new "force bill" that would authorize martial law–type measures akin to Sheridan's plan, including a revival of the power to suspend the writ of habeas corpus. But that provision had always been controversial, and as the days of Republican control of the House of Representatives drew to a close, many party moderates opposed the new force bill as too politically risky. The House ultimately passed the measure, with strong support from Republican Radicals, but the moderates' delaying tactics kept it from reaching the Senate with enough time to be considered before adjournment, and the new force bill met "death by suffocation" in the upper chamber.[5]

Meanwhile, the official release of the House Louisiana subcommittee's report, with its suggestions of White League blamelessness, muted any rallying effect of Grant's message and certainly didn't help the force bill's chances. To quell Republican discontent with the subcommittee's one-sided narrative, the full Louisiana special committee sent its remaining members to New Orleans to redo the investigation. This second panel heard from more of the witnesses recommended by local Republicans, and produced a report acknowledging that White League violence and intimidation had contributed to an 1874 election that "was neither full, free, nor fair."

But the second Louisiana report was also sharply critical of Republican policies in the state, even suggesting that black suffrage had been imposed there prematurely, when most freedmen were illiterate and supposedly prone to political manipulation. The second report reflected the goal of House Republican leaders to create a consensus document as the basis for a political compromise that would move Louisiana off the nation's front pages. Republican leaders asked New York congressman William A. Wheeler, one of the Louisiana committee members sent to conduct the second investigation, to work out a compromise satisfactory to both major factions in the state.

Wheeler's proposed compromise gave Louisiana Democrats control of the state House of Representatives, left Republicans in control of the state Senate, and required Democrats to let Kellogg serve out his term as governor in peace, without impeachments. As the deal took shape, Wheeler sought Grant's opinion and found the president vigorously opposed to the idea of arbitration involving the Louisiana faction allied with the White League. Grant preferred settling the matter "either by the law, or by force, and this was neither one thing or the other," Fish recalled. But as prospects for a new force bill dimmed, Grant changed his mind and told Wheeler he would back the compromise to the hilt. The "Wheeler Adjustment" was ultimately approved by both local factions and took effect on April 17, 1875.

Grant was clearly frustrated as his options for assisting the freedmen narrowed amid vanishing Northern support. Republican lawmakers were unlikely to craft new legal tools for aggressive action against Southern vigilantes if their voters angrily opposed such steps. Grant himself had already been tiptoeing around Northern opinion on these matters. He had vowed the previous December to protect freedmen's rights "with rigor," despite mounting public opposition to federal enforcement efforts, but he initially kept Sheridan's mission to New Orleans and points south hidden from the public—and from most of his cabinet. When Grant pushed for the annexation of Santo Domingo years earlier, viewing it as a possible sanctuary for freedmen, he avoided engaging with the public about that aspect of the plan.

Such tactics didn't always work out. The Santo Domingo annexation push split the Republican Party and severely weakened Reconstruction. Sheridan's Louisiana ramble appeared to be a debacle of that magnitude. The spectacle of bluecoats with bayonets settling election disputes in a Southern state legislature generated "more Northern opposition than any previous federal action in the South," historian Eric Foner reports.

Grant seemed bewildered by the paroxysm of public outrage aimed at the federal government, while Southern atrocities against freedmen went largely overlooked. But he was not ready to surrender. Grant told former Republican senator Benjamin F. Wade that if white Southerners continued to test him, "they will find him a very different customer than Buchanan or Lincoln was to deal with," Wade confided to his wife. Yet months later, Grant's guarded response to another Reconstruction crisis suggested that the public's fury over the Louisiana debacle was still very much in his thoughts.[6]

CHAPTER 14

"PEACEABLY IF POSSIBLE, FORCIBLY IF NECESSARY"

Sheriff Albert T. Morgan saw signs of trouble soon after he began to address the mostly black audience at a Republican political meeting in Yazoo City, Mississippi, on September 1, 1875. As if on cue, "seven or eight of the most substantial white men of the town" abruptly filed into the hall and sat in the first row "immediately in front of me," Morgan recalled.

These men had not come in admiration of Morgan, a member of the scorned "carpetbagger" class who had served in the Union Army and moved to Mississippi from his native Wisconsin after the war in search of his fortune. After struggling to make a living as a cotton farmer on a rented plantation and in various other enterprises, Morgan was elected sheriff of Yazoo County on the Republican ticket, promising to protect the rights of black Mississippians, who now made up a large majority of voters in the county and the state. If this career path was not enough to unhinge many of his white neighbors, Morgan also married a mixed-race woman with "negro blood" and established a school for black children, the first of its kind in Yazoo County.

The late-arriving procession of white men at the Republican meeting reminded Morgan of a peculiar article published weeks earlier in a local Democratic newspaper. The article explained how to disrupt "Radical" political meetings as part of a plan for the decidedly outnumbered Democrats to wrest control of the state from Republicans "peaceably if possible, forcibly if necessary."

The article advised Democrats to send "a committee" of "reputable citizens" to Republican meetings and, when "radical speakers" tried to "mislead the negroes" with "falsehoods," to challenge their assertions and "compel them to tell the truth or quit the stand." As Morgan spoke to the mostly black crowd of about one hundred Republicans, the late-arriving white men seemed to follow the Democratic newspaper's disruptive script.[1]

The leader of the white men, Henry Dixon, left the hall and quickly returned escorting a black man allied with the Democrats, who unleashed "a bitter denunciation of me," Morgan recalled. The Democrats seemed to be trying to provoke the assembled Republicans, evidently seeking an excuse to unholster their weapons in "self-defense." After Morgan resumed his speech, Dixon seized upon some remark that was colorably offensive, drew his pistol, and opened fire. Morgan managed to escape from the hall through a window, though he returned briefly to fire off a few rounds from his own pistol. Meanwhile, others in Dixon's group had also begun firing their weapons and the audience scattered. The chaos spilled into the streets of Yazoo City, now patrolled by armed white men on horseback. Morgan went into hiding.

One Republican was killed and several were wounded in the Yazoo City melee; one of the Democrats was also injured. A few days later, Democrats staged a similar incursion at a Republican political meeting in the nearby town of Clinton in Hinds County, with much more devastating results.

Over two thousand black men, women, and children gathered that Saturday afternoon amid magnolia and pecan trees for a combination barbecue and Republican political rally. The Democratic Party had been invited to send a speaker to facilitate an exchange of ideas. The Democratic speaker arrived at the picnic with a crew of young so-called White Liners carrying concealed weapons.

As the Republican speaker addressed the crowd, a young White Line heckler denounced him for telling "damned lies." A shouting and shoving commotion ensued, followed quickly by gunshots apparently commenced by the White Liners. Soon volleys of White Line gunfire transformed the scene into bedlam, and the black picnickers fled in every direction.

But the vigilantes were far from finished. Companies of heavily armed White Line reinforcements stationed at nearby rail depots now set out to roam the countryside, murdering suspected black political leaders and ransacking their dwellings. In a campaign of terror and retribution that lasted for days, the White Line posses "just hunted the whole county clean out," a black Republican leader recalled.[2]

No precise accounting of casualties associated with the "Clinton Riot" and its aftermath was attempted at the time, but estimates suggest that between thirty and fifty black Republicans were killed. In the days following the episode, hundreds of Hinds County residents sought refuge in nearby Jackson, Mississippi, the state's capital, where a small contingent of U.S. troops was stationed near the federal courthouse. Jackson was also the residence of the state's "carpetbag" governor, Adelbert Ames, a former Union Army general who was elected with overwhelming support from black Mississippians.

The refugees flowing into Jackson brought Ames firsthand accounts of violence against freedmen in Yazoo City and Clinton. He was also fielding reports of similar incidents across the state. Hinds County Sheriff William Harney urgently implored the governor "to use what means there is at your command to stop this slaughter of an innocent and defenseless people."[3]

Ames felt he had little choice but to again call on the federal government for assistance. The Grant administration had refused such a request when White Line violence threatened the Vicksburg municipal elections of August 1874. But when the Republican-controlled state legislature requested federal help in December of that year after the Vicksburg massacre, Grant issued a proclamation authorizing the deployment of U.S. troops to protect Mississippi from domestic violence. After Sheridan set up shop in New Orleans in January 1875, he sent troops to restore Peter Crosby as Warren County sheriff, reversing Crosby's forcible ouster by White Line vigilantes.

In September 1875, it looked as if Mississippi White Liners were trying to replicate the Vicksburg revolt on a much wider scale. "Domestic violence in its most aggravated form exists in certain parts of this state," Ames wired Grant on September 7, alerting the president that "unauthorized armed bodies" were "scouring" the countryside, murdering freedmen and spreading terror. Ames warned that the "necessity of immediate action cannot be overstated." The following day, Ames formally requested federal assistance against domestic violence under Article IV, Section 4 of the U.S. Constitution.

Ames and his wife, Blanche, had decided it would be best for the health of their two young children if she lived with them at the family's home in Lowell, Massachusetts, while he served in Mississippi, which was known for regular outbreaks of yellow fever. But they exchanged letters frequently, and he wrote to Blanche about the importance of securing a deployment of federal troops in Mississippi. "We must have them," he explained, "or the colored voters of the state will be deprived of their rights and liberties, which the amendments of the Constitution expressly stipulate to maintain."

Ames knew his request was replete with peril for Republicans, especially following the politically damaging "banditti" episode involving federal troops in neighboring Louisiana earlier that year. Campaign season was already at hand, in an era when elections were not held all at once in November but spread across the calendar. The most important contest on the Republican calendar, Ohio's election for governor, was at high tide, with balloting only a month away.

"I am fully alive to the fact that my action will be like an exploding shell in the political canvas at the North," Ames wrote to Blanche. Despite such difficulties, he was confident that Grant would respond with an urgency befitting the crisis. "I presume the president will act at once," Ames told his wife.[4]

Grant was vacationing at his family's beachfront cottage in Long Branch, New Jersey, when the governor's telegrams reached him. But he was capable of quick action in such circumstances. The previous September, Grant was packed and ready to depart the White House for a Long Branch holiday when he issued a proclamation addressing the White League revolt in New Orleans—before his cabinet even had time to assemble. But Grant moved much more deliberately in this case. After arranging for sufficient troops to be made ready, he asked his new attorney general, Edwards Pierrepont, to evaluate Ames's request, to determine if a proclamation should be issued and soldiers dispatched to Mississippi.

Pierrepont, a former Democrat, was skeptical of the need for such a deployment. When he informed Ames by telegram that federal troops were at the ready, Pierrepont asked the governor whether they were truly necessary. Was this really the sort of insurrection that "cannot be put down by the State military forces," with help from volunteers among Mississippi's "true citizens"? Pierrepont asked.

The thirty-nine-year-old Ames evinced a bright-eyed, boyish aspect despite his ample paintbrush mustache, but he was hardly known for leaning on others to fight his battles. Barely two months after he graduated from West Point, Ames demonstrated exceptional valor at the July 1861 Battle of Bull Run, for which he would later be awarded the Congressional Medal of Honor. "Everyone who rode with him in battle soon discovered that Ames never hesitated to take desperate chances under fire," a former aide wrote.[5]

Ames had tried to organize a militia of "true citizens" to protect black voters. But white conservatives made the "color line" such an all-consuming issue, he found it impossible to recruit white volunteers for the effort. He considered organizing an all-black militia but dropped the project, believing it could ignite "a war of the races" that could engulf the entire region. The frequent collaborations of violent White Liners and White Leaguers from various Southern states suggested such concerns were hardly alarmist.

Ames wired Pierrepont attempting to explain such Southern realities. Frustrated that "the situation cannot be condensed in a telegram," he still maintained that federal troops would offer "the most complete protection" of the state's black voters.

While Ames pleaded for military assistance, Mississippi Democrats and some of the governor's local Republican foes tried to block it. A Vicksburg Republican wrote to Pierrepont that all was well in their state and any disturbances could be handled by local posses of "good citizens." Federal troops, he warned, would only "aggravate existing difficulties."

Blanche followed newspaper accounts of her husband's struggle to obtain federal military assistance and grew indignant at "Grant's dilatory shilly-shally conduct." But the normally decisive Grant was not finished vacillating.[6]

After he reviewed a report from Pierrepont on the situation in Mississippi, Grant confessed to feeling "somewhat perplexed" about which steps to take. "The whole public are tired out with these annual, autumnal outbreaks in the South," he wrote to Pierrepont, "and there is so much unwholesome lying done by the press and people in regard to the cause & extent of these breaches of the peace that the great majority are ready now to condemn any interference on the part of the government."

Grant wished that "peace and good order" could be restored in Mississippi without a proclamation and the deployment of federal troops. But if that was not possible, "the proclamation must be issued," he told

Pierrepont. And if it came to that, "I shall instruct the Commander of the forces to have no child's play."

Despite his resolute tone, Grant hesitated again, instructing Pierrepont to have a proclamation drawn up in case it was needed later, but not publicized. For now Grant wanted Pierrepont to make sure Ames was truly "exhausting his own resources" before federal help was sent to Mississippi.[7]

Grant's hesitancy apparently involved, at least in part, concerns about the approaching election in Ohio. Both Grant and Pierrepont would have preferred to avoid injecting the explosive issue of troop deployments into the campaign. Pierrepont's next move seemed to be an attempt to sidestep the issue of troops and proclamations altogether, while still addressing Grant's concern that Governor Ames receive all appropriate support.[8]

To convey the president's ambivalent message to Ames, Pierrepont included quotations from Grant's letter in a telegram to the governor, beginning with the memorable observation about dwindling public patience for federal interference in the South: "The whole public are tired out with these annual autumnal outbreaks."

Pierrepont took care to relay Grant's determination that if "peace and good order" were not restored in Mississippi, a proclamation authorizing the deployment of troops "must be issued." But the attorney general also quoted Grant on the need for Ames to recruit volunteers and "strengthen his own position" before receiving such federal help, noting that "every member of the Cabinet who has been consulted" was in "full accord" with the president on this. "We cannot understand why you do not strengthen yourself in the way the president suggests," Pierrepont told Ames. He advised the governor to "let the country see that the citizens of Miss., who are largely favorable to good order, and who are largely Republican, have the courage and the manhood to *fight* for their rights, and to destroy the bloody ruffians who murder the innocent and unoffending freedmen."

In closing, Pierrepont promised Governor Ames that if, after employing all the means at his command, he still could not suppress vigilante violence in his state, "the President will swiftly aid you in crushing these lawless traitors to human rights."[9]

This closing promise of swift aid to crush violent white vigilantes became a crucial part of Pierrepont's strategy to maximize the telegram's impact. Two days after he sent it to Governor Ames, Pierrepont wired Grant to announce: "No proclamation needed."

If no proclamation was issued, there would be no deployment of troops. How was such a quick and painless resolution possible? Pierrepont explained that a delegation of Mississippi Republicans had requested that his telegram to Ames be leaked to the press. Two of Grant's cabinet members, Bristow and Jewell, agreed with the Mississippi visitors. "They all say it will produce quiet," Pierrepont told Grant, then asked the president: "Shall I do it?" Grant's advisors apparently believed that publicizing the telegram, with its presidential promise to "swiftly aid" Governor Ames in suppressing "lawless traitors" if vigilante violence continued, would deter Mississippi White Liners from further outrages, removing the need for proclamations and troop deployments. Grant quickly telegraphed his permission to go ahead with the plan.

Apparently unaware of these stratagems, Ames read Pierrepont's telegram with a combination of anger and disappointment. The attorney general had been "rather severe on us and our party," Ames wrote to Blanche, bristling at Pierrepont's accusation that Mississippi Republicans had taken "no action" to protect themselves. "I have endeavored time and again to organize militia and have utterly failed," Ames told his wife. He confessed that the attorney general's telegram, with its calls for demonstrations of "courage and manhood" by local Republicans, "has quite exasperated me."

Ames spent most of an afternoon composing a reply to Pierrepont, then decided against sending it because his state of mind was "too belligerent." But he poured out his frustrations to Blanche. "What I regret more than anything else is that the North cannot and will not understand the rebellious and barbarous spirit that prevails among the whites here," Ames wrote to his wife. He lamented that Northern ignorance of Southern violence was reinforced by Mississippi Republicans who painted a rosy picture of conditions there to curry favor with local Democrats, placing him and his allies "in a false position."[10]

As Ames cataloged his grievances for Blanche, more than ten days had passed since he urgently requested federal help to put down domestic violence targeting Mississippi freedmen and their allies. His appeal to President Grant had yielded many things in the interim, including a blistering telegram from the attorney general that was also published widely in newspapers. These newspapers ridiculed Ames for having been "disgraced before the country" and "rather neatly snubbed" by Pierrepont, among other humiliations. But the governor's urgent request had not yielded any troops to protect the freedmen.

A group of three hundred Vicksburg freedmen wrote to Ames around that time. They had been following their governor's struggle to obtain a deployment of federal troops and wished to clarify the stakes. "We will ask you to do all you can to get protection, for we have none, and unless we do have, we will tell you we will not carry the next election," the freedmen told Ames. "The colored people will be forced away from the polls and not allowed to vote for fear of being shot down. They are making preparations for it now. They are going around the streets at night dressed in soldiers clothes and making colored people run for their lives."[11]

Ames reluctantly tried again to field a militia, reminding his wife at one point that "all the world agrees I should help myself before calling on the President for troops." His results were little different than before. "None of the white Republicans seem disposed to enter the militia, being intimidated by the white liners," he told Blanche.

As Ames attempted to follow Washington's self-help program, his outlook darkened. On October 12, he wrote to Blanche that the state's atmosphere of violence and threats had by then "thoroughly intimidated" black Mississippians, who probably could not be rallied to the polls "unless we have U.S. troops" for protection, "and it is now too late for that." Even if Grant could be persuaded to order a troop deployment, Ames explained, the time it would take to process an official request for military assistance would leave "hardly a day" for soldiers to reestablish calm before balloting commenced on November 2.

Ames spelled out to his wife the looming consequences for black citizens of unchecked White Line violence and intimidation. "Yes, a revolution has taken place—by force of arms—and a race are disenfranchised—they are to be returned to a condition of serfdom—an era of second slavery. The nation should have acted, but it was 'tired of the annual autumnal outbreaks in the South,'" he wrote, quoting Grant, whose words had evidently stung. "The political death of the Negro will forever release the nation from the weariness," Ames acidly pronounced.[12]

Despite his disappointment, Ames soon managed to rekindle hopes for a better outcome in Mississippi when George K. Chase, an agent of the U.S. Justice Department acting as an emissary for the attorney general, worked out a "peace" deal between the governor and local Democratic leaders. The Democrats promised to suppress political violence and "secure a fair election," while Ames agreed to halt militia recruitment, send existing members home awaiting orders, and to store their weapons under guard in an armory.

Although Ames still felt "sore" at the treatment he had received from the federal government, he wrote Pierrepont to thank the attorney general for Chase's "timely and skillful intervention," through which "a bloody revolution has been averted." But it was soon clear that the Democrats' main motivation for the peace deal was to sweep the all-black militia off the streets, both to ease anxieties among their white constituents and remove the risk that a bloody outrage against the militiamen might reawaken Northern support for U.S. troops to put down vigilante violence. Both sides in Mississippi were well aware that ordering such troop deployments would be much less politically disagreeable for Grant now that the October 13 Ohio election was over and Republican Rutherford B. Hayes had been reelected governor, after serving two consecutive two-year terms in that office from 1868 to 1872. Republicans were already speaking of him as their party's potential presidential nominee in 1876.

Now that Grant had a freer hand, Democrats labored to maintain a surface calm, explaining away reports of violence against freedmen as erroneous or unrelated to politics. But before long, as violent incidents multiplied, even Chase, architect of the peace deal, concluded that the Democrats' promises had been largely empty.[13]

"It is impossible to have a fair election on November 2nd without the aid of U.S. troops," Chase told Pierrepont just four days before the election. Democrats' violent tactics, including "the hanging of several" black leaders, had "so intimidated" the freedmen that they "dare not" engage in politics, and Ames was "powerless" to protect them, Chase reported to his boss. The following day, Pierrepont telegraphed Ames and promised that U.S. troops would intervene if the Democrats failed to keep their pledges to preserve peace and deliver a fair election.

Nearly two months after Ames submitted his urgent request for federal help, pleading that U.S. bluecoats alone could rescue the Mississippi election, Washington at last had tentatively agreed to enter the fray. But now it was much too late for such an intervention to alter the course of events, even if the relatively few troops available on short notice were effectively deployed.[14]

No one knew these unfortunate facts better than Ames. On the day before the election, he wrote to Blanche: "The reports which come to me hourly are truly sickening. Violence, threats of murder and consequent intimidation are co-extensive with the limits of the state. Republican leaders in many localities are hiding in the swamps or have sought refuge beyond the borders of their own counties." As for the eleventh-hour promise of federal assistance, Ames told his wife that "no preparations have been made by a proper disposition of troops to meet the murderous designs of the white-liners."

Election day in Mississippi was not extraordinarily violent; possibly most of the work of intimidating the majority black electorate was complete. But violence remained in the mix. Armed White Liners in Monroe County stalked fords of a river to prevent rural black voters from crossing over to reach their polling place. In Aberdeen, the county seat, a white Democrat warned the Republican sheriff that if the black men who were lined up outside the polling place did not disperse immediately, he and his armed companions would "cover the yard" with their corpses.[15]

Employing such tactics, Democrats swept the 1875 election, winning comfortable majorities in both houses of the state legislature and five of Mississippi's six seats in the U.S. House of Representatives, up from one in the previous election. Mississippi Republicans, who were mostly black, remained a comfortable majority of the state's electorate, but they were now an effectively suppressed majority. In some plantation counties, Republican vote totals actually increased from the previous election. But the party's vote fell off drastically in areas subjected to rampant violence. Yazoo County, with a black majority of two thousand, recorded only seven Republican votes in 1875.[16]

The new Democratic legislature "will be able to do anything it may incline to do," Ames vented to his wife, condemning the election as "worse than a farce." The legislature convened the following January, and by February it was drawing up articles of impeachment against Ames and the state's top three black Republican officials, including Lieutenant Governor Alexander K. Davis.

Eager to leave Mississippi and rejoin his family, Ames cut a deal with the legislature on March 28, 1876, agreeing to resign if Democrats dropped the impeachment charges against him, which he hoped would remove the stain on his reputation. By then, Lieutenant Governor Davis had already resigned following a conviction in his own impeachment, so the president pro tempore of the state Senate, John Marshall Stone, a Democrat, became the governor.

The Democrats' use of violence and intimidation to wrest control of the state government from the Republican majority, soon known as the "Mississippi Plan," energized allies in other states as the 1876 elections approached. The U.S. Supreme Court boosted this momentum on March 27, 1876, with its ruling in *U.S. v. Cruikshank*, which drastically narrowed federal civil rights jurisdiction under the Fourteenth Amendment and gutted the Enforcement Act. *Cruikshank* mostly ratified Justice Joseph Bradley's 1874 circuit court opinion, long seen as fuel for the explosion of white vigilantism across the South that began in the spring and summer of 1874.[17]

Following the Mississippi revolution and *Cruikshank*'s further retrenchment of federal jurisdiction over the protection of black rights, Democrats and their vigilante allies set their sights on the campaign of 1876, and on the last bastions of black majority power in the Southern states: South Carolina and Louisiana.

CHAPTER 15

"OCCASIONALLY THERE WERE A FEW NECKS BROKEN"

Marshall H. Twitchell rode the ferry across the Red River with George King, his lone surviving brother-in-law, on the morning of May 2, 1876, to take care of routine business at the Coushatta courthouse. But looking up from his newspaper as the skiff neared shore, Twitchell saw a strange man in a long coat and black slouch hat standing on the riverbank, aiming a rifle dead at him.

The mysterious gunman might have come to settle any one of a potentially limitless number of grudges against Twitchell, possibly the most loathed carpetbagger in Louisiana. Twitchell had recently been working with federal prosecutors to build cases against local suspects in the Coushatta Massacre, which had claimed the lives of many members of his family. But a lack of witnesses willing to testify had probably erased all hope of bringing the Coushatta killers to justice even before the Supreme Court's *Cruikshank* opinion gutted the Enforcement Act, under which they were charged.

The previous summer, Twitchell had taken a break from turbulent Louisiana to visit his native Vermont, where he promptly bought a house and got reacquainted with a childhood sweetheart, who soon agreed to marry him. But new tumults awaited Twitchell when he returned to Louisiana and took up his duties in the state Senate.

Toward the end of February, as Mississippi Democrats were moving to impeach Governor Ames, Democrats in the Louisiana House of Representatives manufactured articles of impeachment against Governor Kellogg, breaking the deal they had cut with Republicans the previous year to let him serve out his term in peace. But Twitchell, in an adroit parliamentary maneuver, managed to conduct a rushed impeachment trial in the Republican-controlled Senate that cleared Kellogg while the Democratic-controlled House was adjourned to celebrate Mardi Gras. Democrats across the state were furious with Twitchell, "he of the sinister eye, who furnishes most of the backbone to his party," as one local newspaper phrased its condemnation.

During the final Republican caucus after the legislature adjourned, Twitchell advised his party colleagues to stay alert for assassins amid the expected turmoil of the coming campaign. Although he had received many death threats over the years, Twitchell didn't think his political enemies would target him with violence just then, and risk attracting new attention to their suspected role in the Coushatta Massacre and the murders of his family members.

But his suspicions were more than aroused as he rode the ferry across the Red River on May 2 and spotted the gunman on the bank.

"Down in the boat," Twitchell hollered.

A bullet pierced his left thigh and he plunged into the river, clinging to the skiff with one hand. The gunman wheeled on King and shot him in the head, killing him instantly. Then he shot Twitchell twice in the right arm. When Twitchell clung to the boat with his left arm, bullets smashed into his left shoulder.

Floating on his back, blood gushing from his wounds, Twitchell told the ferry operator "to call out that I was dead," he wrote in his memoir. The ferryman obliged, shouting out the news of Twitchell's murder. When it was repeated by observers on the shore, the gunman mounted his horse and left.

The ferryman helped Twitchell onto the boat and moved him to safety. But Twitchell's injuries were devastating. Although he survived, both arms had to be amputated.

The attacker's identity and motives were never proved, but Twitchell had no doubt that the crime was "purely political." Some Northern newspapers agreed, seeing the ambush as the start of a new round of white vigilante terror to subvert the coming election and overthrow Republican rule in Louisiana. But after the recent upheaval in Mississippi, Louisiana Republicans were not expecting much help in suppressing vigilante violence. Even before Twitchell found himself supine and armless in his convalescent bed, many Louisiana Republicans were discouraged by the apparent willingness of their party's leadership to sacrifice them, and the cause of freedom itself, to be rid of the politically perilous issue of Southern intervention.[1]

But the 1876 elections in Louisiana and South Carolina demonstrated that the erosion of Reconstruction was more than a question of raw troop deployments. After a white mob murdered five black men and ransacked the homes of black citizens in Hamburg, South Carolina, the state's Republican governor, Daniel Chamberlain, wrote to President Grant for assistance. The citizens of his majority-black state feared that Democrats were planning to employ a version of the Mississippi Plan during the approaching election campaign, and that "physical violence is to be used to overcome the political will of the people," Chamberlain wrote. Grant fully concurred with the governor on the state's dire emergency. But the Supreme Court's recent *Cruikshank* decision seemed to inject a certain tentativeness in his offer of assistance. "I will give every aid for which I can find law, or constitutional power," Grant promised.

Pursuant to Grant's orders, the U.S. Army stationed more troops in

South Carolina for the 1876 election than at any time since the Civil War. But the soldiers' presence "had little effect" on the state's rampant vigilante violence, according to a top historian of Reconstruction in the state, because "Democratic leaders were well aware of the constitutional, numerical and geographic limitations facing the troops."

South Carolina vigilantes known as Red Shirts drew inspiration from Mississippi White Liners and developed their own program of violent voter suppression. Martin W. Gary, a Democratic candidate for the state Senate who had served as a general in the Civil War, drew up an aggressive blueprint for overcoming the incumbent party's superior numbers. Gary's "No. 1 Plan of Campaign 1876" decreed that every Democrat involved in the effort must be armed with at least a rifle and a pistol, and must "control the vote of at least one Negro, by intimidation, purchase, keeping him away [from the polls] or as each individual may determine, how he may best accomplish it."

Gary's plan motivated many white vigilantes to focus their efforts on the political campaign. A Barnwell County Republican reported that Democrats intended "to kill every leader in the Radical party— and they are going around our houses every night more or less way laying us."

Meanwhile, General Sheridan himself oversaw federal efforts to ensure a peaceful election in Louisiana. From his Chicago headquarters, Sheridan dispatched several extra companies of infantry to the state at the end of August. Under the new U.S. Army commander in the region, General Christopher C. Augur, troops were deployed to more towns and precincts in Louisiana than in any previous election there.

Despite these reinforcements, white vigilantes "terrorized local Republicans almost at will" in districts garrisoned by federal troops, according to a military historian of the period. One of the vigilantes later described how groups of them dealt with freedmen who were resistant to the Democrats' political appeals:

Nothing intimidates a negro so much as mystery. And seeing armed men riding around at night through their quarters on the different plantations set them to thinking.

The work of our little body was done altogether at night and we seldom spent a whole night in our bed. Occasionally there were a few necks broken and straps used among the worst.[2]

Democratic candidates for governor in Louisiana, South Carolina, and Florida claimed victory at the ballot box in the 1876 election. But Republican canvassing boards in each state invalidated enough votes from areas infested by violence and fraud to give victory to the Republicans. A Florida court intervened to seat that state's Democratic candidate for governor, while Democrats in Louisiana and South Carolina simply rejected canvassing board findings in those states, declared themselves the winners, and set up a rival government.

Such things were not unusual in the Reconstruction Era South—Louisiana Democrats still insisted they won the 1872 election for governor. But in 1876, a presidential election to choose Grant's successor was also conducted, and the presidential results in those three states were also disputed when the Republican canvassing boards named the Republican candidate, Ohio governor Rutherford B. Hayes, as the winner after votes tainted by violence were tossed out. Democrats in each of those states insisted that their party's presidential nominee, New York governor Samuel J. Tilden, had actually won. So each of the three states produced two competing sets of Electoral College certificates, with Democrats certifying that the Democrat had won and Republicans certifying the Republican.

Tilden won the popular vote nationally by a comfortable margin. But if Hayes could win the disputed electoral votes in all three Southern states plus Oregon, he would be elected president by a single electoral vote.

With Tilden holding a decisive three percentage point lead in the popular vote, some Southerners threatened violence if he was denied the White House. Republicans countered that Hayes surely would have won easily if Southern elections were conducted honestly, and that Tilden should not gain the presidency with results based on violence, intimidation, and ballot box stuffing. Many feared the intense electoral dispute could ignite a new civil war.

While Congress got to work figuring out who actually won the presidential election, Francis Nicholls, the Democratic candidate for governor of Louisiana, took steps to set up a state government, even though the returning board ruled that he lost the election. On January 9, 1877, Nicholls, a former Confederate general, deployed thousands of White Leaguers, under the command of Frederick Nash Ogden, to seize police stations across New Orleans and the offices of the state Supreme Court. Nicholls also ordered White Leaguers to cordon off Republicans in the statehouse, including Stephen J. Packard, who had been named as the rightful next governor by the Returning Board. Nicholls even appointed his own police department and Supreme Court. South Carolina Democrats set up a similar rival government apparatus led by the Democratic nominee for governor, Wade Hampton.

Republicans in South Carolina and Louisiana sought help from the federal government to discourage rival Democratic claimants to state offices. While in the past federal forces had been employed to help distressed Southern Republicans in similar situations, Grant wanted nothing to do with it this time. When Governor Chamberlain of South Carolina asked General Thomas Ruger, the commander of U.S. forces in the area, to disperse a rival legislature set up by Democrats, Grant forbade the move, in words that recalled the explosive "banditti" episode in the Louisiana legislature two years earlier. "To be plain," Grant wrote to General Ruger, "I want to avoid anything like an unlawful use of the Military and I believe it would be regarded with disfavor if they were used in taking men claiming seats out of the legislative hall."

Grant's refusal to side with the Republican governors of Louisiana and South Carolina in disputes following the 1876 election was among many signs that Reconstruction policy might be about to change even if the Republican Hayes assumed the presidency. Influential Southern Democrats in turn signaled a growing receptivity to Hayes by stressing that they were far more interested in governing their own states than in gaining control of the White House.

Such developments tended to reduce concerns about a violent assault on Washington to install Tilden in the White House as Congress tried to figure out who should be the next president. But Grant reinforced the capital just in case, sending several companies of infantry and batteries of artillery, and ordering a warship to patrol nearby on the Potomac River.

The Constitution provided no real remedies for the electoral impasse so Congress was forced to invent one. The House of Representatives, controlled by Democrats, and the Republican-controlled Senate compromised on the creation of a fifteen-person Electoral Commission, with eight Republican and seven Democratic members. Both chambers had initially planned to select an independent as the fifteenth member, but in the end they settled on Republican Supreme Court justice Joseph Bradley, whose 1874 circuit court opinion in the *Cruikshank* case sharply restricted federal civil rights jurisdiction and was largely upheld by the full U.S. Supreme Court.

After a series of party-line votes, the commission awarded electors from all disputed states to Hayes. Angry Democrats had threatened to tie up the House with procedural delays to interfere with the electoral vote certification, possibly delaying the inauguration. To avoid such unsightly proceedings, Hayes representatives in Washington held talks with Tilden supporters and declared that the new president intended to recognize Democrats Nicholls of Louisiana and Hampton of South Carolina as governors of their respective states, and to adopt a policy of federal noninterference in Southern affairs—in other words, "home rule." Agents of Nicholls and Hampton pledged in turn that the governors would shun reprisals against Republicans and recognize the civil and political equality of black Americans.

The promise to restore home rule in the South, thereby ending Reconstruction, appears to have been the key to lifting the filibuster threat and gaining Democratic acquiescence in a Hayes presidency, although just such a shift in federal policy was likely a foregone conclusion by then. But if a grand "Compromise of 1877" existed, as has long been postulated, its precise terms have proved elusive. In any case, several weeks after Hayes was sworn in as the nineteenth president on March 3, 1877, he enacted a decisive shift in federal Southern policy. President Hayes ordered U.S. troops patrolling the statehouses in Louisiana and South Carolina to stand down, effectively ceding the terrain to White League and Red Shirt vigilantes.

In New Orleans, as Packard and his allies in the legislature prepared to evacuate the statehouse, some Republicans reportedly burned files to prevent White Leaguers from finding evidence for reprisals. Nicholls took official possession of the premises from a White League officer on April 25, amid cheers from "the multitude which was massed in the streets," the *Picayune* reported. South Carolina Democrats also took over the statehouse as Republican claimants withdrew.[3]

For years following the end of Reconstruction in 1877, or the South's so-called redemption, white Southerners continued to use violence, intimidation, and fraud to suppress the votes of black citizens, whose numbers still posed a threat to Democrats' grip on power. But these means of black voter suppression gradually began to seem disagreeable to their beneficiaries, and a sort of reform movement emerged in Mississippi—not to restore effective franchise rights to black people, but to implement a clean and legal way to suppress their votes, to salve the souls of white people.

"The old men of the present generation can't afford to die and leave the election to their children and grand children, with shot guns in their hands, a lie in their mouths and perjury on their lips, in order to defeat the negro," a white Mississippian wrote to his local newspaper in 1890. "I believe the constitution can be made so this will not be necessary."

The nearly all-white delegates to the Mississippi constitutional convention in 1890 rewrote their state's charter to add a literacy test and a poll tax, seen as methods for suppressing the black vote that would not violate the Fifteenth Amendment's prohibition against denying the franchise "on account of race." One convention delegate, a trial court judge, bluntly stated the case for such changes. "Sir, it is no secret that there has not been a full vote and a fair count in Mississippi since 1875, that we have been preserving the ascendancy of the white people by revolutionary methods. In other words, we have been stuffing ballot boxes, committing perjury, and here and there in the state carrying the elections by fraud and violence." The judge believed something had to change. "No man can be in favor of perpetuating the election methods which have prevailed in Mississippi since 1875 who is not a moral idiot," he railed.

Mississippi's new constitution soon produced a cataclysmic decline in black voter participation. On the eve of the state constitutional convention of 1890 there were 189,884 black registered voters in the state. By 1892, after the new constitution was adopted, just 8,615 black men were registered to vote, although black people still constituted a majority of the state's population.

Every other Southern state soon embraced some version of this new Mississippi Plan to implement legal black voter suppression. Delegates to the Louisiana constitutional convention of 1898 adopted a new state charter with voting provisions meant to "perpetuate the supremacy of the Anglo-Saxon race," according to the convention's president. The new provisions, including literacy tests, a poll tax, and property requirements, ravaged black voter registration. In 1896, two years before the new constitution was adopted, 130,334 black voters were registered in Louisiana. By 1900, only 5,320 black voters were registered, and by 1910 registered black voters in Louisiana numbered just 730, less than half a percent of eligible black men.

The dearth of black voices in politics and government left a clear field for the expansion of so-called Jim Crow laws legalizing racial segregation and discrimination across the white-dominated South and beyond. Along the way, the U.S. Supreme Court offered scant resistance. In 1883, the high court struck down the Civil Rights Act of 1875, passed by Republicans in the waning days of Reconstruction, holding that the Thirteenth and Fourteenth amendments did not give Congress the power to curb racial discrimination by private individuals. In *Plessy v. Ferguson* (1896), the court approved state laws mandating racial segregation as long as "separate but equal" facilities were provided, and in *Williams v. Mississippi* (1898), the justices upheld state laws that effectively disenfranchised black voters.[4]

Such decisions helped to sustain racist rules for decades. But in 1954, the Supreme Court of Chief Justice Earl Warren began to dismantle the legal infrastructure of Jim Crow. In *Brown v. Board of Education*, the high court overturned *Plessy v. Ferguson*, ruling that laws imposing racially segregated educational facilities violated the equal-protection clause of the Fourteenth Amendment because "separate educational facilities are inherently unequal." Meanwhile, the political and legislative victories of the civil rights movement established new legal foundations for the Reconstruction-era project of building a multiracial democracy, including the Civil Rights Act of 1964 and the Voting Rights Act of 1965.

"THE WHOLE POWER OF THE GOVERNMENT"

At the height of the 1875 Mississippi crisis, Grant's letter citing public impatience with "these annual, autumnal outbreaks in the South" also captured his own frustration with the nation's flagging resolve to sustain the gains of Reconstruction. But the full measure of Grant's disillusionment in the months following the "banditti" debacle was revealed nearly forty years later in John R. Lynch's 1913 book, *The Facts of Reconstruction*.

Born into slavery, Lynch rose during Reconstruction to become Speaker of the Mississippi House of Representatives at the age of twenty-five, and later won a seat in the U.S. Congress. His book's principal mission was to debunk the flood of lies about Reconstruction and white victimhood that ushered in the Jim Crow era. But he also reflected on his personal experience, including a visit with Grant at the White House weeks after Mississippi White Liners "redeemed" the state with their campaign of violence in 1875. Lynch, then a twenty-eight-year-old Republican congressman from Mississippi, and one of the most promising black leaders in the South, asked Grant to explain why federal troops had not been deployed to put down the lawless White Liners when Governor Ames urgently requested such assistance.

Confronted so forthrightly by his earnest, doe-eyed visitor, Grant accepted full responsibility for withholding the requested troops from Mississippi. He explained the decision as a regrettable but necessary political expedient that had been urged upon him by Ohio Republicans. They believed that such a controversial troop deployment in the thick of an election campaign would have doomed their candidates, even though it would have been insufficient, in their view, to rescue Mississippi from the White Liners.

Lynch recounts his astonishment that Grant acceded to such a "remarkable request," and he chided the president for allowing political considerations to override constitutional duty. "It is the first time I have ever known you to show the white feather," he recalls telling Grant.

Sensitive to his visitor's disappointment, Grant agreed that he should not have yielded to party pressure. But he suggested that his own disappointment with the course of Reconstruction weighed heavily in the decision. Grant explained that he had not intervened in Mississippi because he too was convinced that the state "could not have been saved," and he did not wish to compound the damage by dooming Ohio Republicans with a politically toxic troop deployment.

Why was rescuing Mississippi from the White Liners beyond even the president's power? Grant blamed some of his fellow Republicans who were helping to reverse gains once counted as vital results of the Civil War.

Grant and others believed that enough power had been given to the national government, by postwar amendments and legislation, to protect the rights of former slaves, and that any rebalancing of traditional federalism these efforts involved had been part of the Civil War settlement approved by former Confederate states to gain readmission to the union. The legal tools created within this new arrangement had been potent enough to crush the Klan a few years earlier. But Grant told Lynch that "leading and influential Republicans" started using their institutional power and sway over public opinion to "cripple" the president so he could not enforce the Constitution and laws along the lines established after the war. He did not name names, but the *Slaughterhouse* ruling and the Bradley opinion, which narrowed federal authority, were both written by Republicans; and moderate congressional Republicans, unsettled by election losses and the "banditti" scandal—stoked by renegade Republican Carl Schurz—blocked an attempt to bolster federal authority with a new force bill in the spring of 1875.

Grant worried that setbacks such as these were reversing gains once counted as indispensable results of the North's Civil War victory. Yes, slavery had been abolished forever, and the indissolubility of the federal union had been firmly established. But the hoped-for diminishment of state sovereignty had apparently not been accomplished after all; nor had the creation of a national sovereignty with sufficient power vested in the federal government to protect individual citizens against personal violence when their states failed, refused, or neglected to do so.

Whatever the motives of the men who drove these developments, "future mischief of a very serious nature is bound to be the result," Grant told Lynch, forecasting that the federal government would soon be "at a great disadvantage" and "the results of the war of the rebellion will have been in a large measure lost." Citing "the lack of power of enforcement" in the federal government, Grant predicted: "What you have just passed through in the State of Mississippi is only the beginning of what is sure to follow."

Governor Ames perhaps had gotten a glimpse of this hobbled federal enforcement presence weeks earlier, when federal troops finally showed up in Mississippi at the tail end of the 1875 campaign, too late to reverse the designs of violent White Liners in any case, and operating under constraints that Ames found remarkable. "I have copies of the orders of the troops," he wrote to his wife. Soldiers were only "to be used to 'prevent bloodshed in case of disorders,'" Ames told Blanche, while explaining that they evidently could not be used "to prevent disorders nor to prevent intimidation nor to secure to all men their political rights." Ames could hardly see the point of such a deployment. "What a mockery are such orders," he scoffed.

After the U.S. Supreme Court, in *United States v. Cruikshank*, adopted the Bradley opinion's narrowed scope of federal authority the following March, troops deployed for election duty in South Carolina and Louisiana later that year were again seen to be oddly feckless.[1]

Tepid public support and a more confining legal landscape gradually restrained Grant's impulse to enforce the rights of freedmen "with rigor," as he had vowed to do. But after his presidency ended, he learned that not all domestic deployments of federal troops were condemned as threats to the soul of the Republic—only those, apparently, that were intended to protect the interests of black Americans.

When railroad strikes convulsed several states outside the South in 1877, inspiring miners and steelworkers to stage sympathy work stoppages and producing numerous clashes with authorities and significant property damage, local law enforcement was often unable, or unwilling, to restore order. President Hayes had withdrawn troops from the South to turn the page from Grant's Reconstruction policy, but he did not hesitate to deploy soldiers as strikebreakers at the behest of rattled governors and railroad executives, with few guidelines to keep the troops in harness. Instead of acting as neutral peacekeepers, soldiers reopened rail lines and blocked union meetings.

Shortly after Grant left the White House, he and his wife, Julia, embarked on an extensive world tour, but he made an effort to keep up with news from home. Foreign papers "have been full of the great railroad strike," he wrote from London to an American friend in August 1877. Grant supported the federal government's exertions to "put down" any lawless demonstrations, but one thing about the episode struck him as "a little queer":

During my two terms of office, the whole Democratic press, and the morbidly honest and "reformatory" portion of the Republican press, thought it horrible to keep U.S. troops stationed in the Southern States, and when they were called upon to protect the lives of negroes—as much citizens under the Constitution as if their skins were white—the country was scarcely large enough to hold the sound of indignation belched forth by them for some years. Now, however, there is no hesitation about exhausting the whole power of the government to suppress a strike on the slightest intimation that danger threatens. All parties agree that this is right, and so do I. If a negro insurrection should arise in South Carolina, Mississippi, or Louisiana, or if the negroes in either of these States—where they are in a large majority—should intimidate the whites from going to the polls, or from exercising any of the rights of American citizens, there would be no division of sentiment as to the duty of the President. It does seem the rule should work both ways.[2]

ACKNOWLEDGMENTS

My sincere thanks to the people who gave generously of their time and insights to help in the production of this little book. My old friend Russell Shorto, author of many popular narrative histories, read the manuscript at various stages and offered valuable suggestions everywhere along the way. My friend and literary agent, Anne Edelstein, contributed vital input as she reviewed the evolving manuscript, and her enduring faith in the project was essential. Karen Houppert, my advisor and teacher at the Johns Hopkins master's in writing program, contributed penetrating feedback on early chapters.

I'm indebted to Eva Shorto, for her fastidious research assistance in the archives of New Orleans; to Nolan Eller, for help navigating the Marshall Harvey Twitchell Papers at Louisiana Tech University; and to Paul Carnahan of the Vermont Historical Society, for guiding me to the Twitchell holdings in their collection. Many thanks also to Lori Schexnayder of Howard-Tilton Memorial Library in New Orleans, and to Nick Okrent and the staff of the University of Pennsylvania libraries. And I'm very grateful to Jonathan Jao and David Howe at HarperCollins for their peerless editing and abundant patience.

NOTES

PROLOGUE: THE BEST, THE BRAVEST, AND THE PUREST

1. *Daily Picayune*, January 1, 5, 1875; *New York Herald*, June 3, 1875; Joseph Wheelan, *Terrible Swift Sword: The Life of General Philip H. Sheridan* (Boston: Da Capo, 2012), 121–22; Grant to Sheridan, August 26, 1864, John Y. Simon, ed., *The Papers of Ulysses S. Grant*, 28 vols. (Carbondale: Southern Illinois University Press, 1967–2005), 12: 96–97; William Hepworth Dixon, *White Conquest*, vol. 2 (London: Chatto & Windus, 1876), 38; Paul Andrew Hutton, *Phil Sheridan & His Army* (Norman: University of Oklahoma Press, 2013), 23; Philip Henry Sheridan, *Personal Memoirs*, vol. 2 (New York: Webster, 1888), 262; *Daily Picayune*, December 28, 1874.

2. *Platform of the Crescent City White League*, in *New Orleans Bulletin*, July 1, 1874; Eric Foner, *Reconstruction: America's Unfinished Revolution* (New York: Harper & Row, 1988), 294–95; Ted Tunnell, "The Propaganda of History: Southern Editors and the Origins of Carpetbagger and Scalawag," *Journal of Southern History* (November 2006): 792–93, 798–99, 800–806.

3. Mark Grimsley, "Wars for the American South: The First and Second Reconstructions Considered as Insurgencies," *Civil War History* (March 2012): 16; *Vicksburg Troubles*, House Report 265, 43rd Congress, 2nd Session, 11.

4. Ulysses S. Grant, *Sixth Annual Message*, December 7, 1874; *Affairs in Louisiana*, Senate Executive Documents No. 13, 43rd Congress, 2nd Session, 19–20; James Ford Rhodes, *History of the United States from the Compromise of 1850*, vol. 7 (London: Macmillan, 1906), 132; William Gillette, *Retreat from Reconstruction, 1869–1879* (Baton Rouge: Louisiana State University Press, 1982), 237.

5. James M. McPherson, *Battle Cy of Freedom: The Civil War Era* (New York: Oxford University Press, 2003), 756–78; Sheridan, *Personal Memoirs*, vol. 1, 500; Adam Badeau, *Grant in Peace: From Appomattox to Mount McGregor: A Personal Memoir* (Hartford, CT: S. S. Scranton, 1887), 98; Roy Morris, *Sheridan: The Life and Wars of General Phil Sheridan* (New York: Crown, 1992), 182–84.

6. *Platform of the Crescent City White League*; *Affairs in Louisiana*, Senate Executive Documents No. 13, 43rd Congress, 2nd Session, 28; Sheridan to Belknap,

January 4, 1875, and January 9, 1875, Sheridan Papers, Manuscript Division, Library of Congress, Washington, D.C.

7.   Sheridan to Belknap, January 5, 1875, in *Affairs in Louisiana*, Senate Executive Documents No. 13, 23; *Daily Picayune*, January 6, 1875; *New Orleans Bulletin*, January 6, 1875; *New York Times*, January 6, 1875; *New York World*, January 6, 1875, quoted in *New York Herald*, January 7, 1875; *New-York Tribune*, January 7, 1875.

8.   Allen C. Guelzo, *Reconstruction: A Concise History* (New York: Oxford University Press, 2018), 11–12; Grimsley, "Wars for the American South"; *Foreign Policy*, December 1, 2017; *Washington Post*, May 6, 2019.

9.   *Inter-Ocean*, December 14, 1874; *New Orleans Republican*, October 14, 1874.

10.   *National Republican*, December 21, 1874; Elaine-Frantz Parsons, "Klan Skepticism and Denial in Reconstruction-Era Public Discourse," *Journal of Southern History* (February 2011): 53–54; Ulysses S. Grant, *Sixth Annual Message*, December 7, 1874.

11.   *Congressional Globe*, January 10, 1861, 309; *The Life of Henry A. Wise of Virginia, 1806–1876* (New York: Macmillan, 1899), 68, 267.

12.   *New National Era*, April 6, 1871.

13.   *National Republican*, January 8, 1875; Ted Tunnell, *Edge of the Sword: The Ordeal of Carpetbagger Marshall H. Twitchell in the Civil War and Reconstruction* (Baton Rouge: Louisiana State University Press, 2001), 191–92; *Daily Picayune*, September 15, 1874; *Brooklyn Daily Eagle*, August 10, October 15, 1874; *Louisiana Democrat*, November 3, 1874.

14.   *Washington Chronicle*, quoted in *New Orleans Republican*, December 29, 1874; *National Republican*, November 23, December 26, 1874.

15.   Richard Zuczek, ed., *Encyclopedia of the Reconstruction Era* (Westport, CT: Greenwood, 2006), Appendix 3; Campbell Gibson and Kay Jung, *Historical Census Statistics on Population Totals by Race, 1790 to 1990, and by Hispanic Origin, 1790 to 1990, for the United States, Regions, Divisions, and States* (Washington, D.C.: U.S. Census Bureau, 2002), Table A-18, Race for the United States, Regions, Divisions, and States: 1870; Foner, *Reconstruction*, 422–23; Melinda M. Hennessey, "Reconstruction Politics and the Military— Eufaula Riot of 1874," *Alabama Historical Quarterly* 38, no. 2 (1976): 118–23; *National Republican*, December 21, 1874.

16.   S. G. F. Spackman, "American Federalism and the Civil Rights Act of 1875," *Journal of American Studies* 10, no. 3 (1976): 315; *National Republican*, December 21, 1874; Lamar to Edward Donaldson Clark, December 23, 1874, in "L. Q. C. Lamar's Letters to Edward Donaldson Clark, 1868–1885, Part II: 1874–1878," *Journal of Mississippi History*, May 1975, 191.

17.   Lawrence N. Powell, "Why Louisiana Mattered," *Louisiana History* 53, no. 4 (2012): 394; Foner, *Reconstruction*, 437; David Herbert Donald, *Lincoln* (New York: Simon & Schuster, 2011), 484–87.

CHAPTER 1: THERE IS LOVE ENOUGH

1. Richard Campanella, "Three Exposition Halls, Three Fates," *Preservation in Print*, November 2014, 14; *New Orleans Times*, May 7, 1872; Edwin L. Jewell, *Jewell's Crescent City Illustrated: The Commercial, Social, Political and General History of New Orleans, Including Biographical Sketches of Its Distinguished Citizens* (New Orleans, 1874), 88; William A. Jordan, United States patent 129,480, "Improvement in Earth Closets," July 16, 1872.

2. *New Orleans Times*, July 16, 1873; *Daily Picayune*, July 16, 1873; T. Harry Williams, "The Louisiana Unification Movement of 1873," *Journal of Southern History* (August 1945): 349–69; Foner, *Reconstruction*, 263, 437.

3. *Daily Picayune*, July 13, 1873; *Jewell's Crescent City Illustrated 1873*, 128; T. Harry Williams, "The Politics of Reconstruction," in *Romance and Realism in Southern Politics* (Athens: University of Georgia Press, 1961), 34; *New Orleans Times*, July 16, 1873.

4. *Daily Picayune*, July 13, 1873.

5. *New Orleans Times*, July 16, 1873; Louis R. Harlan, "Desegregation in New Orleans Public Schools During Reconstruction," *American Historical Review* 67, no. 3 (1962): 663–67; Roger A. Fischer, *The Segregation Struggle in Louisiana, 1862–1877* (Urbana: University of Illinois Press, 1974), 113–20; *Daily Picayune*, September 29, 1872.

6. *New Orleans Times*, June 6, 1873; *New Orleans Republican*, June 4, 1873.

7. *Daily Picayune*, June 8, 1873.

8. *New Orleans Republican*, June 19, 1873.

9. *Ouachita Telegraph*, June 21, 1873; *Shreveport Times*, June 26 and 28, 1873; *New Orleans Republican*, July 3, 1873.

10. T. Harry Williams, *PGT Beauregard: Napoleon in Gray* (Baton Rouge: Louisiana State University Press, 1955), 52, 259; Julia Ellen Le Grand Waitz, *The Journal of Julia Le Grand, New Orleans, 1862–1863* (Richmond, VA: Everett Waddey, 1911), 163.

11. Williams, *PGT Beauregard*, 54, 60, 93.

12. Ibid., 92; Waitz, *The Journal of Julia Le Grand*, 269; *New Orleans Crescent*, July 21, 1866.

13. Williams, *PGT Beauregard*, 268–69; *Raleigh Weekly Sentinel*, July 29, 1873; *Ouachita Telegraph*, June 21, 1873; *Morning Star and Catholic Messenger*, June 29, 1873.

14. *Daily Picayune*, July 1, 1873; Williams, *PGT Beauregard*, 266.

15. *New Orleans Times*, May 28, 1873; Williams, "The Louisiana Unification Movement of 1873," 355.

16. Foner, *Reconstruction*, 47; David C. Rankin, "The Origins of Black Leadership in New Orleans During Reconstruction," *Journal of Southern History* 40, no. 3 (1974): 427; Ira Berlin, *Slaves without Masters: The Free Negro in the Antebellum South* (New York: New Press, 1974), 108–9; Caryn Cossé Bell, "The Common

Wind's Creole Visionary: Dr. Louis Charles Roudanez," *South Atlantic Review* 73, no. 2 (2008): 13; Jean-Charles Houzeau and David C. Rankin, *My Passage at the New Orleans Tribune: A Memoir of the Civil War Era* (Baton Rouge: Louisiana State University Press, 1984), 25n34, 27, 34; Laura Foner, "The Free People of Color in Louisiana and St. Domingue: A Comparative Portrait of Two Three-Caste Slave Societies," *Journal of Social History* (1970): 407; Loren Schweninger, "Prosperous Blacks in the South, 1790–1880," *American Historical Review* 95, no. 1 (1990): 34–35, 39; David C. Rankin, "The Impact of the Civil War on the Free Colored Community of New Orleans," *Perspectives in American History* 11 (1977–78), Charles Warren Center for Studies in American History, Harvard University, 382; Berlin, *Slaves without Masters*, 136; Donald E. Everett, "Demands of the New Orleans Free Colored Population for Political Equality," *Louisiana Historical Quarterly* 38 (1955): 44; Williams, *PGT Beauregard*, 257; *New Orleans Times*, May 28, 1873.

17. Williams, "The Louisiana Unification Movement of 1873," 364; *New Orleans Times*, July 16, 1873.

18. *Daily Picayune*, July 16, 1873. Edwin L. Jewell, *Jewell's Crescent City Illustrated*, 120–21; Williams, *PGT Beauregard*, 5, 39, 51.

19. *New Orleans Times*, July 16, 1873; ibid., June 3, 1873.

20. Howard C. Westwood, "Benjamin Butler's Enlistment of Black Troops in New Orleans in 1862," *Louisiana History* 26, no. 1 (1985): 8, 14; James G. Hollandsworth Jr., *Louisiana Native Guards: The Black Military Experience During the Civil War* (Baton Rouge: Louisiana State University Press, 1995), 17; Rodolphe Lucien Desdunes, *Our People and Our History: Fifty Creole Portraits*, trans. and ed. Dorothea Olga McCants (Baton Rouge: Louisiana State University Press, 1973), 132–33; Bell, "The Common Wind's Creole Visionary," 10; *L'Union*, September 27, October 12, 1862, quoted in David Connell Rankin, "The Forgotten People: Free People of Color in New Orleans, 1850–1870" (PhD diss., Johns Hopkins University, 1976), 212.

21. Houzeau and Rankin, *My Passage at the New Orleans Tribune*, 71–72.

22. *L'Union*, September 27, 1862, quoted in Caryn Cossé Bell, *Revolution, Romanticism, and the Afro Creole Protest Tradition in Louisiana, 1718–1868* (Baton Rouge: Louisiana State University Press, 1997), 223; Rankin, *The Forgotten People*, 213; Lincoln to Banks, November 5, 1863, in *Lincoln, Collected Works*, vol. 7; *L'Union*, April 11, 1863, quoted in Rankin, *The Forgotten People*, 214.

23. *New Orleans Times*, November 6, 1863; *Liberator*, April 1, 1864; Rankin, *The Forgotten People*, 217–18.

24. Rankin, *The Forgotten People*, 218–19; *Anglo-African*, April 16, 1864; *Liberator*, April 15, 1864; Everett, "Demands of the New Orleans Free Colored Population," 50; Louis Ruchames, "William Lloyd Garrison and the Negro Franchise," *Journal of Negro History* 50, no. 1 (1965): 44; *New York Times*, June 23, 1865; Fred Harvey Harrington, *Fighting Politician: Major General*

N. P. Banks (Philadelphia: University of Pennsylvania Press, 1948), 148; *Daily Picayune*, May 11, 1864; *Debates in the Convention for the Revision and Amendment of the Constitution of the State of Louisiana, 1864*, 450.

25. Rankin, *The Forgotten People*, 225.

26. *L'Union*, November 15, 1862; April 14, 1864; May 26, 1864, quoted in Rankin, *The Forgotten People*, 223, 225–26.

27. *New Orleans Tribune*, July 28, 1864; Houzeau and Rankin, *My Passage at the New Orleans Tribune*, 23; *New Orleans Tribune*, July 21, 1864, quoted in Kristi Richard Melancon, "An African American Discourse Community in Black & White: The New Orleans Tribune" (PhD diss., Louisiana State University, 2011), 38.

28. Houzeau and Rankin, *My Passage at the New Orleans Tribune*, 5–34; David C. Rankin, "The Politics of Caste: Free Colored Leadership in New Orleans During the Civil War," in *Louisiana's Black Heritage*, ed. Robert R. Macdonald, John R. Kemp, and Edward F. Haas (New Orleans: Louisiana State Museum, 1979), 132; Jean-Charles Houzeau, *La Terreur Blanche au Texas et Mon Evasion* (Brussels: Ve Parent & Fils, 1862), 59; Jean-Charles Houzeau, *La Question de l'Esclavage* (Brussels: Ve Parent & Fils, 1863), XII, 98.

29. Houzeau and Rankin, *My Passage at the New Orleans Tribune*, 78–81.

30. Ibid., 29, 34; John Rose Ficklen, *History of Reconstruction in Louisiana, Through 1868* (Baltimore: Johns Hopkins University Press, 1910), 142–43.

31. Houzeau and Rankin, *My Passage at the New Orleans Tribune*, 36–37; Lincoln to Banks, August 5 and November 5, 1863, in Lincoln, *Collected Works*, vols. 6 and 7; Rankin, "The Politics of Caste," 135; Houzeau, 121; *New Orleans Tribune*, December 8–9, 1864, and January 24, 1865, quoted in Ted Tunnell, *Crucible of Reconstruction: War, Radicalism, and Race in Louisiana, 1862–1877* (Baton Rouge: Louisiana State University Press, 1984), 83–85; William P. Connor, "Reconstruction Rebels: The New Orleans Tribune in Post-War Louisiana," *Louisiana History* (1980): 166.

32. William Edward Burghardt Du Bois, *Black Reconstruction in America: An Essay Toward a History of the Part Which Black Folk Played in the Attempt to Reconstruct Democracy in America, 1860–1880* (New York: Harcourt, Brace, 1935), 153, 456; Peyton McCrary, *Abraham Lincoln and Reconstruction: The Louisiana Experiment* (Princeton, NJ: Princeton University Press, 2015), 298–302; *Congressional Globe*, February 27, 1865, 1129; *Washington Evening Star*, April 12, 1865; David Herbert Donald, *Lincoln* (New York: Simon & Schuster, 2011), 585–88, 597.

33. *New Orleans Tribune*, May 6, 1865; James G. Hollandsworth Jr., *An Absolute Massacre: The New Orleans Race Riot of July 30, 1866* (Baton Rouge: Louisiana State University Press, 2004), 30–32; Foner, *Reconstruction*, 159; Tunnell, *Crucible of Reconstruction*, 95, 100; Mark W. Summers, "The Moderates' Last Chance: The Louisiana Election of 1865," *Louisiana History* 24, no. 1 (1983):

55; *New Orleans Tribune*, May 17, 1865, cited in Summers, "The Moderates' Last Chance," 55.

34. Foner, *Reconstruction*, 268, 272, 276; Tunnell, *Crucible of Reconstruction*, 97–99, 100–104; House Ex. Doc No. 30, 44th Congress, 2nd Session, 409–10; *New Orleans Tribune*, December 13, 1865; Select Committee on the New Orleans Riots, House Report No. 16, 39th Congress, 2nd Session, 525.

35. Tunnell, *Crucible of Reconstruction*, 96–100; C. Peter Ripley, *Slaves and Freedmen in Civil War Louisiana* (Baton Rouge: Louisiana State University Press, 1976), 190–92; Hollandsworth, *An Absolute Massacre*, 34–35; Houzeau and Rankin, *My Passage at the New Orleans Tribune*, 44; *Civil Code of the State of Louisiana, with the Statutory Amendments from 1825 to 1866 Inclusive* (New Orleans: Bloomfield, 1867), 28; Joe Gray Taylor, *Louisiana Reconstructed 1863–1877* (Baton Rouge: Louisiana State University Press, 1974), 102; *New Orleans Tribune*, November 28, 1865.

36. Taylor, *Louisiana Reconstructed 1863–1877*, 102–3; Foner, *Reconstruction*, 241–44, 471.

37. Foner, *Reconstruction*, 247–55, 263; Tunnell, *Crucible of Reconstruction*, 100–104; Summers, "The Moderates' Last Chance," 58, 62; Hollandsworth, *An Absolute Massacre*, 36.

38. *Daily Picayune*, July 28, 1866; Houzeau and Rankin, *My Passage at the New Orleans Tribune*, 124.

39. Hollandsworth, *An Absolute Massacre*, 67; Donald E. Reynolds, "The New Orleans Riot of 1866, Reconsidered," *Louisiana History* 5, no. 1 (1964): 9.

40. Tunnell, *Crucible of Reconstruction*, 104–5; Hollandsworth, *An Absolute Massacre*, 87–89, 48.

41. Tunnell, *Crucible of Reconstruction*, 104–5; Select Committee on the New Orleans Riots, 79–80; Hollandsworth, *An Absolute Massacre*, 75, 102.

42. Hollandsworth, *An Absolute Massacre*, 104–6; *New Orleans Tribune*, cited in *Philadelphia Evening Telegraph*, August 7, 1866; Tunnell, *Crucible of Reconstruction*, 104–9; Houzeau and Rankin, *My Passage at the New Orleans Tribune*, 127.

43. Tunnell, *Crucible of Reconstruction*, 106; Select Committee on the New Orleans Riots, 176.

44. *New Orleans Times*, July 31, 1866; Sheridan to Grant, August 2, 1866, in *The New-Orleans Riot: Its Official History: The Dispatches of Gens. Sheridan, Grant, and Baird*, Murray Pamphlet Collection, Library of Congress, retrieved from https://www.loc.gov/item/03004157/; Taylor, *Louisiana Reconstructed 1863-1877*, 111; House Executive Documents, 39th Congress, 2nd Session, No. 68, 40; Select Committee on the New Orleans Riots, 326; House Executive Documents No. 68, 40.

45. Reynolds, "The New Orleans Riot of 1866, Reconsidered," 5; Eric L.

McKitrick, *Andrew Johnson and Reconstruction* (New York: Oxford University Press, 1988), 427; Foner, *Reconstruction*, 262–67; *Nation*, October 15, 1866.

46. Houzeau and Rankin, *My Passage at the New Orleans Tribune*, 127–33, 159; *Evening Telegraph*, August 7, 1866.

47. Houzeau and Rankin, *My Passage at the New Orleans Tribune*, 127, 133; Foner, *Reconstruction*, 275–77.

48. Joseph G. Dawson III, *Army Generals and Reconstruction* (Baton Rouge: Louisiana State University Press, 1982), 46–58; Andrew Johnson to Grant, August 19, 1867, in *The Papers of Ulysses S. Grant*, 17: 280.

49. Charles Vincent, "Negro Leadership and Programs in the Louisiana Constitutional Convention of 1868," *Louisiana History* 10, no. 4 (1969): 341–47; Taylor, *Louisiana Reconstructed 1863–1877*, 139, 143–44, 151; Tunnell, *Crucible of Reconstruction*, 113; Houzeau and Rankin, *My Passage at the New Orleans Tribune*, 144–45.

50. Houzeau and Rankin, *My Passage at the New Orleans Tribune*, 51; Tunnell, *Crucible of Reconstruction*, 135; F. Wayne Binning, "Carpetbaggers' Triumph: The Louisiana State Election of 1868," *Louisiana History* (1973): 21, 32–34; *New Orleans Times*, January 16, 1868; Francis Byers Harris, "Henry Clay Warmoth, Reconstruction Governor of Louisiana," Louisiana Historical Quarterly 30, no. 2 (April 1947): 548; Tunnell, *Crucible of Reconstruction*, 145; Berlin, *Slaves without Masters*, 138–41; *New Orleans Tribune*, July 2, 1867.

51. Tunnell, *Crucible of Reconstruction*, 24, 135, 145; *New Orleans Republican*, January 31, 1868; Binning, "Carpetbaggers' Triumph," 35; Houzeau and Rankin, *My Passage at the New Orleans Tribune*, 48–50.

52. Binning, "Carpetbaggers' Triumph," 38–39; Marcus B. Christian, "The Theory of the Poisoning of Oscar J. Dunn," *Phylon (1940–1956)* 6, no. 3 (1945): 255; Joseph Logsdon and Caryn Cossé Bell, "The Americanization of Black New Orleans," in Arnold R. Hirsch and Joseph Logsdon, eds., *Creole New Orleans: Race and Americanization* (Baton Rouge: Louisiana State University Press, 1992), 249; Tunnell, *Crucible of Reconstruction*, 135; Houzeau and Rankin, *My Passage at the New Orleans Tribune*, 55–56; Taylor, *Louisiana Reconstructed*, 156–57, 187–202; Lawrence Powell, "Centralization and Its Discontents in Reconstruction Louisiana," *Studies in American Political Development* 20, no. 2 (2006): 115; Tunnell, *Crucible of Reconstruction*, 164–69; Henry Clay Warmoth, *War Politics and Reconstruction: Stormy Days in Louisiana* (Gretna, LA: Pelican, 2001), 51.

53. Powell, "Centralization and Its Discontents," 121, 125–30; Tunnell, *Crucible of Reconstruction*, 170; Taylor, *Louisiana Reconstructed*, 233–34.

54. Charles McClain, "California Carpetbagger: The Career of Henry Dibble," *Quinnipiac Law Review* 28 (2009): 920–22; *Rapides Gazette*, August 2, 1872; Senate Reports, 42nd Congress, 3rd Session, No. 457, XLIV, XVIII, XX; House Exec. Doc. No. 91, 42nd Congress, 3rd Session, 152; Ella Lonn, *Reconstruction*

in Louisiana After 1868 (New York: Putnam's, 1918), 184–96; Taylor, *Louisiana Reconstructed*, 243–47; Senate Executive Documents No. 47, 42nd Congress, 3rd Session, 1–2.

55. Taylor, *Louisiana Reconstructed*, 241–45; Tunnell, *Crucible of Reconstruction*, 171; *Daily Picayune*, January 14, 1873; Senate Reports, 42nd Congress, 3rd Session, No. 457, XLV; Senate Executive Documents No. 47, 42nd Congress, 3rd Session, 1–2; "Republican Albatross: The Louisiana Question, National Politics, and the Failure of Reconstruction," *Louisiana History* (Spring 1982): 112–13.

56. *Daily Picayune*, February 28, 1873; Taylor, *Louisiana Reconstructed*, 254–55; Tunnell, *Crucible of Reconstruction*, 171; Hogue, *Uncivil War*, 104–6.

57. Tunnell, *Crucible of Reconstruction*, 171; Hogue, *Uncivil War*, 104–6; Joel M. Sipress, "From the Barrel of a Gun: The Politics of Murder in Grant Parish," *Louisiana History* 42, no. 3 (2001): 305, 311–13.

58. Tunnell, *Crucible of Reconstruction*, 189–93; Hogue, *Uncivil War*, 109–12; Sipress, "From the Barrel of a Gun," 305; Charles Lane, *The Day Freedom Died: The Colfax Massacre, the Supreme Court and the Betrayal of Reconstruction* (New York: Henry Holt, 2008), 99, 104–7, 265–66.

59. Taylor, *Louisiana Reconstructed*, 270–72; *Leavenworth Daily Commercial*, April 19, 1873; McPherson, *Battle Cry of Freedom*, 793–94; *New Orleans Republican*, reprinted in *Minneapolis Daily Tribune*, April 20, 1873; *Daily Picayune*, July 6, 1873; Tunnell, *Crucible of Reconstruction*, 193.

60. Hogue, *Uncivil War*, 139–40; *Cleveland Leader*, June 27, 1873, in *New Orleans Republican*, July 3, 1873.

61. *Daily Picayune*, July 12, 1873; Williams, "The Louisiana Unification Movement of 1873," 363; Heather Cox Richardson, *The Death of Reconstruction* (Cambridge, MA: Harvard University Press, 2009), 60; Williams, "The Louisiana Unification Movement of 1873," 359; *New Orleans Times*, June 17, July 16, 1873; *New Orleans Republican*, July 16, 1873.

62. Williams, "The Louisiana Unification Movement of 1873," 366; *Daily Picayune*, July 18, 1873; *New Orleans Republican*, July 17, 1873; Williams, "The Louisiana Unification Movement of 1873," 367.

63. *American Citizen*, August 30, 1873; *Louisiana Affairs*, House Report 261, 43rd Congress, 2nd Session, 1031–32.

CHAPTER 2: "THE SWING OF OLD SOLDIERS"

1. John Y. Simon, ed., *The Papers of Ulysses S. Grant*, 28 vols. (Carbondale: Southern Illinois University Press, 1967–2005), 25: 218–20.

2. Ibid., 219.

3. *New York Herald*, September 19, 1874, 3.

4. Henry Adams Testimony, *Senate Report 693*, 46th Congress, 2nd Session, 2: 101–2; Foner, *Reconstruction*, 289.

5.   Henry Adams Testimony, *Senate Report 693*, 2: 103.

6.   Ibid., 101–2.

7.   *The Papers of Ulysses S. Grant*, 25: 218.

8.   Andrew Currie Testimony, *Senate Report 693*, 3: 81; Henry Adams Testimony, *Senate Report 693*, 2: 114.

9.   *The Papers of Ulysses S. Grant*, 25: 218–19; Henry Adams Testimony, *Senate Report 693*, 2: 104.

10. Eric T. L. Love, *Race Over Empire* (Chapel Hill: University of North Carolina Press, 2004), 27–72.

11. *The Papers of Ulysses S. Grant*, 25: 219.

12. Rev. John Boyd et al., *Committee of 1000 Men*, to Ulysses S. Grant, Washington, D.C., September 5, 1874, General Records of the Department of Justice, Records Group 60.

13. *New Orleans Republican*, September 15, 1874, 1; *Daily Picayune*, September 22, 1874, 9; Hogue, *Uncivil War*, 127.

14. *New Orleans Times*, March 19, 1867; William L. Richter, "James Longstreet: From Rebel to Scalawag," *Louisiana History* (1970): 215–17.

15. Hogue, *Uncivil War*, 135; Alfred Rudolph Waud, *Sketch of an African American Policeman*, 1871, Historic New Orleans Collection; John Whiteclay Chambers, *The Oxford Companion to American Military History* (New York: Oxford University Press, 1999), 593–94.

16. Hogue, *Uncivil War*, 74, 89; Lane, *The Day Freedom Died*, 104–5.

17. Robert J. Kaczorowski, *The Politics of Judicial Interpretation: The Federal Courts, Department of Justice, and Civil Rights, 1866–1876* (New York: Fordham University Press, 2005), 143–49; Lane, *The Day Freedom Died*, 204–12.

18. *Louisiana Affairs*, House Report 261, 43rd Congress, 2nd Session, 246; Taylor, *Louisiana Reconstructed*, 284–85.

19. Ted Tunnell, "The Propaganda of History: Southern Editors and the Origins of Carpetbagger and Scalawag," *Journal of Southern History* (November 2006): 792; *Daily Picayune*, September 22, 1874, 9; Stuart Omer Landry, *The Battle of Liberty Place: The Overthrow of Carpet-Bag Rule in New Orleans, September 14, 1874* (New Orleans: Pelican, 1955), 83, 88; Taylor, *Louisiana Reconstructed*, 297.

20. *Daily Picayune*, September 22, 1874, 9; *Affairs in Louisiana*, Senate Executive Documents No. 13, 3.

21. *Daily Picayune*, September 22, 1874, 9; Taylor, *Louisiana Reconstructed*, 285–91; Judith K. Schafer, "The Battle of Liberty Place: A Matter of Historical Perception," unpublished lecture delivered to Louisiana Historical Society, New Orleans, October 13, 1992, 15; Hogue, *Uncivil War*, 131.

22. *Daily Picayune*, September 22, 1874, 9; *New Orleans Republican*, September 15, 1874, 1.

23. Hogue, *Uncivil War*, 135; *Daily Picayune*, July 29, 1885, 2.

24. Hogue, *Uncivil War*, 135; Landry, *The Battle of Liberty Place*, 92–94, 96; Frank L. Richardson, "My Recollections of the Battle of the Fourteenth of September, 1874, in New Orleans, Louisiana," *Louisiana Historical Quarterly* 3 (October 1920): 498–501.

25. Hogue, *Uncivil War*, 131; *Daily Picayune*, September 22, 1874, 9; Richardson, "My Recollections," 499; Landry, *The Battle of Liberty Place*, 125–27.

26. Landry, *The Battle of Liberty Place*, 125–27; Richardson, "My Recollections," 500.

27. Landry, *The Battle of Liberty Place*, 125–26.

28. *New Orleans Republican*, September 15, 1874, 1; Landry, *The Battle of Liberty Place*, 125–27; Hogue, *Uncivil War*, 137.

29. *Uncivil War*, 137–38; Taylor, *Louisiana Reconstructed*, 294.

30. *Daily Picayune*, September 15, 1874, 1.

31. Ibid.

32. *Weekly Clarion*, Jackson, MS, September 24, 1874.

CHAPTER 3: YANKEE PANKY

1. Marshall Harvey Twitchell, *Carpetbagger from Vermont: The Autobiography of Marshall Harvey Twitchell* (Baton Rouge: Louisiana State University Press, 1989), 148–49; Tunnell, *Edge of the Sword*, 214–15; *New Orleans Times*, September 16, 1874, 7; *Daily Picayune*, September 16, 1874, 1.

2. Twitchell, *Carpetbagger from Vermont*, 139–40; Tunnell, *Edge of the Sword*, 192–95.

3. Testimony of Marshall Twitchell, *Louisiana Affairs*, House Report 261, 392; Tunnell, *Edge of the Sword*, 192–93.

4. Twitchell, *Carpetbagger from Vermont*, 137–38.

5. Ibid., 19–20; Tunnell, *Edge of the Sword*, 15.

6. Twitchell, *Carpetbagger from Vermont*, 24–30;

7. Tunnell, *Edge of the Sword*, 72–82; Twitchell, *Carpetbagger from Vermont*, 61–62, 75.

8. Twitchell, 81–82; Tunnell, *Edge of the Sword*, 84.

9. Twitchell, *Carpetbagger from Vermont*, 61–62, 75; Tunnell, *Edge of the Sword*, 72–82.

10. Twitchell, *Carpetbagger from Vermont*, 86–98; Tunnell, *Edge of the Sword*, 96.

11. Twitchell, *Carpetbagger from Vermont*, 99–116; *Edge of the Sword*, 115, 135–40.

12. Louisiana Affairs, House Report 261, 385; Tunnell, *Edge of the Sword*, 152; *Carpetbagger from Vermont*, 129.

13. Tunnell, *Edge of the Sword*, 192–209; Twitchell, *Carpetbagger from Vermont*, 140–42, 148.

14. Twitchell, *Carpetbagger from Vermont*, 148–49; Tunnell, *Edge of the Sword*, 214–15.

CHAPTER 4: SYMPATHY FOR THE JUNTA

1. *The Papers of Ulysses S. Grant*, 25: 222–24; Hamlin Garland, *Ulysses S. Grant: His Life and Character* (New York: Doubleday, 1898), 425; Hamilton Fish diary entry for September 16, 1874, Reel 1, Hamilton Fish Papers, Manuscript Division, Library of Congress, Washington, D.C.; Grant Proclamation 220, September 15, 1874: "Law and Order in the State of Louisiana."

2. *Personal Memoirs of Ulysses S. Grant* (New York: Cosimo Classics, 2007) 193; White House Historical Association, text retrieved from https://www .whitehousehistory.org/photos/green-room-during-president-grants-administration; *Wilmington Journal*, Wilmington, NC, June 14, 1872, 2.

3. Grant to William Tecumseh Sherman, June 21, 1868, in *The Papers of Ulysses S. Grant*, 18: 292; Geoffrey Perret, *Ulysses S. Grant: Soldier & President* (New York: Random House, 1997), 434; *Daily Phoenix*, Columbia, SC, March 26, 1872, 2.

4. *National Republican*, March 18, 1874; Tunnell, *Crucible of Reconstruction*, 160–61; Taylor, *Louisiana Reconstructed*, 241–49; George Rable, "Republican Albatross: The Louisiana Question, National Politics, and the Failure of Reconstruction," *Louisiana History* (Spring 1982): 112–13, 118–19.

5. *New Orleans Bulletin*, September 18, 1874, 1; *The Papers of Ulysses S. Grant*, 25: 223–24; Fish diary entry for September 16, 1874; Hogue, *Uncivil War*, 141.

6. *New Orleans Times*, September 20, 1874, 1.

7. Dawson, *Army Generals and Reconstruction*, 179–80.

8. *The Papers of Ulysses S. Grant*, 25: 224.

9. *Nation*, September 24, 1874, 198; *New-York Tribune*, September 18, 1874, 4.

10. Jewell to Elihu B. Washburne, September 19, 1874, in *The Papers of Ulysses S. Grant*, 25: 226; *National Republican*, September 17, 1874, 1.

11. Taylor, *Louisiana Reconstructed*, 296; Adelbert Ames to Blanche Butler Ames, November 4, 1874, in *Chronicles from the Nineteenth Century* (privately issued, Clinton, MA, 1957), ii, 52.

CHAPTER 5: INVADERS

1. *Vicksburg Troubles*, House Report 265, 43rd Congress, 2nd Session, 75–76, 80–81.

2. Ibid., 175–76.

3. Ibid., 14–16; 438.

4. Ibid., iii; William C. Harris, *The Day of the Carpetbagger: Republican Reconstruction in Mississippi* (Baton Rouge: Louisiana State University Press, 1974), 634–36.

5. Eric Foner, *Freedom's Lawmakers: A Directory of Black Officeholders During Reconstruction* (New York: Oxford University Press, 1993), 54; James Wilford

Garner, *Reconstruction in Mississippi* (New York: Macmillan, 1902), 331; *Vicksburg Troubles*, iv.

6. *Vicksburg Troubles*, 145, 109, 80, 467, viii.

7. Ibid., ix, x, 169–71.

8. Ibid., x, 295–97.

9. Ibid., 178.

10. Harris, *The Day of the Carpetbagger*, 648; *Vicksburg Troubles*, 176.

11. *Daily Picayune*, December 8, 1874, 1; Mark Wahlgren Summers, *The Press Gang: Newspapers and Politics, 1865–1878* (Chapel Hill: University of North Carolina Press, 1994), 223–24.

12. *Vicksburg Troubles*, ix, 481.

13. *Cincinnati Commercial*, December 11, 1874, reprinted in *New York Times*, December 14, 1874; *Vicksburg Troubles*, ii; *Inter-Ocean*, October 6, 1874; Grimsley, "Wars for the American South," 9; John S. McNeily, "Climax and Collapse of Reconstruction in Mississippi," *Publications of the Mississippi Historical Society* 12 (1912): 299; Taylor, *Louisiana Reconstructed*, 283.

14. McNeily, "Climax and Collapse of Reconstruction in Mississippi," 301–3; *Cincinnati Commercial*, December 11, 1874, reprinted in *New York Times*, December 14, 1874.

CHAPTER 6: FEAR OF A BLACK STATE

1. Fish diary entry for December 22, 1874, Reel 2; *National Republican*, December 23, 1874, 4; William N. Armstrong, *Around the World with a King* (New York: Frederick A. Stokes, 1904), 9; "Hawaiian Song," Library of Congress, https://www.loc.gov/item/ihas.200197484/.

2. *Chicago Times*, December 13, 1874, 3; *New Orleans Bulletin*, December 29, 1874, 6; *Inter-Ocean*, December 23, 1874, 2; Ruth M. Tabrah, *Hawaii: A History* (New York: Norton, 1984), 84; *Cincinnati Daily Gazette*, December 14, 1874, 2.

3. *Cincinnati Commercial*, December 27, 1872, 2.

4. *New National Era*, April 3, 1872, 2.

5. *The Papers of Ulysses S. Grant*, 25: 295.

6. *Vicksburg Troubles*, ii; *Affairs in Alabama*, House Reports 262, 43rd Congress, 2nd Sess, 1074.

7. Christine Kreiser, "Royal Visit," *American History*, February 1, 2013, 19.

8. U.S. Department of State, *Papers Related to the Foreign Relations of the United States, 1875–1876*, 669–70; *Sacramento Daily Union*, December 3, 1874, 2; *National Republican*, December 14, 1874, 1; *Washington Evening Star*, December 12, 1874, 1.

9. *Spirit of Jefferson*, Charles Town, WV, January 26, 1875, 1; *Papers Related to the Foreign Relations of the United States, 1894*, 17, 163.

10. *Inter-Ocean*, December 14, 1874, 1; *Daily Picayune*, December 22, 1874, 8; Grant, Second Inaugural Address, March 4, 1873; *Personal Memoirs of Ulysses S. Grant*, 461.

11. *The Papers of Ulysses S. Grant*, 20: 74–76; M. G. Norman to Hamilton Fish, October 2, 1869, quoted in Brooks D. Simpson, *The Reconstruction Presidents* (Lawrence: University Press of Kansas, 1998), 146.

12. Simpson, *The Reconstruction Presidents*, 144–46.

13. *Congressional Globe*, 41st Congress, 3rd Session, 225.

14. Ibid., app.: 30.

15. *London Spectator*, January 29, 1871, in *Littell's Living Age*, 104: 635–36.

16. Simpson, *The Reconstruction Presidents*, 145–48.

CHAPTER 7: "A TRIP SOUTH MIGHT BE AGREEABLE"

1. *The Papers of Ulysses S. Grant*, 25: 339–41.

2. William F. G. Shanks, *Personal Recollections of Distinguished Generals* (New York: Harper, 1866), xx, 131–32, 156–58, 162; Moritz Busch, *Bismarck: Some Secret Pages of His History* (New York: Macmillan, 1898) I: 128.

3. U. S. Grant to General H. W. Halleck, July 14, 1864, in *The Papers of Ulysses S. Grant*, 11: 242–43; Jean Edward Smith, *Grant* (New York: Simon & Schuster, 2001), 294, 87–117; Morris, *Sheridan*, 21–22; Hutton, *Phil Sheridan & His Army*, 4–6; Wheelan, *Terrible Swift Sword*, 51–55.

4. George F. Hoar, *Autobiography of Seventy Years Vol. I* (New York: Scribner's, 1903), 209.

5. *New York Herald*, December 24, 1874, 10; *Affairs in Louisiana*, Senate Executive Documents No. 13, 19–20; *Chicago Daily Tribune*, December 29, 1874, 1.

6. William S. McFeely, *Grant* (New York: Norton, 1982), 418.

7. Fish diary entry for December 29, 1874, Reel 2.

CHAPTER 8: A LOCAL CLUB

1. *Daily Picayune*, January 1, 1875; *New-York Tribune*, January 1, 1875; *Congressional Record*, 43rd Congress, 2nd Session, 6.

2. *Daily Picayune*, July 1, September 15, 1874; Taylor, *Louisiana Reconstructed*, 283–84; Justin A. Nystrom, *New Orleans after the Civil War: Race, Politics, and a New Birth of Freedom* (Baltimore: Johns Hopkins University Press, 2010), 296fn24; House Reports 101, Part 2, 43rd Congress, 2nd Session, 206–9, 218–19, 210–13, 193–95; Hogue, *Uncivil War*, 127; *Daily Picayune*, July 2, 1874.

3. Nystrom, *New Orleans After the Civil War*, 163–64; *Daily Picayune*, June 30, 1874.

4. Nicholas Lemann, *Redemption: The Last Battle of the Civil War* (New York: Farrar, Straus & Giroux, 2006), 190–91; *Daily Picayune*, July 1, 1874; House Reports 101, Part 2, 43rd Congress, 2nd Session, 189, 211.

5. *Daily Picayune*, December 21, 27, 1874; Andrew L. Slap, *The Doom of Reconstruction: The Liberal Republicans in the Civil War Era* (New York: Fordham University Press, 2006), xiii–xiv, 191–92, 227–28; Foner, *Reconstruction*, 503; Gillette, *Retreat from Reconstruction*, 134; William B. Hesseltine, *Ulysses S. Grant, Politician* (New York: Dodd, Mead, 1935), 373–76; James T. Otten, "The Wheeler Adjustment in Louisiana: National Republicans Begin to Reappraise Their Reconstruction Policy," *Louisiana History* 13, no. 4 (1972): 356, 359; *New Orleans Times*, December 17, 1874.

6. *National Republican*, December 19, 1874; January 8, 1875; *Daily Inter-Ocean*, January 1, 1875; House Reports 101, 43rd Congress, 2nd Session, 1; Nystrom, *New Orleans After the Civil War*, 11, 66, 76–77; Taylor, *Louisiana Reconstructed*, 163; "The Origin and Activities of the 'White League' in New Orleans (Reminiscences of a Participant in the Movement)," *Louisiana Historical Quarterly* 23 (April 1940): 532; *Daily Picayune*, July 2, 1874; House Reports 101, 43rd Congress, 2nd Session, Part II, 209, 211–12; Nystrom, *New Orleans After the Civil War*, 169.

7. House Reports 101, 43rd Congress, 2nd Session, 9, 5–6; *New Orleans Bulletin*, July 18, 1874; Tunnell, *Crucible of Reconstruction*, 204; House Reports 101, 43rd Congress, 2nd Session, Part II, 75; Lou Falkner Williams, *The Great South Carolina Ku Klux Klan Trials, 1871–1872* (Athens: University of Georgia Press, 2004), 45; *Daily Inter-Ocean*, January 1, 1875.

8. House Reports 101, 43rd Congress, 2nd Session, 1; Gillette, *Retreat from Reconstruction*, 135.

CHAPTER 9: KANGAROO QUORUM

1. Marie Caroline Post, *The Life and Mémoirs of Comte Régis de Trobriand, Major-General in the Army of the United States* (New York: Dutton, 1910), 445–46, 452.

2. Smith, *Grant*, 565; *Daily Picayune*, January 1, 1875, 1; Dawson, *Army Generals and Reconstruction*, 203; *Inter-Ocean*, January 1, 1875, 1.

3. *Inter-Ocean*, December 30 and December 31, 1874, 4; 4.

4. Dawson, *Army Generals and Reconstruction*, 203–4; Post, *Life and Mémoirs of Comte Régis de Trobriand*, 446; *Inter-Ocean*, January 4, 1; Grace Elizabeth King, *New Orleans: The Place and the People* (New York: Macmillan, 1917), 320; *Affairs in Louisiana*, Senate Executive Documents No. 13, 27.

5. *Affairs in Louisiana*, Senate Executive Documents No. 13, 27–28.

6. *Inter-Ocean*, January 5, 1875, 1; *Affairs in Louisiana*, Senate Executive Documents No. 13, 27–28.

7. *Inter-Ocean*, January 5, 1875, 1; *Affairs in Louisiana*, Senate Executive Documents No. 13, 27–28.

8. Dawson, *Army Generals and Reconstruction*, 205.

9. Post, *Life and Mémoirs of Comte Régis de Trobriand*, 450–54.

10. *Visitor's Guide to New Orleans* (New Orleans: J. Curtis Waldo, 1875), 157.

11. *Cincinnati Commercial*, September 25, 1874, 7; *Inter-Ocean*, September 26, 1874, 1.

12. Post, *Life and Mémoirs of Comte Régis de Trobriand*, 450–51.

13. *Affairs in Louisiana*, Senate Executive Documents No. 13, 21.

14. *Inter-Ocean*, January 5, 1875, 1.

15. *Affairs in Louisiana*, Senate Executive Documents No. 13, 20.

CHAPTER 10: "THE GENIUS OF SMALLNESS"

1.   *Memphis Daily Appeal*, January 5, 1875; *Richmond Whig*, quoted in *Chicago Tribune*, January 11, 1875; *New-York Tribune*, January 12, 1875; Carl Schurz, "Why Anti-Grant and Pro-Greeley," *Speeches, Correspondence and Political Papers of Carl Schurz*, vol. 2 (New York: Putnam's, 1913), 397–98; James M. McPherson, "Grant or Greeley? The Abolitionist Dilemma in the Election of 1872," *American Historical Review* 71, no. 1 (1965): 44, 47; Slap, *The Doom of Reconstruction*, xiii–xv.

2.   Schurz, "Why Anti-Grant and Pro-Greeley," 394–99.

3.   *Congressional Record*, 43rd Congress, 2nd Session, 365–71; *New-York Tribune*, January 12, 1875.

4.   Hans L. Trefousse, *Carl Schurz: A Biography* (New York: Fordham University Press, 1982), 3, 14–28, 32–36, 40–42, 55, 64, 71, 81, 87–102, 109–59; Carl Schurz et al., *The Reminiscences of Carl Schurz*, vol. 3 (New York: McClure, 1907), 158; Hans L. Trefousse, "Carl Schurz's 1865 Southern Tour: A Reassessment," *Prospects* 2 (1977): 294–96; Senate Executive Documents, 39th Congress, 1st Session, No. 2, 1–2, 20, 82, 45–46, 30.

5.   Schurz et al., *The Reminiscences of Carl Schurz*, vol. 3, 191; Trefousse, "Carl Schurz's 1865 Southern Tour," 298–301; Schurz et al., *Reminiscences*, vol. 3, 202; Brooks D. Simpson, "Grant's Tour of the South Revisited," *Journal of Southern History* 54, no. 3 (1988): 426, 439–42; Senate Executive Documents, 39th Congress, 1st Session, No. 2, 106–8.

6.   Trefousse, "Carl Schurz's 1865 Southern Tour," 304; Simpson, "Grant's Tour of the South Revisited," 443; Senate Executive Documents, 39th Congress, 1st Session, No. 2, 4, 48; *New-York Tribune*, December 23, 1865.

7.   Simpson, "Grant's Tour of the South Revisited," 441–42, 443, 444n45.

8.   *New-York Tribune*, January 12, 1875; *New Orleans Bulletin*, January 12, 1875; *Chicago Tribune*, March 29, 1871; Trefousse, *Carl Schurz*, 195.

9.   *New York Herald*, September 25, 1877; *The Papers of Ulysses S. Grant*, 28: 259; Trefousse, *Carl Schurz*, 170–71, 188; *New National Era*, December 22, 1870; August 1, 1872; Foner, *Reconstruction*, 500; *Congressional Record*, 43rd Congress, 2nd Session, 367; *New-York Tribune*, January 12, 1875.

10. *Congressional Record*, 43rd Congress, 2nd Session, 365; *National Republican*, January 12, 1875; *New York Herald*, January 12, 1875; Hogue, *Uncivil War*,

151–52; Senate Executive Documents No. 13, 43rd Congress, 2nd Session, 25, 21; *Congressional Record*, 43rd Congress, 2nd Session, 365–68.

11. *New York Herald*, January 12, 1875; *New-York Tribune*, January 11–14, 1875.

CHAPTER 11: WAR IN PEACETIME

1. Allan Nevins, *Hamilton Fish: The Inner History of the Grant Administration*, vol. 2 (New York: Dodd, Mead, 1936), 751; Fish diary, January 8, 1875; Belknap to Sheridan, January 6, 1875, in Senate Executive Documents No. 13, 43rd Congress, 2nd Session, 25; Ron Chernow, *Grant* (New York: Penguin, 2017), 723; Amos Elwood Corning, *Hamilton Fish* (New York: Lamere, 1918), 58.

2. Fish diary, November 24, 1871; January 8, 1875; *New-York Tribune*, January 11, 1875; Fish diary, January 8, 1875; Bristow to J. M. Harlan, January 11, 1875, Bristow Papers, Library of Congress; Bristow to G. C. Wharton, January 14, 1875; Bristow to Harlan, January 11, 1875; Fish diary, January 10, 1875.

3. Ross A. Webb, "Benjamin H. Bristow: Civil Rights Champion, 1866–1872," *Civil War History* 15, no. 1 (1969): 39–40; Robert J. Kaczorowski, "Federal Enforcement of Civil Rights During the First Reconstruction," *Fordham Urban Law Journal* 23 (1995): 158–60; Bristow to J. M. Harlan, January 11, 1875; Bristow to G. C. Wharton, January 14, 1875.

4. Robert J. Kaczorowski, "Revolutionary Constitutionalism in the Era of the Civil War and Reconstruction," *New York University Law Review* 61 (1986): 939; Everette Swinney, "Enforcing the Fifteenth Amendment, 1870–1877," *Journal of Southern History* 28, no. 2 (1962): 202–4; Kaczorowski, "Federal Enforcement of Civil Rights During the First Reconstruction," 159; *Statutes at Large of the United States*, XVII, 1871, 13–15.

5. Kaczorowski, "Federal Enforcement of Civil Rights During the First Reconstruction," 160–62, 179–83; Herbert Shapiro, "The Ku Klux Klan During Reconstruction: The South Carolina Episode," *Journal of Negro History* 1 (1964): 46; *Richmond Dispatch*, February 11, 1873.

6. Michael A. Ross, "Obstructing Reconstruction: John Archibald Campbell and the Legal Campaign Against Louisiana's Republican Government, 1868–1873," *Civil War History* 49, no. 3 (2003): 249–50; Michael A. Ross, "Justice Miller's Reconstruction: The Slaughter-House Cases, Health Codes, and Civil Rights in New Orleans, 1861–1873," *Journal of Southern History* 64, no. 4 (1998): 649–52; Akhil Reed Amar, "The Bill of Rights and the Fourteenth Amendment," *Yale Law Journal* 101 (April 1992): 1259; *The Slaughter-House Cases*, 83 U.S. 36 (1873), 77, 96; Wilson R. Huhn, "The Legacy of Slaughterhouse, Bradwell, and Cruikshank in Constitutional Interpretation," *Akron Law Review* 42 (2009): 1053–54; Charles Calhoun, *Conceiving a New Republic: The Republican Party and the Southern Question, 1869–1900* (Lawrence: University Press of Kansas, 2006), 52.

7. Robert J. Kaczorowski, *The Politics of Judicial Interpretation: The Federal Courts, Department of Justice, and Civil Rights, 1866–1876* (New York: Fordham

University Press, 2005), 106–7, 140–48; *Daily Picayune*, June 28, 1874; *New Orleans Bulletin*, June 30, July 12, 1874; *Times*, Shreveport LA, August 6, 1874; Lane, *The Day Freedom Died*, 214.

8. *National Republican*, December 21, 1874; *Philadelphia Inquirer*, January 6, 1875; *Congressional Record*, 43rd Congress, 2nd Session, 331; Fish diary, January 11, January 8, 1875; *The Papers of Ulysses S. Grant*, 26: 22; *New York Times*, January 22, 1875.

CHAPTER 12: MAKING MARTYRS

1. *New Orleans Times*, January 6, 1875; *New Orleans Bulletin*, January 7, 1875; *Daily Picayune*, January 6, 11, 1875; Hoar, *Autobiography of Seventy Years Vol. I*, 208; *New York Times*, January 22, 1875; Sheridan to Belknap, January 9, 1875, in *The Papers of Ulysses S. Grant*, 26: 22; *New-York Tribune*, January 7, 1875.

2. Sheridan to Belknap, January 9, 1875, in *The Papers of Ulysses S. Grant*, 26: 22; *New Orleans Times*, January 11, 1875; Sheridan to Belknap, January 7, 1875, Senate Executive Documents No. 13, 43rd Congress, 2nd Session, 25; *New Orleans Bulletin*, January 9, 1875; Sheridan to Belknap, January 9, 1875, Senate Executive Documents No. 13, 43rd Congress, 2nd Session, 27; *New York Herald*, January 10, 1875.

3. Senate Executive Documents No. 13, 43rd Congress, 2nd Session, 29–31; David Dixon, *Hero of Beecher Island: The Life and Military Career of George A. Forsyth* (Lincoln: University of Nebraska Press, 1994), 119; House Executive Documents No. 30, 44th Congress, 2nd Session, 409–16; Senate Report 693, 46th Congress, 2nd Session, Part II, 128.

4. House Executive Documents No. 30, 44th Congress, 2nd Session, 410–14; Senate Executive Documents No. 13, 43rd Congress, 2nd Session, 30; Sheridan to Belknap, January 7, 1875, Senate Executive Documents No. 13, 43rd Congress, 2nd Session, 25; *New York Times*, January 22, 1875; *North Star*, Danville, VT, June 25, 1875; *Daily Picayune*, January 7, 1875; *New York Herald*, January 6, 10, 1875; *Detroit Free Press*, January 7, 1875; Hoar, *Autobiography of Seventy Years Vol. I*, 208.

5. Taylor, *Louisiana Reconstructed 1863–1877*, 307; Kaczorowski, "Federal Enforcement of Civil Rights During the First Reconstruction," 159; *Cincinnati Gazette*, January 5, 1875, quoted in *Daily Picayune*, January 6, 1875.

6. *Daily Picayune*, January 12, 1875; *Weekly Louisianian*, January 16, 1875; *New Orleans Republican*, January 10, 12, 17, 1875.

CHAPTER 13: "A REPROACH UPON THE STATE AND COUNTRY"

1. William Hepworth Dixon, *White Conquest*, vol. 2 (London: Chatto & Windus, 1876), 112–15; Sheridan to Belknap, January 5, 1875, in *Affairs in Louisiana*, Senate Executive Documents No. 13, 43rd Congress, 2nd Session, 23; *New-York Tribune*, January 12 and 13, 1875.

2. *Congressional Record*, 43rd Congress, 2nd Session, 6; *Detroit Free Press*, January 7, 1875; Fish diary, January 11, 1875; *New York Times*, January 13, 1875; *Daily Picayune*, January 12, 1875.

3. Fish diary, January 11, 1875; Senate Executive Documents No. 13, 43rd Congress, 2nd Session, 6, 1; Carolyn E. Delatte, "The St. Landry Riot: A Forgotten Incident of Reconstruction Violence," *Louisiana History* 17, no. 1 (1976): 48–49.

4. Senate Executive Documents No. 13, 43rd Congress, 2nd Session, 1–6; *New-York Tribune*, January 6, 1875; Senate Executive Documents No. 13, 7.

5. *Daily Picayune*, January 14, 1875; Dixon, *White Conquest*, vol. 1, dedication page; vol. 2, 142, 113–22; *National Republican*, January 15, 1875; Rable, "Republican Albatross," 125–27; Simpson, *The Reconstruction Presidents*, 180–81; *Chicago Tribune*, March 5, 1875.

6. James T. Otten, "The Wheeler Adjustment in Louisiana," 358–63; *Louisiana Affairs*, House Report 261, 8, 19; Fish diary, February 2, 1875; Foner, *Reconstruction*, 554; Benjamin F. Wade to his wife, February 27, 1875, quoted in Simpson, *The Reconstruction Presidents*, 181.

CHAPTER 14: "PEACEABLY IF POSSIBLE, FORCIBLY IF NECESSARY"

1. Albert Talmon Morgan, *Yazoo: or, On the Picket Line of Freedom in the South: A Personal Narrative* (Washington, D.C., self-published, 1884), 465, 457–58; Lemann, *Redemption*, 100–101; *Mississippi in 1875*, Senate Report No. 527, 44th Congress, 1st Session, xiii; *Raymond Gazette*, August 4, 1875, quoted in *Weekly Mississippi Pilot*, September 11, 1875.

2. Lemann, *Redemption*, 108–14; *Mississippi in 1875*, Part 1, 494.

3. Lemann, *Redemption*, 117–19; Harney to Ames, September 6, 1875, in *The Papers of Ulysses S. Grant*, 26: 293.

4. Grant, Proclamation 223, *Law and Order in the State of Mississippi*, December 21, 1874; Ames to Grant, September 7 and September 8, 1875, in *The Papers of Ulysses S. Grant*, 26: 293, 296; Lemann, *Redemption*, 70; Adelbert Ames to Blanche Butler Ames, September 8 and 9, 1875, in *Chronicles from the Nineteenth Century*, 2: 167–69, 98.

5. Lemann, *Redemption*, 121; *The Papers of Ulysses S. Grant*, 26: 296–97; Henry C. Lockwood, *A Man from Maine: A True History of the Army at Fort Fisher* (Rockland: Maine Association, 1894), 40.

6. Ames to Pierrepont, September 11, 1875, in *The Papers of Ulysses S. Grant*, 26: 297; Harris, *The Day of the Carpetbagger*, 665; Blanche Ames to Adelbert Ames, September 10, 1875, in *Chronicles from the Nineteenth Century*, 2: 171.

7. Grant to Pierrepont, September 13, 1875, in *The Papers of Ulysses S. Grant*, 26: 312–13.

8. John Roy Lynch, *The Facts of Reconstruction* (New York: Neale, 1913), 151; Charles W. Calhoun, *Conceiving a New Republic: The Republican Party and the Southern Question, 1869–1900* (Lawrence: University Press of Kansas, 2006), 85–87.

9. Pierrepont to Ames, September 14, 1875, in *Boston Globe*, September 17, 1875.

10. Calhoun, *Conceiving a New Republic*, 86; Pierrepont to Grant, September 16, 1875, in *The Papers of Ulysses S. Grant*, 26: 314; Adelbert Ames to Blanche Ames, September 17 and 19, 1875, in *Chronicles from the Nineteenth Century*, 2: 183, 186.

11. *Norfolk Virginian*, September 17, 1875; *Daily Picayune*, September 17, 1875; Three Hundred Voters, Vicksburg, Miss., to Ames, September 14, 1875, in *Mississippi in 1875*, Part 2, 87.

12. Adelbert Ames to Blanche Ames, October 9 and 12, 1875, in *Chronicles from the Nineteenth Century*, 2: 211, 216.

13. Adelbert Ames to Blanche Ames, October 9, 12, 14, 18, 1875, in *Chronicles from the Nineteenth Century*, 2: 211, 216, 217, 224; Ames to Pierrepont, October 16, 1875, in *The Papers of Ulysses S. Grant*, 26: 335; Lemann, *Redemption*, 126–28, 138.

14. *The Papers of Ulysses S. Grant*, 26: 336; Adelbert Ames to Blanche Ames, October 28, 1875, in *Chronicles from the Nineteenth Century*, 2: 244; Lemann, *Redemption*, 145–46.

15. Adelbert Ames to Blanche Ames, November 1, 1875, in *Chronicles from the Nineteenth Century*, 2: 248; Harris, *The Day of the Carpetbagger*, 684–85; Lemann, *Redemption*, 152–53.

16. Foner, *Reconstruction*, 561–62; Garner, *Reconstruction in Mississippi*, 395; Lemann, *Redemption*, 154.

17. Adelbert Ames to Blanche Ames, November 4, 1875, in *Chronicles from the Nineteenth Century*, 2: 249; Lemann, *Redemption*, 162–64, 170–71; *United States v. Cruikshank*, 92 U.S. 542, 23 L. Ed. 588, 23 S. Ct. 511 (1876).

CHAPTER 15: "OCCASIONALLY THERE WERE A FEW NECKS BROKEN"

1. Tunnell, *Edge of the Sword*, 219–25, 232–52; 260; Twitchell, *Carpetbagger from Vermont*, 162, 169–74.

2. Daniel H. Chamberlain to Grant, July 22, 1876, and Grant to Chamberlain, July 26, 1876, in *The Papers of Ulysses S. Grant*, 27: 199–200; Richard Zuczek, "The Last Campaign of the Civil War: South Carolina and the Revolution of 1876," *Civil War History* 42, no. 1 (1996): 19–26; William Arthur Sheppard, *Red Shirts Remembered: Southern Brigadiers of the Reconstruction Period* (Atlanta: Ruralist Press, 1940), 46–47; Zuczek, "The Last Campaign of the Civil War," 24; Dawson, *Army Generals and Reconstruction*, 232–34; Charles M. Barrow to Fanny Z. Lovell Bone in Bone, "Louisiana in the Disputed Election of 1876," *Louisiana Historical Quarterly* 15 (1932): Appendix C-6, 100–101.

3. Foner, *Reconstruction*, 575–82; Hogue, *Uncivil War*, 165–67; Brooks D. Simpson, "Ulysses S. Grant and the Electoral Crisis of 1876–77," *Hayes History Journal* 11 (1992): 3, 14–16; *Daily Picayune*, April 26, 1877; Hogue, *Uncivil War*, 176, 185–86.

4. *Weekly Jackson Clarion*, May 8, 1890; Vernon Lane Wharton, *The Negro in Mississippi, 1865–1890* (Chapel Hill: University of North Carolina Press, 1965), 206–7; Richard H. Pildes, "Democracy, Anti-Democracy, and the Canon," *Constitutional Commentary* 893 (2000): 300fn18, 301–3; M. Isabel Medina, "The Missing and Misplaced History in Shelby County, *Alabama v. Holder*—Through the Lens of the Louisiana Experience with Jim Crow and Voting Rights in the 1890s," *Mississippi College Law Review* 33 (2014): 202, 211–12; *The Civil Rights Cases*, 109 U.S. 3 (1883); *Plessy v. Ferguson*, 163 U.S. 537 (1896); *Williams v. Mississippi*, 170 U.S. 213 (1898).

EPILOGUE: "THE WHOLE POWER OF THE GOVERNMENT"

1. Lynch, *The Facts of Reconstruction*, 150–55; Adelbert Ames to Blanche Ames, November 1, 1875, in *Chronicles from the Nineteenth Century*, 2: 248; Grant to Chamberlain, July 26, 1876; Zuczek, "The Last Campaign of the Civil War."

2. Foner, *Reconstruction*, 582–85; Grant to Commodore D. Ammen, August 28, 1877, in Daniel Ammen, *The Old Navy and the New*, vol. 2 (Philadelphia: Lippincott, 1891), 537–38.

INDEX

ABOUT THE AUTHOR

Robert Cwiklik is the author of *House Rules*, which chronicles a year in the life of a freshman congressman, as well as several books for children and young adults. He was an editor at the *Wall Street Journal* for more than fifteen years and lives in Philadelphia.